Making Trouble

DESIGNING IN DARK TIMES/RADICAL THINKERS IN DESIGN

Edited by Clive Dilnot and Eduardo Staszowski

These two series push at the boundaries of contemporary design thinking, responding to the world's current and pressing social, economic, and environmental challenges and crises.

Exploring the interaction of design with critical thought and social research and presenting both modes of thought (models, concepts, arguments) and courses of action (scenarios, strategies, proposals, works), titles engage polemically with the opportunities now presented to rethink what acting in the world and designing might be.

DESIGNING IN DARK TIMES

Politics of the Everyday, Ezio Manzini
Designing in Dark Times: An Arendtian Lexicon,
edited by Eduardo Staszowski and Virginia Tassinari
Making Trouble: Design and Material Activism,
Otto von Busch

FORTHCOMING

Designing for Interdependence: A Poetics of Relating,
Martín Ávila
Design Education and Democracy at the Edge of Collapse,
Zoy Anastassakis and Marcos Martins
Design and the Social Imagination, Matthew DelSesto
Designing Relationally: Making and Restor(y)ing Life,
Arturo Escobar, Michal Osterweil, and Kriti Sharma
The Possibility of the Artificial, Clive Dilnot

"*Making Trouble* is a timely and sincere investigation of how simple, small, low-tech craft skills may help to bring about change. Otto von Busch has written—and made—an important contribution to how each of us may learn to understand empowerment through craft."

—Jessica Hemmings, Professor of Crafts,
University of Gothenburg, Sweden

"This book is something so unusual as a practical creative counter-design handbook, a high-level theory analysis, of design, of society and its relations of domination, and most importantly, how we can, literally, make justice. This book outlines numerous examples of how we can make our creative redesigning of things matter, by hacking the machines, objects, and different constructions in our society. Even in the way it is written and organized, this book is inspirational, practical, theoretical, political, radical, and very creative."

—Stellan Vinthagen, Endowed Chair in the
Study of Nonviolent Direct Action and
Civil Resistance and Professor of Sociology at
University of Massachusetts, Amherst, USA

"von Busch's intellectual project is a very sophisticated one in which the argument concerning the importance of material activism is embedded within a deep knowledge of wide-ranging intellectual terrain. The range is amazing, extending from political theory, through literature, to art and design. What is especially impressive is the way in which von Busch braids these works together with a very light touch. The narrative voice throughout the manuscript is fantastic. The book is a pleasure to read. It is a powerful mix of lucidity and sophistication—an all too rare combination. I can pay no higher compliment to a writer than to say that I genuinely wanted to read on!"

—Victoria Hattam, Professor of Politics,
New School for Social Research, New York, USA

"Full of good energy, this book conveys a sense of excitement through its spirit of provocation, pace, and imaginative imagery: a 'page turner' both practical and affirmative. Even though it leans upon some difficult academic sources, it has a directness and clarity. The book's radicalism is measured and implicit, rather than reckless. It will speak to students and teachers and challenge orthodoxies in a learned but informal way."

—John Wood, Professor Emeritus at Goldsmiths,
University of London, UK, and Professor of
Design at University of Wales, Trinity Saint David, UK

Making Trouble

Design and Material Activism

Otto von Busch

BLOOMSBURY VISUAL ARTS
LONDON • NEW YORK • OXFORD • NEW DELHI • SYDNEY

BLOOMSBURY VISUAL ARTS
Bloomsbury Publishing Plc
50 Bedford Square, London, WC1B 3DP, UK
1385 Broadway, New York, NY 10018, USA
29 Earlsfort Terrace, Dublin 2, Ireland

BLOOMSBURY, BLOOMSBURY VISUAL ARTS and the Diana logo are trademarks
of Bloomsbury Publishing Plc

First published in Great Britain 2022

Cover design: Andrew LeClair and Chris Wu of Wkshps

A catalogue record for this book is available from the British Library.

Library of Congress Cataloging-in-Publication Data
Names: Busch, Otto von, 1975– author.
Title: Making trouble : design and material activism / Otto von Busch.
Description: London ; New York : Bloomsbury Visual Arts, 2022. |
Series: Designing in dark times | Includes bibliographical references.
Identifiers: LCCN 2021040305 (print) | LCCN 2021040306 (ebook) |
ISBN 9781350162549 (paperback) | ISBN 9781350162556 (hardback) |
ISBN 9781350162563 (epub) | ISBN 9781350162570 (pdf) | ISBN 9781350162587
Subjects: LCSH: Design–Political aspects. | Industrial arts–Political aspects. |
Social justice. Classification: LCC NK1520 .B85 2022 (print) |
LCC NK1520 (ebook) | DDC 745.4–dc23
LC record available at https://lccn.loc.gov/2021040305
LC ebook record available at https://lccn.loc.gov/2021040306

ISBN: HB: 978-1-3501-6255-6
PB: 978-1-3501-6254-9
ePDF: 978-1-3501-6257-0
eBook: 978-1-3501-6256-3

Series: Designing in Dark Times

Typeset by Newgen KnowledgeWorks Pvt. Ltd., Chennai, India

To find out more about our authors and books visit www.bloomsbury.com
and sign up for our newsletters.

"What is more splendid than gold?," asked the king. "The light," replied the serpent. "What is more refreshing than light?," the former asked. "Conversation," the latter said.

—Goethe, "The Fairy Tale"

To the workshop teachers and techs, for the conversations by the workbench, and with great thanks to the reader who took time to make something out of my ramblings.

CONTENTS

Dear Reader,

Writing is a craft, and so is reading. A book taken seriously is material to engage. It should be handled, measured, picked apart, and built upon. When you take notes, it should be the plan of a heist. You break into a book and leave the pages with the valuables, if there are any.

Even a smash-and-grab requires attention and observation, and you probably do so best with a pencil in hand. Like any drawing, one has to dare to make the first line, break through the drywalls of the white page. You can't get any work done if you don't <u>engage the matter.</u>

A JUSTICE MACHINE

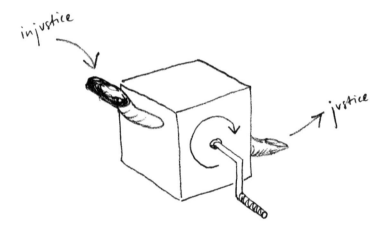

injustice

justice

PREFACE

How do you build a justice machine? How does it work? This is its simple workings: You put in a manifestation of injustice, pull the crank, and out comes something more just. Any ideas? Here are some of the suggestions: You put in a sword and two plowshares come out. You put in a gold medal and out come a hundred coins. You put in a bullet and out come coins in the amount it cost to produce it. You put in a cookie, and it comes out split into two halves, cut with surgical precision. Or, as a more cynical participant suggested, you put in a cookie, and you crank and crank, and nothing comes out. Great ideas—now you have three hours to build a working prototype. Here's a box of mixed materials: the workshop is yours. Have fun.

The making workshop of a design school is often a confusing place. The hype of innovative making easily overshadows the mundane possibilities of what an undergrad student can accomplish in the few hours at their disposal with rudimentary crafts and simple tools. And no matter how much designers claim theory and practice is one and the same, I often find it challenging to create studio experiences where the two convincingly overlap: how do I apply object-oriented ontologies, the carpentry of things, tool-being, or the material turn when I try to teach the basics of woodturning? I tell my students the importance of working with sharp tools, but my thinking turns blunt; even putting Latour and the lathe in the same sentence makes my head spin.

This book aims to add a perspective to the making practice that one may typically find at academic design institutions. Common in foundation courses, this is most often basic manipulations of materials, creating models from wood and soft metals, plastic and fabric, using simple hand tools and cheap or found materials. In these settings, matter is shaped through primitive making. Seen from the outside, it may resemble a shop class of middle school, but with more emphasis on form and aesthetics. But with design being called to face increasingly urgent challenges, from global injustices to climate change, the simple tools of shop class may need sharper edges to cut into everyday materials in other ways.

Bringing theoretical texts to the workshop is not always working well. Sometimes it seems text and hand can lack good coordination, that models of thought do not always translate well into clay or cardboard. Analytical distinctions and models can suffer in their translation to matter, just like the surfaces on a mitered half lap joint do not match as well as I thought, something I notice after cutting the pieces. It's easy to get disappointed, as they seemed to fit perfectly on my drawing. Similarly, I often find that abstract concepts are not so easily translated into a simple material form that a student can build with the tools available in the model shop. This is where the justice machine comes in as such a playful challenge—an abstract concept, almost metaphysical, such as justice has to be made concrete. And not only that, something quite "meta" has to be made in matter, or *made to matter*. Or, as I jokingly have phrased the challenge to students, *justice will have to be made.*

Throughout the iterations of the assignment, justice has so far worked as the best example of something "meta." It is a concept many have some ideas around, yet seldom has predefined articulations. Using word plays like "making justice" also draws in assorted movie references, which often get the students discussing narratives if and where examples of justice are the outcome of actions. Are the actions of the hero just? What tools are used? This makes it a great conversation starter. Also, a concept such as justice has a designerly element to it. It could be seen through what philosopher Gianni Vattimo calls "pensiero debole" (weak thought) as pointing to *what might be* rather than what is fully realized, a concept that whispers of potential more than staking out a claim. Thoughts that seek compassion more than assert their rights.[1] This general direction of *what might be* positions the discrepancy between design (planning) and making (manifesting) into the spotlight: what a design *points toward* and what it *makes real.*

[1] Vattimo (2012: 51).

These are directions that seldom overlap. It is the sad reality of design work; the initial idealism is almost always betrayed by reality.

This is the challenge I find myself facing. The design workshop, or making space, of design school is a place to engage and practice the skills of shaping matter. Most often, these are material samples, mock-ups, models, and prototypes. You need earplugs and protective glasses. Don't wear jewelry. And don't wear your best sandals (don't wear them at all!). It is a space where you deal not so much with the fine arts but the dirty arts of matter. Even if the dean may tell you otherwise, in the Chain of Being, or *scala naturae*, that permeates design schools, matter is low, whereas ideas and systems all appear higher. Not only are the workshops placed near ground level in the buildings, often even in the basement, but they are also low ranking in the status hierarchy of academic labor. The shop-techs and assistants are surely respected, but they sit by themselves in the cafeteria, in their own sphere in between the academic staff and the students. The professors have to spend their time doing admin and lecture about design thinking, wicked problems, cultures of change, and the modes of existence. If they can carve out the time, they try to keep up with their reading and publishing, to fulfill the criteria to keep themselves employed and respected, and not least keep the university ranking up. As much as making is at the heart of design school, it is no wonder you seldom see the full professors by the sewing machines and belt sanders. Their labor is badly needed elsewhere. Even when it is supposed to be of concern, there is just so little time to get into the workshop and make *matter* matter.

Most of my colleagues agree this is a shame. Design scholars seem to share a hunger to experiment in the workshops and make things. Even if the world is text or not, designed objects stabilize social relations. Things interact with politics, coloniality, aesthetics, and all kinds of abstract subjects, as their very materiality makes asymmetric power relations have real physical effects. Objects have the power to affect our decisions. And yes, design, as a profession, has a propensity to run the errands of its client or master, the one who pays for the work. Designers thus make the power relations between client and users concrete, and they have significant influence in the work of aligning societal struggles into the invisible habits of everyday life. Theorists and practitioners agree; the matter of design is powerful.

BACK TO MATTER

But as my design students encounter and embrace theoretical perspectives that emphasize the agency of matter, or the politics of objects and nonhuman actors, this also seems to coincide with a decentering of the practical labor in the design workshop from the curriculum. Much time is spent on getting the vocabulary and ideology right. How a thing is made is complemented with why it is needed in the first place and who it serves. It can be a bit scary building a model as it makes such an irrevocable statement: what if the model is too normative or manifests unintended politics? A worried student finds it undoubtedly safer to read a bit more before getting one's hands dirty.

This tendency exposes a paradox in how designers approach the tension between the making and matter of the workshop and the theory and meta of the seminar. It is reflected in much of current design practice. On the one hand, facing social, political, and environmental turmoil on a global scale, building another chair may seem futile or even an insult to those who suffer. The issues are systemic, and a product can hardly be relevant on that scale. Yet, simultaneously, the agency of matter can be almost overwhelming in that it makes an indisputable material statement. Once you make something, its presence is concrete. That statement is hard to obscure with the elaborate techniques of discursive and cynical masking in the meta seminars. It seems the more designers read of the thing-power and political agency of objects, the lesser claims to matter designers do. They instead retreat into speculation, critique, and discursive exercises, with Lilliputian projects ending up as diagrams, power points, workshops, and zines (yes, much of my own practice has fallen victim to this).

This is a challenge. As the physical and political effects of design become explicit in social injustices, geopolitical struggles, and climate change, there is simultaneously confusion about which agency really matters in which context. As I design a shovel, and I negotiate the brief, the users and stakeholders seem to include everybody from minerals and worms, subaltern and disabled, laborers and users, miners and logistical workers, victory gardens and agribusiness, and somewhere far off, the client who will pay me for the work to make some more money. It can be confusing. But just because it is confusing doesn't mean we should discuss this only in the graduate seminars. Making, even if only simple models, can help us shift between several perspectives.

As they may appear pretty straightforward, the essential skills for making are still entangled in their academic context. Even if I try to embrace post-human inclusion and the thing-power of the stuff around me, I find it hard to negotiate by the workbench. It is hard getting away from the fact that the tool is in *my hand*. The workshop is designed that way. Human agency gets priority. The mistakes are mine. Only the amateur blames the material for the errors of the hand. So even if this is a book about design and matter, the human actor is privileged. Like so many others, in the end, I present my Power-Points to other academics, and this book to you, dear reader. My material audience, and the nonhuman agencies I try to include, asks few questions I am yet trained to address. This book is just text on paper. No wood or tools come with it. It is written for a human reader. So you may rightly ask, whatever happened to the "nothing about us without us?" I stand guilty as charged.

Yet let me defend myself. My challenge is to try to bring the models of thought behind this book as close to their material expressions as possible. Like most designers, I use my sketches to expose how I see, imagine, and handle the things around me. I try to show the workings of materials and how I distinguish concepts from each other. While not concrete enough to tap on, test, and evaluate, these sketches are invitations to come closer to how I see the many material agencies interact in the processes of primitive making. I try to use a language we can share by the workbench.

ACTIVIST MAKING

Ok, so far so good. So what is it we will examine here by the workbench then? It is not just any form of making I explore in this book. As the title suggests, the book centers around the troubles of making, and specifically how matter is mobilized in design activism. On the streets, the questions of activism increasingly rupture the previous tacit consensus as protesters call for justice across the world. Heavily equipped police use teargas and military-grade equipment as they clash with demonstrators who in turn use improvised defenses, ready-made everyday objects turned into political props. It may range from umbrellas, bicycle helmets, leaf blowers, and whatever may come in handy. Vigilantes and militias sometimes join in, and things escalate and get rough. Two (or more) sides wield material tools to strengthen their position in the current disputed societal vision. Here, the complex issues and negotiations of perspectives and priorities around justice take physical shape. The quest for justice appears everywhere, rendered practical by designed matter, through spontaneous or primitive forms of making. It can be an improvised gas mask made from a plastic bottle, mitigating the effects of the tear gas. It can be a homemade radio transmitter broadcasting news about protests as the internet gets blocked by authorities. Or an improvised club or shield.

Activist struggles for justice take physical shape in flags and barricades, in street theater puppets and slogans painted on umbrellas, in slingshots and soup kitchens. Sometimes the function of these objects is primarily symbolic. Other times they reply to force and serve life-saving purposes for protesters. Used to disrupt the status quo, they extend the agency of their users and become primitive justice machines at work, depending on their context. Yet, simultaneously, other types of protests materialize in complex justice-*evading* machines, similarly disrupting the status quo—in exquisite smuggling tunnels, offshore tax accounts, cryptocurrency schemes, homemade weapons, and narco-subs. All sides claim the priority of their perspective and purpose. Nobody said justice was any more straightforward matter than a mitered half lap joint.

When we encounter material activism in this book, I emphasize how the making of primitive objects comes to *matter in social conflict.* I will especially examine how this conflict stands in contrast to the state. In most cases, justice is administered by the state, to put it simply. Making, in taking the form of justice machines, is powerful when it comes to face the state (or is needed to evade the state). The material activism we will encounter focuses on making that is administered, regulated, or forbidden by the state, as it interferes with how the state presides over its protocols of justice.

The material activism we will meet is practices of making that stand in proximity to, trespass into, or even challenge how state administration aligns and organizes the agency of its population. It is a making that manifests struggles for justice, facing up against state boundaries, laws, and institutions. These may be innocent or sometimes more daring or even destructive, but we also have a lot to learn from the more dangerous forms of making: they expose the boundaries making measures its power against.

Even if I use the idea of justice machines in relation to making, the purpose here is not to debate the principles of justice. But it is essential to recognize that a call for justice stands behind almost all forms of activism. The experience of being mistreated, be it by siblings, people in power, or by fate, acts as the foundation of social struggles. Activism highlights the contestation between the visions of what each side considers fair. A justice machine is a way to make such struggles tangible through matter. Throughout the text, these machines will appear to set light on how matter and making are put to use in political conflict, making positions more concrete, and amplified through various forms of activism. With practical examples, I will introduce what I see as helpful ways to think about the agency and power that comes with dealing with matter in primitive making.

The struggles for justice often involve confrontations with the status quo expressed in hierarchies, customs, and the law. The purpose is to unpack how making, as a creative process, adds material agency to contended deliberations. Thus, this is not a book on the legality or legitimacy of disobedience and dissent, nor the dilemmas around decrees of moral sentiment (perhaps start with *Antigone* for that). Just as objects help make social relationships more permanent, material repurposing can twist and displace the hierarchical arrangements that cement what we consider just or unjust. I hope to show that making can be an intrinsic part of renegotiating these social protocols and relations.

It is crucial to notice how material struggles around justice differ widely between various states, and the boundaries are unevenly dispersed or upheld between cultures, dictatorships, or democracies. The examples are primarily from the North, from democracies and consumer societies. But to take an example, making alcohol may not be much of a problem in one culture, while certainly so in another. And similarly, making weapons to arm a community in a civil war is different than preparing a bomb for an act of terror. We will not dive into the ethical minefields of such practices, but I hope to suggest a lens through which designers can think of their making, activism, and material powers more generally.

Making takes place around the world in different shapes, in various contexts, and from different situations and needs. Similarly, the struggles for justice take on varied concerns around the globe, and their means and ends diverge. Hyped as a garage and hackerspace practice, making may appear radical among privileged groups in Western consumer societies, but not to the majority of the world where it is a means for survival or a struggle for dignity. Yet the setting of this book is in the Western design school workshop, where the tacit understanding has long been that modernism and consumerism set the general ontology of where and why design happens. Even if much design education has diversified over the last decades to address a more comprehensive global scope, the idea of progress, as defined in design education, is still primarily the journey along the paved roads of modernism. Design is still modeled to support, or at least act within or toward, consumer societies. In this book, I am primarily speaking to the context of the design school workshop, like at Parsons, where I teach. I hope these thoughts can make sense elsewhere too, and I encourage you to tweak these ideas to your setting and struggle.

AFFIRMATIVE MAKING

As will be further explored, primitive making concerns making the most straightforward possible contraptions, or what we could playfully refer to as minor justice machines. As we will see along the way, they consist of everything from a wooden chair or a repurposed metal cookie box, a knitted wool balaclava, or a carved linoleum stamp. On a technological level and the tools involved, these are things that draw connotations more to middle school shop class than engineering and disruptive innovation. Yet, even if so simple, a crude or primitive object may still disrupt the arrangements of the injustices addressed. Minor, and in many cases somewhat naïve, these types of making may still be so powerful they must in some instances be banned by the state!

This is where we get with this inquiry: primitive making can still be powerful enough to be controversial and forbidden. It is here, in the "forbidden crafts," where we may find some seeds to the realist power of making and craft. This is making that establishes a contested claim to power, suggesting forms of living and being that stand in contrast to those designated and negotiated through the state. It *makes* one world that threatens to bypass, or even *unmake*, another. From here, the workshop at design school can become another arena in education to discuss the politics and power of making. Hopefully, it can be done in a practical and engaging way, where students take part in *touching power*.

This is also why the focus is on simple workshop objects. Over the last decades, as more of public life has become medialized or moved online, technological and digital activism has come to the forefront, not least with practices such as tactical media and hacking. Similarly, political campaigning and awareness-raising may seem ever present in the mailboxes and social media feeds. But the primitive objects are everywhere and often out of sight and out of mind. The primitive forms of making in the workshop are not nostalgic. They have the potential to expose the importance of these neglected objects and help us *unlearn* how we take their physical attributes, affordances, and alignments for granted. A provocative remaking of these simple objects makes these controversies concrete. It is precisely by being a bit forbidden, or even on the boundaries of sabotage, that we come to inquire and touch the controversy.

An essential part of the making experience is producing something tangible. A day's work is anchored in a tangible reality we can share with others. While it is not unique to making, there is a fundamental element of pride and pleasure that should not be underestimated. In line with this experience, I hope to offer a ludic as much as applied thinking by the workbench. I see it as a constructive, affirmative, and playful way to think of activism in the making. This is a book for those who like to build things. Whereas, as philosopher Peter Sloterdijk warns, in the footsteps of the Enlightenment, much academic inquiry turns "complex and sad," I have aimed to engage a way of making that can echo some of the joy that comes with practicing with tools and materials. Here, the affirmative pleasure of building does not stand in contrast to critique. Indeed, no objects on the workbench can save the world, and only very few can even make a modest contribution to even a minor betterment. But an inquiry with the fresh eyes, sharp tools, and the dirty hands of the workshop can at least push the handy to take practical steps in repairing what is obviously broken.

It is my experience that every hands-on assignment also calls for courage. Even when you measure twice before the cut, it requires a daring mix of both calculations as well as happy naivete to finally carve into the material. Safe cynicism builds few new models of the worlds we need in the future. Don't turn your making complex and downcast (or sadly militant), but develop skill, thought, and desire with the intrinsic pride and pleasures that emerge from building primitive things. Don't submit the joy of making under the hunger to achieve, update your social media or CV. Allow yourself to explore and experiment and make mistakes to escape the vicious circle of servitude. Use practical action and your workbench tools to find forms of political action that render new futures discussable and tangible. Making is not all fun and games, and not all domination can be broken by insurgent repair, but such practice can balance some of the fearful bitterness of everyday life. Some forms of making can be dangerous or even illegal, but we may learn and manifest the civics of care anew from it. I hope some encouragement and joy can come from this book, and you get back to the workshop soon enough. I look forward to seeing you there.

1 Power in the Making

I often hear people claiming that design and making are "powerful" and "political"—but in what way? The design of a missile or fighter jet is undoubtedly powerful and also political. Their use even more so. An industrial machine, a car, or a vacuum cleaner is too. A lock, a bench, and a chair? Or a PET bottle, a cookie jar, and some tape? It seems the intensity differs.

Machines, products, and objects all manifest tangible relationships. Tools interfere in the connections people make with their surroundings, modifying the bodily capacities of those who have access and use them. By manipulating the immediate surroundings, our agency shapes matter, which influences us back. In a very practical way, the process and outcomes of making affect the distribution of agency across the social field. Who has the power in making, who becomes more powerful, and how does matter play a part in this process?

This becomes especially clear when making becomes part of conflicts. One example can be street protests, where the voices and bodies of people turn to the public to express their views. Sometimes these means are amplified with signs, flags, and megaphones. Attention is needed to a political issue. Tensions may rise as protesters try to increase their impact, using their bodies to interfere with other public functions, traffic, or infrastructure. Typically, the police force appears to preserve the status quo as protesters now start breaking laws that are set to keep order. Fences, uniforms, nightsticks, handcuffs, tear gas, and water cannons become means to break up the protest. The conflict between the parts is heightened. It is a typical scene that emerges all over the world; sophisticated tools for riot control are set against the ill-protected bodies of protesters who are calling for their voice to be heard.

Yet, also protesters prepare themselves for what they know is coming. An example can be the improvised armors of the Spanish activist group Las Agencias, a collection of reinforced garments they jokingly call "Pret-a-resister." Here, plastic water bottles are rigged with tape to the body, to the chest, shoulders, and arms, protecting against the blows of the nightsticks. One type of street-level citizen-making, with materials from the local deli, is set against the police force's sophisticated design, equipment, and training. There is an uneven power relationship in such conflict, and by making a water bottle armor, Las Agencias highlights the vulnerability of the protesters.

As posited by craft theorist Jessica Hemmings, when tracing the political impact of craft or making, one should pay attention to how the *powerlessness* of craft is a factor for its perceived power.[1] The domesticity of craft appears very different than the political power manifested in public. For example, domestic crafts that comment on war create another form of tension than a movie, a poster, or a flag. A war-rug, body count mittens, or embroidered slogans, all highlight the tension between the tranquility and softness that craft connotes and the harsh reality they appear in.

A similar tension appears when we encounter simple repurposed domestic products in protests worldwide. From the simple umbrellas in Hong Kong and primitive riot shields made from cut-apart plastic trash bins with duct tape handles, to more sophisticated gas masks made from plastic PET bottles,

---

[1] Hemmings (2018).

iconic from the Taksim Square protests in Istanbul. When street protests repurpose peaceful everyday products, the proportions of conflict are heightened. Something happens when bringing these materials into street protests, especially when set against police forces' militarized equipment and violent tactics.

The improvised crafts for street protests may seem like an extreme, or at least an exception, when it comes to making practices, but start making, and you immediately run into trouble. Making seems to attract all kinds of trouble. On the one hand, materials just don't want to do what the drawing so elegantly suggests, and ideas don't render so ideal as the maker wants it. But also, just put your new creation out on the street, and people will react in unpredicted ways. As you start making, don't ask for permission, as you may soon find social protocols, laws, and regulations that point out just how disruptive your new thing really is, even if it is unpretentious and plain. Building regulations, warranties, insurance policies; the confines of craft start coming out of the woodwork as soon as you get carving into the everyday.

PRIMITIVE MAKING

What interests me is the trouble of everyday and straightforward things. Drawing from Eric Hobsbawm's classic study on the political agency of social bandits and peasant organizations, whom he calls *primitive rebels*, what a reader will find in this book is a journey through some of the material agency and insurgency of *primitive makers*.[2] It is primitive because it is the making with elementary hand tools often found at home, using the ubiquitous materials of the introductory design workshop, and not requiring any advanced skills. Like in Hobsbawm's study, the primitive signifies a more fluid than hierarchically institutionalized practice, organized while not necessarily structured or incorporated. It should not be confused with

[2] Hobsbawm (1959).

"primitive arts" and does not imply the othering of indigenous practices or a romantic perspective of a less mediated connection with the world.

Primitive making also signifies a relationship to the more popular connotation between making in general and the strand of do-it-yourself (DIY) practices that have emerged under the term *maker culture*. Over the past decades, what were previously amateur DIY practices have been infused with Design Thinking buzz and have become maker culture, made popular with *Make* magazine's launch in 2005, and celebrated as a "Third Industrial Revolution" or an "entrepreneurial revolution" of garage tinkering.[3] Marked with a special Maker Faire event at the White House on June 18, 2014, this cultural phenomenon aligns well with the Silicon Valley startup culture. It has long also taken on political language. For example, in the efforts to bring a DIY mindset to technology like in the "Maker's bill of rights" published in *Make* magazine in 2005, a political tone is set to the act of making, yet simultaneously aligning it within a realm of unregulated and free/open labor, binding this type of practice to unpaid volunteering. Today, this type of entrepreneurial making and hacking can be found in ubiquitous hackathons, seductive training grounds for precarious labor, that frame cultural expectations around the labor of making as "innovative" and "cool," and thus rightfully paid little and without any chance for organization or unionization.[4]

---

[3] The idea of a new industrial revolution is common within the narrative of the maker movement, emphasizing making with a tilt toward digital tools, the production of artifacts using digital manufacturing technologies, distributed systems, spaces, and services (Anderson 2012).

[4] A labor perspective of hackathons is made explicit in Zukin and Papadantonakis (2017). In a similar vein, the editors of *Journal of Peer Production* (issue 5, 2014) offer an executive summary of the hype around maker culture:

> Shared Machine Shops are not new. Fab Labs are not about technology. Sharing is not happening. Hackerspaces are not open. Technology is not neutral. Hackerspaces are not solving problems. Fab Labs are not the seeds of a revolution.

The reason to focus on primitive making is to mitigate a drift toward technological tendencies in the branded "making" where the term increasingly connotes microcontrollers, robots, drones, and the prolific gadget-centered consumer-making of Silicon Valley. I thus use primitive to limit a technological drift where, for example, "critical making" primarily deals with technologies commonly used in hackerspaces. Yet, these efforts are certainly praiseworthy, and I subscribe to their radical pragmatic position of possibility, breaking through structures, that I also see inherent to design work: a can-do pragmatism emphasizing that *things can be different!*[5]

It is in relation to the technological and abstract drift I emphasize the primitive; it is about the appropriate technology for the introductory workshop course. As we will see further on, the primitive element also signifies an ascetic use of technology in teaching for the educational purpose of getting closer to the material properties and the recalcitrance of matter—its potential to align as well as *resist*. But again, we can also use the term to think of an ascetic use of technology in the Greek meaning of ascetic, as a form of "exercise," a training or practice to find the appropriate levels of effort and use to reach the intended goal. It is primitive and appropriate because it does not waste or produce surplus; it uses minimal surplus technology, minimal surplus metaphysical abstraction, and minimal surplus subordination. We will come back to some of this later.

Concerning the more corporate parts of maker culture, the term primitive can also help emphasize social and historical conditions that necessitate creativity and the dignity of survival. Making is a practice beyond the commodity-centric hypes framed by mainstream maker culture. It suggests an agency,

---

[5] In this way, I find this exploration of primitive making aligning well with Ratto (2011), Ratto and Boler (2014), and Marres et al. (2018), even if these titles put more focus on the types of making and design that emphasize digital technologies, systems, and media. Similarly, Ian Bogost (2012) takes on to address artifacts that *practice philosophy*, yet also these are primarily digital.

inventiveness, and ingenuity that emerge from basic tooling, the possibility of an egalitarian inclusiveness that comes from tight circumstances.[6] In line with Hobsbawm, the primitive in making signifies a sense of uninstitutionalized, or even undomesticated, potential of bottom-up appropriation—that making can be a "wild thing" in the sense of design historian Judy Attfield's classic study of the unruly life of objects.[7] If wild things are "things with attitude" (as Attfield has it), primitive making is a *making with attitude* (disrespectful to the hagiographic tendencies of design)—an attitude not to be domesticated but to learn and build from.

But before we move on, let's take a step back. In its most rudimentary form, we can imagine a scenario of primitive making. A ball has gotten stuck up in the tree, just a few feet higher than I can reach with my hands. A primitive tool is needed, and I search around on the ground to find a fallen branch I can use to extend my arm's reach to poke the ball so it falls down. Some branches are too short or too thin to do the work. But I soon find one to use. However, it a bit too wide, has many small twigs and leaves, so it gets stuck on the other tree branches as I try to reach the ball. To make the branch less cumbersome, I start breaking off the twigs until only the core branch remains, and with this I can finally reach the ball. Even without building anything new, the task has been accomplished with straightforward means, repurposing a fallen branch into a poking-a-ball-out-of-a-tree-stick.

---

[6] For a more thorough critique of gender, race, and privilege in maker culture, see Vossoughi et al. (2016). Using the terminology of James Scott (1990), I would suggest primitive making is one of the weapons of the weak, at work on the level of the *infrapolitical*, everyday operations occurring beneath the surface or under the radar of the more debated and scrutinized power politics.

[7] Attfield (2000), but one could also interpret a "practice of the wild" in Gary Snyder's terms (1990: 11), as the energy and richness, the uncontrolled wilderness of sweets, which implies "chaos, eros, the unknown, realms of taboo, the habitat of both the ecstatic and the demonic ... it is a place of archetypical power, teaching, and challenge."

MATTERS AND MATERIALS

What has happened along the way in the scenario above is that I have turned the matter of found wood into the material of a stick. The wood is the same matter, but as I twisted off the twigs and leaves, I infused the properties of the branch with my human intention, refining it to align with my objective of getting the ball out of the tree. Without these modifications, I could not have used the branch to reach into the tree to poke the ball down. Or, to be a bit clearer in the definition, the *matter* of the branch (the raw substance of the tree) became the *material* of the stick (the matter in relation to human agency and intentions). To put it differently, matter is the wild part of "raw material," before it is domesticated into cultured materials, aligned with human purpose.

When I build things, I most often engage materials. For example, the wood I use in the workshop is planted, nursed, cultivated, harvested, and milled into a format that aligns with the standard use of the material, even if it is just a rough sawn two-by-four (often called "construction lumber," a term that reveals its purpose). A particular type of tree is selected, planted, and grown in conditions deemed favorable for its use, flitch cut, cut for grade, or quartered. The tree is cut down when it has reached the right height. It is then milled to bring out the best properties of the matter for its use as material (for wood lengthwise along the fibers). The properties of the matter are in league with the intended practices of its use, which relates not only to its practical use but also to transport, environmental regulations, trade agreements, and price; all parameters are part of domesticating matter into material. Even if I just need a plank to use as an improvised cutting board, the wood I will find in my local hardware store will probably be pine or cedar, not ebony or sandalwood.

Matter is subjected to the power of human intentions, harvested, refined, and modified under a regime of use and purpose. Yet, as is often apparent at the workbench, even if cultured, materials are frequently feral; they "have their own will." As I work on a piece of matter with my tools, using it as material, the matter fights back. The wood split from an unseen crack, the textile fibers curl up with the moisture of my hands, or I may encounter a law of physics unknown to my experience (such as when introduced to heat-treating and quenching when hardening metal). A theory of matter does not always match its handing; causation can seem intuitive yet remains unarticulated or unknown. These feral properties of materials are central to crafts. When it comes to matter, anthropocentric models of thought always put agency and control in the maker's hands (human or god). But it is not always so simple. Anthropologist Tim Ingold points out how the process of making cannot be about imposing mental models for direct translation onto matter (the idea of "hylomorphism") but rather a "gestural dance" of contrapositions, between the maker and recalcitrant materials. The clash of this hylomorphic model is apparent, for example, in chopping wood with an axe (or whittling), where the fibers of the wood guide the force of the edge. In such conditions, a form cannot be univocally imposed on matter, but the emerging shape is "more topological than geometrical" and answers to the latent variables of the material itself (i.e., the matter stays recalcitrant). When it comes to dealing with matter, form is emergent rather than imposed.[8]

But, with the word *design*, human intentions and plans take the front seat. While some properties of matter are welcome, too much recalcitrance interferes with the plans. Materials are used that specifically limit the insubordinate elements of matter. For example, as the humidity affects the properties of massive wood, the use of plywood, chipboard, or MDF—materials made to limit the movement of the fibers—can be of great help to take shortcuts. A cabinet drawer made from massive wood requires a lot of knowledge of the wood's properties, whereas the equivalent made from plywood less so. In the relationship between matter and materials, one can spot a common

---

[8] For a more detailed discussion, see Ingold (2013, 25–6, 44–5). For example, woodworker and studio furnituremaker James Krenov preferred the term *composing* to design, as making is reacting to the wood, in continuous reevaluation and improvisation, where the maker must remain open to wherever the wood takes the composer.

delineation between the fields of design and craft. Designers usually want less recalcitrance in their materials. Unpredictable matter is cumbersome when trying to align complex plans with industrial production, and designers often treat their materials as they treat their laborers. Predictable standards are needed.

On the other hand, craft practitioners can take another approach to their materials, aligning more with the feral properties of matter. With more experience and time, they can turn recalcitrant wood, such as twisted branches, into unique objects that bring out the best properties of that specific piece of material. To return to the example of the ball stuck in the tree, we can see a continuum between matter and material. As I work with my branch and break off the twigs to reach the ball, I step by step turn the recalcitrant matter into material, working along with my will to reach the ball. From being a piece of matter in alignment with the strivings of the tree (to life), I manipulate to design the branch into material to align with my intentions.

Working with matter deals with control: whose will that comes to the front. And to shape the world according to one's will is at the heart of magic. Thus, it is no surprise that there is a long tradition in connecting the practice of making to magic and trickery, or the cunning will of the craftsman manipulating things to change the course of events. Many ancient, as well as more recent, myths concern the creation of objects with magical powers, from magical weapons of gods, like Mjolnir, armors of heroes like Achilles and Beowulf, to objects such as wands, rings, grails, helskor, and seven-league boots, to cursed or poisoned gifts of the underworld. They are a ubiquitous element in religion and myth, in fantasy and sci-fi. The more recent histories of nationalism, modernism, progress, and entrepreneurship are full of similar mythical things, presented in history books and displayed as reified objects at design museums, each endowed with fantastical powers of progress or disruptive innovation.[9]

---

[9] There is also an affective grounding in sociomaterial objects that evokes the enchantment of making. The "homemade" signifies a certain form of

Like the historical narratives, the mythical practices of contemporary design are gendered and favor certain hands over others: heroic values over care, cultured over nomadic techniques, creation and violence over objects of domesticity and repair.[10] Being a profession that has historically been at the service of mass production, this also influences the foundational courses of design school, where techniques and workshop environments have traditionally been masculine and concern creation more than maintenance and restoration. The more holistic and civic perspectives of craft, which were central to the pedagogical ideas of *Sloyd* education of Uno Cygnaeus and Otto Salomon at the end of the nineteenth century, quickly turned subservient to the ideals of productivity, industriousness, and innovation.

Making is thus a process of handling matter and materials that are never neutral. It emerges from the intentions of the maker as well as institutional, societal, cultural, and economical designs. As much as it is grounded in matter, tools, and the workbench, the techniques of making instill matter with the more immaterial or even metaphysical properties of values and plans for use.

MAKING BETWEEN MATTER AND META

Making makes a claim to power: it suggests the designer can control and shape matter in ways that also reproduce control to users or clients. Making a garment gives the user the authority

connotation to material meaning, not yet alienated. It is not least captured by D. H. Lawrence in the poem "Things Men Have Made," first published in the American magazine *The Dial* in 1929:

> Things men have made with wakened hands, and put soft life into are awake through years with transferred touch, and go on glowing for long years. And for this reason, some old things are lovely warm still with the life of forgotten men who made them.

[10] For an extensive discussion on the cultures, virtues, and struggles over repair, see Spelman (2002).

to adjust body temperature and aesthetic expression. Making a spoon will help the user control the drinking of the soup, and designing it for mass production will help the client create and sell more spoons. This is a territory designers have dealt with over the past century.

As design takes on more complex issues, systems, and social tensions, the material matters of making seem further and further removed from the immediate task at hand. Experiences, services, and conflicts are not easily addressed with the standard tools of the workshop. The physical models seem far removed from, and even less real than, the urgent suffering under the shadows of the unjust distribution of agency across the world. Mind maps and diagrams seem more applicable to values, cultures, hyperobjects, wicked problems, and more-than-human entanglements. When going from being a maker to a change agent, it can be hard to find the suitable instruments in the tool shed to grasp visions, policies, systems, and strategies, or relationships such as poverty, subordination, empowerment, or liberation.

If we return to the ball stuck in the tree, we saw how the wild matter of the branch was turned into the material of the stick. With the stick we could reach up and poke down the ball. But we could also turn toward human activities to get the ball down, such as getting a bunch of people to shake the tree, or build a human pyramid to reach higher. This would require some basic organization. We may need to set a rhythm in order to shake the tree, or decide how the lighter person should stand on the shoulders of the stronger if they are to reach higher. Language and values get involved in the simple task of getting the ball down. Organizing these activities turns more abstract, or more meta, than poking down the ball with a stick. Meta seems to be *beyond* matter, as it gets us entangled in hierarchies, values, laws, and customs.

To deal with complex issues like these, designers have to go meta or draw out mental models, organizational diagrams, and flowcharts of decision hierarchies. They use conceptual tools to connect, draw, and give shape to these models. The meta seems disconnected from the limitations of matter. It concerns supply

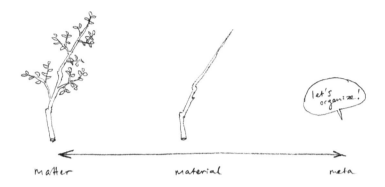

and demand, divisions of labor, global production chains, work culture, theories of change, and so on, all the many seemingly untouchable layers of intentions that are not only more abstract but also have their plans discussed and plotted higher up in organizational hierarchies.

This elevation of abstraction is nothing new but emerges from the classic Chain of Being, with the minerals at the bottom and the divine at the top of the hierarchy. With the heavy heritage of the Gnostics, it seems easy to separate the flawed matter of the workshop from the imperceptible, yet more critical, aether of meta. Matter is the object, artifact, product, or model. It is imperfect, unsustainable, and commodified, while the meta is the societal, cultural, political, and philosophical.[11] A similar division is also made in esotericism and occulture (and the planes of manifestation), where low magic (or magick) deals with the material properties of potions, and higher, or ceremonial, magic deals with astral projections, thought forms, and angels.

These historical hierarchies have implications when turning theory into physical models in the workshop. In working with meta, design is further and further detached from the

---

[11] Matter is tangible, grounded, but also deceitful, the thing the cunning Demiurge manipulates "with fraudulent dexterity" (Herzog 2006: 71) using the tools of the workshop, whereas to address the meta you need more discursive devices to make sensible the highest, unknowable God.

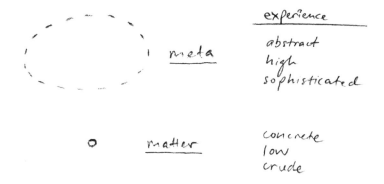

experience

abstract
high
sophisticated

meta

matter

concrete
low
crude

matters of making. The immediate situation of use, as tested by the workbench, does not seem to be enough. More layers of expertise and theoretical tools are needed to make sure the right questions are asked and the most appropriate method used to reach approximations that reside in future evaluations and data. Strategies and more elaborate plans of action are needed to engage a multitude of users, institutions, and policies. The goals are often vague and contested. It is a realm of design that is very far removed from the immediate situation of wanting to poke down a ball from a tree. The intellectual esteem and social impact are higher with meta than with matter, and so is the pay grade. When we all stand there, having built our human pyramid to reach up into the tree, simply poking down the ball with a stick becomes almost a form of cheating.

However, the meta of cultural values or organizations is not devoid of physical manifestations. It is an in-between sphere full of contested relations yet simultaneously stabilized through protocols, policies, and political arrangements. These arrangements form an unnoticed presence that enables its systemic workings, a cosmological aether of sorts. The types of relationships are the *dark matter* of culture.[12] Like

---

[12] Gregory Sholette (2010) seeks the missing masses of the art world and uses the term to put attention to the majority of ignored or dismissed artistic practices that uphold the cultural field, such as amateurs, street

its cosmic equivalent, it is an abundant yet nebulous systemic presence that stays in the shadows, scaffolds, and upholds a system's fundamental workings. Design strategist Dan Hill suggests dark matter is the unseen organizing matter behind a product, service, or artifact. It is the choreography of relationships, the unlit cosmos in which design exists. Hill continues:

> Dark matter is the substrate that produces. A particular BMW car is an outcome of the company's corporate culture, the legislative frameworks it works within, the business models it creates, the wider cultural habits it senses and shapes, the trade relationships, logistics and supply networks that reproduce it, the particular design philosophies that underpin its performance and possibilities, the path dependencies in the history of northern Europe, and so on. This is all dark matter; the car is the matter it produces. ... The dark matter of strategic designers is organizational culture, policy environments, market mechanisms, legislation, finance models and other incentives, governance structures, tradition and habits, local culture and national identity, the habitats, situations and events that decisions are produced within.[13]

For Hill, dark matter is the background presence that produces the tangible types of design we usually take for granted. It is the systemic mass within an organization that designers hardly perceive, yet that affects the outcome of every decision. Hill continues:

> For the strategic designer, the relationship between observable physical matter and the imperceptible dark matter

and subcultures, the noncommercial sector, the crypts and basements of culture's dwelling places, from which the institutional art world extracts its riches. Latour (1992) argues similarly for the missing masses, the nonhuman, that upholds society and social relations.
[13] Hill (2012: 82, 83).

is indeed symbiotic and essential as it may be to the cosmos. Manipulating one both enables and affects the other.[14]

Yet, from my perspective, I would like to accentuate how dark matter is bound to *matter*. While there are certainly occasions the dark matter stays as vague meta, as in informal agreements, an atmosphere in meetings, and so on, I want to put focus on how, in most cases, dark matter is *matter*. Dark matter is the physical arrangement of matter that manifests meta, that translates meta into societal effects. Hierarchies and values are made present in tweed suits, glass buildings, and office designs. Logistical networks and policies can be touched in standardized containers and loading docks. The importance of the speaker is manifested in the arrangement of the chairs in the room. Fences, doors, keys, and passports manifest boundaries circumscribed by laws and customs; these are things of matter that make meta real.

Don't think of matter and meta as opposites that by necessity exclude each other. They co-exist along a continuum of human intentions and organization. There is a long stretch of various mixtures and materials in between, where matter and meta reach into each other. While meta may in many ways be imperceptible, it is full of dark matter that arranges and makes social relations stable. The meta is made up of relationships made durable through material means. While the visions, goals, and culture of an organization may be abstract, shifting the perspective from the smallest to largest scales may reveal meta being housed in the dark matter of a headquarters building or expressed in organizational charts, white papers, reports, and policy documents; in excel sheets and internet protocols; processed and shipped over the height of loading docks and size of shopping carts; implemented in team-building merchandise and corner offices. While the meta may seem abstract, it is most often housed or reflected in matter.

[14] Ibid., 84, 85.

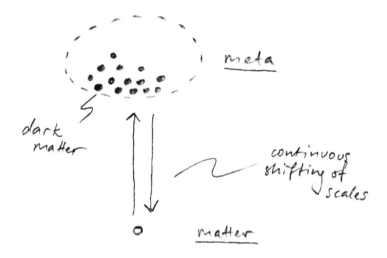

To "go meta" seems to be the fate of design when you start addressing societal or conceptual issues. After reading some serious social theory, it is hard to go back and build something. Even if students are encouraged to continuously switch between matter and meta, go up and down in scales, jump from the specific to the abstract and quickly back, it is usually the matter you deal with in the workshop that suffers in the long end. Not only is matter low, but it is also vapid and banal when held in contrast to meta. Paradoxically, the more designers take on a theoretical perspective of the "the material turn," studying how technologies and things have agency, the less inclined they seem to actually wield this thing-power. Indeed, it may seem absurd to turn to matter, hand tools, and the making or tweaking of small discreet objects when our planet is challenged by hyperobjects of the Anthropocene, Capitalocene, Plantationocene, Chthulucene, more-than-human politics, not to mention global, racial, economic, gendered injustices and violence, and so on. Everything urgent, global, and political seems to be meta. Yet all these meta events are made up of discreet parts, "knotted" together, by matter and small acts of making: discrete actions that reproduce the meta through the means of matter.[15]

As suggested in the opening assignment of the justice machine, I have over the past decade or so been trying to push my basic design studios to grapple and engage with a designerly relationship between matter and meta. The process I have been attempting to puzzle out aims to show how the meta is always present in matter. The meta-perspective can be manipulated in the workshop as much as in the diagrams; that meta is not necessarily "above" the matter. Meta can be concrete: sometimes as dispersed dark matter, but also highly present in simple everyday matter. You can touch the meta in the workshop.

As described in the introduction, I have invited students to build justice machines to experience how meta can be made present in matter. But we have also tested this perspective in making provocative products, corrupt chairs, political pockets, or cardboard contraptions that start revolutions. And most often, after a bit of confusion, concepts that appeared as construed got materialized into forms that spoke a language many of the young designers felt at home with, rendered in fabric, plywood, cardboard, and other typical materials from the school's workshop. In my experience, getting physical with meta-abstractions also helps level the field across the class, between the well-read and more practically inclined students, or between introverts and extroverts, and where perspectives and cultures come to speak in their own material dialects. And almost in all cases, students suggested that using the common tools of the workshop to take on abstract or theoretical issues helped making the meta more concrete. Indeed, cutting and gluing some plywood is always rewarding after a hard day of deterritorialization.

---

[15] I like Kim Stanley Robinson's (2012) description of this time "The Dithering," as a state of indecisive, seemingly random, agitation. This uncertainty of meta manifests in each little bit or matter, dithering and distributed unevenly, and with different intensity, yet these parts are everywhere.

2   State Metaxu

In 2008, I attended a panel on design at the European Social Forum in Malmo. The overall theme of the forum was "Another World Is Possible," and I was there to discuss the role design could play in demonstrations or protests, and how this could help make other worlds possible. It became a lively discussion about all kinds of possible worlds and if designers have the means and interests to make such worlds possible or not. Some designers thought they could fix anything with the right thinking. Others were more skeptical: in the end, isn't design, per definition, a pawn to the status quo? I spoke at length with a protester, and we didn't agree on everything. But I left the arguments with some very powerful perspectives on ways to think and work with design.

One thing that stood out to me was how the protester in a very animated spirit argued that what was so powerful about street demonstrations was that one could, at the moment of confrontation with the riot shields of the police, actually "touch power." When pushing against the plastic barrier, intangible state decrees became palpable. As much as it was an idealist enterprise in confronting the police for a cause he considered just, the protester argued that the confrontation made the political contestation between visions very real. The boundaries between the status quo and a new possible world were made physical, and the obstacle that held the vision of the future back was a riot shield. The challenge for design, the protester posited, was to make the experience of constructing alternatives as real as the riot shield while also making sure this alternative was pushing against the government's status quo.

There are many types of interfaces between the people and their government. But it is only through a handful of these that citizens can interact with the functionings of the state. The government speaks through laws, media, or decrees, and citizens respond through forms, surveys, and votes. The riot shield is another interface of the state, a more physical and intensive embodiment. The shield manifests how design stands in relation to the state's tangible material power and how, typically, these aspects are designed to disappear from our senses to blend into everyday habits or unquestioned obedience. With this transparent plastic and impact-proof separator between them, two opposing subjects come face to face. The state representative operates from one side. The other side is for the unruly public. Most people don't encounter this interface until the day they are the ones who are considered disorderly.

The fence, the cell wall, the riot shield: these are surfaces that act as membranes of power. They give shape to the state. It is matter that makes the abstract meta of statehood touch and align physical bodies. The state often remains abstract in design briefs. It acts in the background. Yet, on the material plane of the riot shield, the state appears in a form highly relatable to the making of the workbench. It is an infrastructure of control and domination that is accessible with the average hand tools of the workshop. When we place it on the workbench, the state can be touched and examined like an artifact of design, easily detectable to the senses.

As the discussant pointed out, the opposition is no longer abstract in the clash with that rigid plastic shield. State order is felt on the skin, in opposing hands pushing the riot shield in two incompatible directions: on one side a protester, and on the other a police officer. Compared to the stable matter of a wall, fence, or barbed wire, the shield is caught in the dynamics between two bodies. Both parts push the transparent but hard surface of the shield as a boundary between two opposing organizations of meta. On one side, "Law and Order." On the other, "Anarchy." State regulation versus disruptive and recalcitrant civics. The meta of cosmos versus chaos. And the boundary is, in this case, made from 4-mm-thick transparent polycarbonate plastic.[1]

METAXU

Whose order, whose law, we may ask? And how does this order manifest itself? In the case of the shield, it is a designed artifact made for precisely this occasion. The shield shapes users toward particular possibilities and paths of action: the officer on

---

[1] As part of many direct-action movements, the dichotomy between the opposing sides of a wall or fence is an essential part of visioning as much as practicing nonviolent forms of togetherness, in opposition to the violence on the other side. This can be exemplified not least in the Greenham Common Women's Peace Camp throughout the 1980s and 1990s, an example that also used to contrast the opposition between the military–industrial–scientific complex versus the domestic and caring spheres, to explicitly use care and motherhood to challenge the violent purpose of the base (Rose 1983). Cook and Kirk (1983: 5) note:

> Greenham Common women's peace camp has existed now [June 1983] for 21 months, maintaining an unbroken presence outside the air base, despite two bad winters and continual harassment by the authorities [the camp would last uninterruptedly for 19 years, disbanded in 2000]. The ideas and vitality exemplified by the peace camp are in dramatic contrast to the bleakness and dreadful purpose of the base-two opposing value systems right next to one another but on opposite sides of the fence. The peace camp is a remarkable manifestation of women's determination and vision, an inspiration to many thousands of people in this country and abroad. As well as being around-the-clock protest against cruise missiles, it is also a resource—a women's space in which to try to live our ideals of feminism and nonviolence, a focus for information and ideas, a meeting place, and a vital context for women to express their beliefs and feelings.

one side, the protester on the other. In line with Sara Ahmed's suggestion that objects always come with specific *orientations* that align the interactions between matter and subject, making certain actions find themselves "in place," the shield separates two arguing sides across a hard but mobile plastic divide, an individual screen, but also a portable wall.[2]

On the level of the riot shield, the state appears in resonance with Simone Weil's concept of "metaxu," a surface in between that is dividing while also uniting. To Weil, metaxu is a barrier that draws together, such as:

> Two prisoners whose cells adjoin communicate with each other by knocking on the wall. The wall is the thing which separates them, but it is also their means of communication … every separation is a link.[3]

In the riot shield, as in the prison cell walls, metaxu is material. The surface stops bodies from touching and makes them inseparable: the membrane touches and unites opposing sides. *The shield is a meta membrane made from matter.* The surface guides and aligns behaviors, pushes bodies, and orients possibilities. Like the cell, the shield is not neutral; it embodies an asymmetry. The warden has the key. The prisoner does not. The riot shield has handles on one side and is smooth on the other. It is made to be operated from the police officer's side and pushed against the protester on the other. By design, it limits agency from one end but enables it from the other. These

---

[2] Ahmed (2010: 235). In Langdon Winner's famous argument, artifacts enact special forms of politics through their "arrangements of power and authority in human associations as well as the activities that take place within those arrangements" (1980: 123). Along similar lines, Madelaine Akrich (1992: 208) argues objects have certain designated "scripts," which she defines, "like a film script, [by which] technical objects define a framework of action together with the actors and the space in which they are supposed to act."

[3] Weil (2002: 145). Weil's use of metaxu (μεταξύ—"intermediary" or "in between") is spiritual as much as physical, used to unpack the relationship between god and humans and also to notice a Platonic understanding of a betweenness that is also a "distance between the necessary and the good."

are material orientations that embody the meta. In its use, the shield is an artifact that physically manifests what Raymond Geuss argues is the foundational political question: *who does what to whom for whose benefit?*[4]

Geuss's political question brings together four distinct variables; (1) Who? (2) What? (3) To whom? (4) For whose benefit? It is a valuable tool for unpacking the political contestations around matter, or how design distributes agency across populations. As Geuss states, "To think politically is to think about agency, power, and interests, and the relations among these." Yet the course of action and use of agency must also relate to embodied as well as perceived powers, to the *ability* to do, that is, "who *could* do what to whom for whose benefit," that is, also taking incitement and threat of enforcement into account. When engaging with making, the *could* point to the *capacity* of matter to act in alignment with political power, affecting or forcing itself upon bodies to execute the ability/threat. That is, if the foundational political question of Geuss may first seem abstract, it can help us trace how matter aligns and enforces the political relations at work in creating obedience and servitude.

The riot shield is a device that divides up the political space. While made from widely available plastic, a material many designers are accustomed to, a primitive object such as a riot shield exposes an essential lesson for designers: matter is drawn into trouble. Matter interfaces the state and does so more intensely in some instances than in others. State meta is not an abstract container but takes physical shape. It will bash against your body if you disagree with its designations.

The transparent plastic of the riot shield also exposes how we encounter state meta. The state is not big or located in the capital. It is small and everywhere, unevenly distributed, and of varying intensity. You can bang your hand against it. But you can also manipulate it with your average hand tools. Everywhere this conflict is designed. Sometimes its matter overshadows

---

[4] Geuss (2008: 25–7).

human subjects, like in a border wall, a prison, in airports, and highway viaducts. But most often, it is small, and we come in touch with it by mere habit: invisible and thus unnoticed, yet the way it aligns us with government designations is very tangible.

The riot shield is a powerful artifact that distributes agency, allowing agency from one side through the handles while refusing access on the other with its smooth surface. It *amplifies* agency on one side while *displacing* agency on the other. To understand governmental distributions of agency from this perspective means to seek the mechanisms that facilitate the reproduction of subordination and obedience among the interactions between people and matter. These designs are all the small everyday components that contribute in a material way to what Foucault calls the "dispositive" or "apparatus" of discipline and control.[5] Here, the shield forms the hard interface of the state apparatus. It acts with the muscle power of the officer while also with material means—in this case, explicitly *in the hands* of a state representative.

But pushing a shield only provides so many dimensions of action, even if some ju-jitsu can reorient and respond to the opposing forces in dynamic ways. On the other hand, making may tune and manipulate the force of the membrane between matter and meta differently. New dimensions and interfaces may open; new connections and forces be enacted. When finding the right metaxu with the state, making can affect how we interact with political systems. But in the clash, we may also run into trouble.

STATE SPACE–STATE MATTER

It is not only the police using shields that appear at demonstrations, but similar props have become ubiquitous

---

[5] For a longer discussion on these definitions, see Agamben (2009) and Bussoloni (2010).

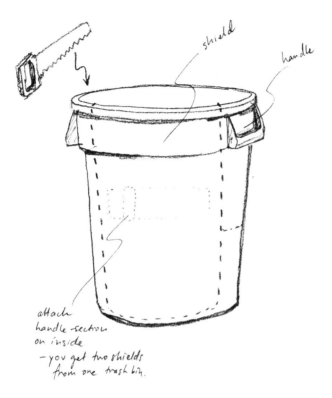

shield

handle

attach
handle section
on inside
– you get two shields
from one trash bin.

riot gear among many protesters too. Homemade shields make practical Roman-looking props for the right-wing marchers, giving connotations to the shield and sword of patriotism. The improvised and rough-looking equivalents can speak of the grassroots spontaneity of the "99 percent." When I first saw improvised riot shields from cut-apart plastic trash bins, I thought it was a fascinating twist of public infrastructure. Cutting a trash can into half and attaching a handle with zip ties and duct tape was not only a smart repurposing of materials, making a light, sturdy shield from a material available everywhere, it was also a material repurposing of one type of barely visible state infrastructure, our waste management systems, into DIY riot gear. It was a savvy prop used to raise an issue that has also been invisible and handled like low and insignificant.

A cut-apart trash bin with improvised handles becomes a shield for street protesters. It is a fascinating twist of how matter and primitive making are employed in the political life of the city.

Whereas riot shields make conflict apparent, it can be hard to find the places to touch and intervene into the meta with primitive making. The trouble with manipulating meta is that it appears in most cases intangible, and even its dark matter slides into the background of our attention. It is hard to find the places where the meta is most intensely present in matter, and where it can effectively be gripped and tuned. Yet messing with the dark matter in instances where it is firmly bound to the meta means that the practice of making comes into proximity to and in friction with the meta. This is also when making starts running into trouble, when making starts interfering with the dark matter backed up by the state.

While a discussion of politics cannot but deal with the state, the purpose of this book is not to dive into the details or debate around the operations of administration, policy, or state power. But I will suggest a framework through which the state is seen, touched, and confronted through everyday matter. In these instances, manipulation and making clash with the official or state-designated distribution of interfaces between people and state functions. This happens primarily in the functions of sorting, in what Scott calls "state space," where the state makes its presence known, governs, appropriates, and assigns an order to populations and practices, where

> the modern state, through its officials, attempts with varying success to create a terrain and a population with precisely those standardized characteristics that will be easiest to monitor, count, assess and manage. The utopian, immanent and continually frustrated goal of the modern state is to reduce the chaotic, disorderly, constantly changing social

reality beneath it to something more closely resembling the administrative grid of its observation.[6]

Scott's concept of "state space" signifies the territories where the state manages to project its power: in the range of the cannons from the fort, the roads across which the taxman and his mercenaries travel, the space of logistics where infrastructure supports troops, and so on.

Just like state space is not black/white, it is not evenly distributed, but fluctuates with the seasons, depends on governmental intrigues and the servitude or unruliness of the domesticated populations. Some interests favor more state presence in certain areas and services, while others want its reconfiguration; it is a matter of endless political debate.

For makers, state space is of interest, as the state *takes place* in matter. In proximity to state space, we could find the dispersal of *state matter*. Here, some matter manifests the meta-organization of the state more intensely than others, for example, in borders and barbed wire, weapons and bullets, tax forms and ledgers, money and registers, in buildings like castles, courts, parliaments, and prisons. Through the lens of the state, matter arranges subjects into domestication and *state being*, making participatory subordination tangible, symbiotic, and more permanent.[7]

However, the power of the state is not total, but instead quite fragile. It is unevenly distributed, of various intensity and in uncertain flux, continuously contested from below and torn between rivaling ambitions, fractions, parties, and institutions. Adversarial states undermine their opponents, while large

---

[6] Scott (1998: 81–2). For a longer discussion on "state space" as zones of governance, extraction, and appropriation, see Scott (2009). Note that the distribution of state space is uneven and in continuous negotiation; some spaces may have too much or little state presence depending on these negotiations (e.g., in infrastructure, maintenance, services, policing); there is always some power at work; the question is how it is negotiated.

[7] Following DeLanda (1997), some matter is high-density statehood, and in these instances, we encounter the *crystallization of statehood*.

corporations command global networks of public and private industries and institutions. These corporations wield power through lobbying, but even more so through the economic resources of investments and labor, which in turn affects the decisions of governments. It is in the power of corporations to reward loyalty, on the one hand, or impose material hardship on the economy, on the other, undermining the rulings of governments. However, on different scales, traditions, communities, and informal networks play just as important roles in the running of everyday life. So the state's role should not be seen as a totalizing entity, and neither should it be held as the perpetual adversary to freedom.

Yet, for the type of design activism that will be further examined here, the state is an essential factor. It is the entity that draws up and enforces the boundaries of legal versus illegal practices. It is also the entity many activist propositions stand in conflict with, through policies and legal frameworks. The state is a meta-organization with abstract functions attempting to align subjects to its purpose. In state space, societal relationships of domination and subjugation are made more permanent and become present in extractive practices, structural hierarchies, and truth regimes. These, in alliance with mechanisms of their enforcement, manifest and cement relationships that regulate the freedoms and flourishings of subjects. Specifically, the state facilitates and also sets boundaries around the accessibility and distribution of matter, materials, goods, commodities, as well as practices of making; how subjects are encouraged or discouraged to practice and make things in specific contexts and situations. As elaborated on by Elaine Scarry, practices of making and unmaking shape the foundation of how conceptions of social organization and justice become manifest in our world. As Scarry posits, "An understanding of political justice may require that we first arrive at an understanding of making and unmaking."[8] To use Scarry's concepts, the two sides clash between visions and practices of *making* and *unmaking*

---

[8] As Scarry (1985: 279) points out, medicine and law, health and torture are interfaces between bodies and the state, regulated as separate while always

contrasting worlds, and often the boundary is drawn between the state and the body, in institutional frameworks that guide legal makings versus illegal makings, what are just interventions into bodies (medicine) and what are unjust interventions (torture).

The purpose here is not to moralize the state, to say that it is good or bad. The properties of the state are unevenly distributed. They manifest in various levels of intensity, and it is crucial not to forget that the state is very often a dominant force in everyday life. I may live in a way or in a place where I encounter very little of the state, yet it can ultimately demand and enforce citizens to kill others and also prepare them to die themselves. It is the state that has the power to invite or evict people from its territory and create and execute policies that affect most of the subjects within and beyond its boundaries. Thus, somehow addressing the state is necessary, and also to engage in the struggle over the control over its operational resources—perhaps even challenge the parliament or politicians to address an injustice or a current issue at hand. A thousand paths and flowers may bloom, but their distribution and strategic position in relation to the state makes a huge difference. The player who captures the state, or sets up a structure that rivals the state, has a potent tool at hand. Ignoring it can be fatal.

With its manifestations, the state appears to us a container, framed by border walls, and what is within is our shared society. The capital is the center, and from here, from buildings locked to most people, the state authority speaks its decrees. It is also here people look for orders to be given and where they bring grievances and petitions. If people want change, they try to change things in the capital since that is where power resides and the formal interfaces open up.

This perspective of the state also affects when designers engage with meta. If a designer is to address the meta, one seeks to influence it in certain places: in the parliament, the ministries of politicians, judges, state bureaucrats, lobby groups, and

also flowing into each other. They are "institutional elaborations of body and state" (42).

NGOs. This is where power emanates from, where policies are made, opposition is defined, and news are broadcast from. If protesters want change, they go out on the streets, turn toward the capital, and address the authorities: "Listen politicians, we want change!"

The process often called "modernization" produces a symbiotic relationship between the state and its subjects, the government and the governed. The elements of statehood infuse themselves into the notion of continuity and stability; it is in names, identities, bank accounts, and houses, dispersed yet made up of matter. Its meta crystallizes in ledgers, sewers, and computer systems, inconsistent yet present in matter *where it matters* to uphold state space. Value and boundaries, hierarchies and subjecthood are translated into identity and housing, sleeping and eating, work and leisure. This, in turn, is manifested in matter through money and keys, water and sewage pipes, roads and bridges, electricity cables, and appliances.[9]

Artifacts, technologies, and infrastructure make social relationships and distributions of agency more permanent, to the degree they and the errands they run for the state seem to disappear. Social scientists have adopted this perspective to challenge human-centeredness and instead account for the "missing masses" that also make up the society, while it is "embedded" into social life, sunk to disappear into technologies, structures, and social arrangements. Historically, infrastructure is instrumental in bringing about the modern world through technical systems.[10] For example, Jo Guldi underscores how the *rule* of law is accompanied by infrastructure as plain and

---

[9]   Thrift (2004) suggests everyday infrastructure is our "epistemic wallpaper." It is just there, but we barely recognize it. As Larkin (2013) posits, the politics of infrastructure resides exactly in its invisibility.

[10] Latour (1992) searches the "missing masses" in social inquiry, while Star (1999) points out how matter is "embedded" into guiding social arrangements. Infrastructure is not permanent but requires activation and maintenance to ensure the stability of organization over time, fighting against constant entropic decay, yet noticing how such work is unevenly distributed and deliberately foreclosed (Graham and Thrift 2007).

simple, yet essential, as the *road* of law. Whereas premodern states were dependent on fluctuating routes of trade, carrying commerce, stories, and religion, but also precarious victims of migration, disease, and rebellion, the modern state is built on the construction, control, and maintenance of roads. The creation of the modern state goes hand in hand with the construction of centralized infrastructure systems to smoothen logistics that serve the flows of matter, energy, and agency of control. As Guldi posits, "Modern governments in developed nations have mediated the relationship between individuals and infrastructure technology for so long that the role of the state in designing ports, sidewalks, and bus lines is nowadays taken for granted."[11] This is also why much political activism happens along, on, or in roads: the struggle is in the street, in the public, in the logistic nodes, and underneath the asphalt, the beach.[12]

STATE META IN THE MATTER

Yet like the possible sandcastles under the street paving, we seldom see the meta under the surface of matter. The meta of the state manifests in regulations and constructions, in the standards of zoning, codes, laws, schemes, copyrights, libel, and tort, which give material as well as immaterial shape to the speeds, directions, and momentum of movements of matter, energy, information, and agency. The forms of infrastructure affect surveillance, administration, and projection of power, all meta mechanisms for centralized government "colonizing at home."[13]

---

[11] Guldi (2012: 4).
[12] Also opposition to certain state designations blend into the background in a similar way that state does. What is "countercultural" becomes everyday, without necessarily being co-opted: a food co-op, a voluntary community, an alternative power grid, they all become simply ways of living that seldom come into conflict with the dominant alignment of collective behaviors.
[13] Guldi (2012: 79).

The creation of infrastructure is ridden by ideological struggles, even if they seldom become apparent when utilizing such systems. For example, idealists may see road construction as a paved path toward increased commerce and communication, building toward a peaceful coexistence between previously isolated and rivaling nations and clans. Transport produces codependence and peace. The same idealism echoes today in the discourse around broadband, universal internet access, and infrastructure set up to facilitate free movement of goods and people. Simultaneously, infrastructure also increases competition and rivalry between social groups and regions, with very diverse interests in the nation competing for its construction, use, and maintenance. In contrast, other interests try to block it and divert its flows in efforts to administer and control rivals and populations. Infrastructure and self-determination are intrinsically entwined.[14]

The crystallization and dispersion of the meta of statehood through dark matter has implications for making practices in general, and especially when thinking about political activism. If one is to address or interfere with meta in a hands-on manner, it is crucial to find out how it manifests power asymmetries, smooths out resistance, and makes permanent arrangements of control. In such cases, the meta resides in the designation of agency within the commonplace: the meta is contained within matter.

It may be easy to grasp how the electric power grid, highways, servers, or subway or railway systems may be essential components of a state, and that each of them has what political scientist Jane Bennett calls "thing power."[15] But state arrangements are present in smaller, more dispersed,

---

[14] Guldi (2012: 22) points to how historical infrastructure projects in the United Kingdom was an essential part in systems of centralized control:

> That competition did not make a more social or peaceful nation. Rather, political struggles created a world where the rich policed the poor, where landowners smarted against the powers of the state, and where the economic success of a poor region like Scotland could collapse the moment its lobby for infrastructure weakened.

[15] Bennett (2004).

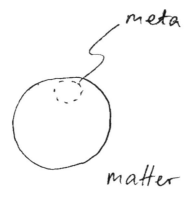

and quotidian objects. State negotiations of control present themselves in food containers, insurance forms, power plugs, service elevators, plastic bags, and in your cup of coffee. They all intend to align the user's agency with its designated use. It may be easy to think of the meta as mostly shaping matter in the form of patents, copyrights, and regulations, and in objects that we closely associate with state power and violence; in the ditches and gallows, barbed wire and spikes, uniforms, and bombs, prison keys and passports. But it is also present in the stamp on your birth certificate, in the "both parents must sign" permission slip, in the categories on your driver's license, in the boot that locks your wheel to immobilize your car, in the technocratic language on the form even a native speaker struggles to understand, in the fine print at the bottom of your court documents, in the fine lines that make up the dead ruler's face on the bills you have to hand over to pay for your parking fine. Some of this matter acts on you in more symbolic than physical ways, yet they all distribute and align agency, sort and cement decisions, and intensify the affective incarnation of something as meta as the state. The meta is in the matter; things are designed that way.[16]

---

[16] Mike Monteiro (2019) offers an angry and entertaining rant about the lack of ethics in design and the failures of education to critically engage with the many damages design is responsible for. The basic premise is that designers

Even if matter makes arrangements more stable and permanent, they are also in continuous disintegration. Decay and entropy are natural processes that also affect state matter. This makes material aspects unstable and in constant renegotiation with social conflict. What should be maintained, serviced, and repaired? It is easy to recognize how new products rearrange social relationships, but so do various forms of maintenance as it cements certain positions and interests. Care and repair are not necessarily neutral and virtuous but also caught in a conflict between the state-aligned designations in matter and the governed subject.

The meta in the matter can also disintegrate. Borders that were once contended can lose their intensity and turn insignificant. Old coins can be left useless for transactions, and the barbwire let to rust. State processes put their attention elsewhere, and the old arrangements are not as urgent.

Buckminster Fuller famously argues that you never change things by fighting the existing reality; to change something, we must build a new model that makes the existing one obsolete. While it may be easy to build new things, the tricky part is the second part of the sentence—how to make "the existing model obsolete." Here, the making I am trying to articulate comes in the *active displacement* of an old reality, an unjust arrangement, to make it obsolete. It is a rearrangement of matter that can mobilize behaviors that challenge and displace existing distributions of power.

A homemade riot shield, made from a trash can, does not displace the power of the professional plastic shield, yet it does more than merely shift perspectives. It redistributes agency along the contested boundary between parts, the police, and protesters. It does not necessarily escalate the conflict by weaponizing the contested border, yet it clearly sets agencies and interests against each other.

Two riot shields set against each other do not reveal any new possibilities, while they effectively *make present* that in

created or at least contributed essentially to the mess we are in: it was designed that way.

some instances reality is down to a zero-sum game. However, other forms of primitive making offer alternative forms of living, *remaking* the world. This can be a more effective way to renegotiate arrangements or displace state meta from matter. In such cases, the process of making sets out to make the riot shields obsolete in a way that deescalates or even short-circuits conflict, and this is what we should explore more. There can be stealthy ways to suggest and make alternative forms of living possible while probing to find leverage points to make such arrangements as powerful as those of the status quo. In such cases, primitive making does not seek conflict but probes the holes of the membrane to suggest ways in which the old model can become obsolete. It is our task ahead to set out to find such ways.

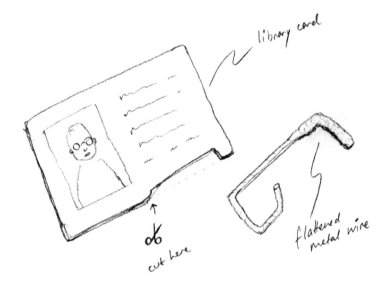

library card

cut here

flattened metal wire

3   Making Matters

In high school, my friends and I faced something we felt was unfair. In the chilling winter, the teachers encouraged us to be outside in the fresh air for the breaks between classes and locked the classrooms to ensure we were not staying inside. The smokers occupied the area by the doors that had a small roof, and their territory was staked out with a coolness that was not inviting to awkward seventh graders like me. This meant only very few had access to the dry spots at the schoolyard, which were very coveted on south Sweden's cold and damp west coast.

The challenge was on; there must be ways to open the classrooms and sneak back in. Blocking the latch bolt with a piece of tape could stop the door from locking if the departing teacher didn't look twice when leaving the classroom. But it was an imperfect technique. Some of us tried to figure out how to open the latch. We found that the spring-loaded latch bolt in the lock could be manipulated from the outside by cutting a rectangular slot in our thin plastic library card, sliding the card in between the door and the frame, and pulling back the latch bolt. But often, the plastic was too flimsy to pull the latch out of the strike hole in the door frame. However, in shop class, new techniques quickly spread and I managed to make a simple improved device by cutting a piece of wire from a metal hanger, bending it into a hook, and then hammering it flat on the anvil. This slightly refined instrument proved to be a much more successful design. Finally, the uncool nonsmokers had a dry space to hide. Left in the cold rain, we felt we had been treated unfairly, and we now had access to a primitive justice machine.

But the success was short-lived. It was easier to manipulate the lock than the observing eyes of the teachers. They quickly got suspicious if we failed to leave the classroom before the next class and got caught inside. We tried to say the previous teacher had forgotten to lock the door. But if the same teacher came back who had left the classroom locked, he or she was not convinced. The plan started to falter. Too late, we realized the need to plan and coordinate what times and classrooms to open to avoid detection. Instead, soon enough, a decree from the administration instructed the teachers to also lock the deadbolt when leaving the classrooms, and we were once again left out to shudder in the rain.

But for a while, a renewed interest in shop class united my classmates and me. A practical world opened beyond the butter knives and birdhouses we had to carve and build as part of the traditional *Sloyd* curriculum, the Scandinavian system of handicraft-based education. After having finished what was expected from class curriculum, the teacher could let us do some cool things, like cutting out "ninja stars" from sheet metal, or making throwing knives (disguised as "letter openers"), or turning a classic baseball bat. But the simple little hook for manipulating the lock captured our imagination of what useful things could be made in class. It was beyond our reach to address the meta of school schedules or changing the Nordic hard-spirited culture that a bit of cold does you good, so it was the material works that opened the passage inside. The skills from the shop class proved practically useful in ways no other subject in school did.

There were several lessons learned from the simple flat metal hook. A fundamental anti-authoritarian spirit can help you stay dry. Being clever with your hands can get you respect from the cool crew. And direct action gets the goods.

But there is also a very material level of understanding the lessons learned. There is immense power in the lived experience of how a massive and heavy door, inaccessible to the force of a body, has such minimal surface and mechanism to shut it closed. Finding its weak spot and producing a primitive tool to manipulate it seemed mind-blowing. When design theorist Vilem Flusser argues the lever is the most primitive yet powerful design, I always think back on my primitive flat wire hook. To me it was a lever. Primitive making can be a practical attitude, a way to be free.

Means and ends are close in primitive making. Complexity is reduced and made tangible. I can find a similar fascination when encountering videos online on repairing things, or using primitive technologies, or homesteaders showing how to build tiny homes on a budget.

Primitive making reduces mediation. It unlearns delegation and, in many cases, even consumerism. It is where design meets the immediate gratification of direct action.

MAKING LEVERAGE

But what my friends and I dearly missed in our seventh-grade door-hacking was a bit of *strategic thinking*. Planning ahead was not really our thing. If you had told me then, I would just have said it sound complicated. It would also have disconnected us from the immediacy of our actions. But the strategic thinking I am after here is plainly about seeing connections and placing action at the right time and place, and with appropriate effort. Or simply get a bit of overview and think a few steps ahead. If we had been a bit more strategic in our making of the hooks, applying the technique with moderation and on the rainy and cold days where it mattered most, rather than in a scattered manner, our aims would have been better realized. But we were too immersed in our immediate results, a thrill common in the process of making, and got caught far too soon.

Being absorbed by the magic of making does not necessarily exclude a strategic overview of the situation. We could have used our time by the anvil to not only bend and flatten the wire but also plan our next moves in the upcoming heist for a warm classroom. We should have done a bit more *strategic making*—merging making with some strategic planning. Or perhaps a bit wordier, a primitive making that manipulates matter at the right strategic time and context for the intended leverage. On a more practical level, strategic making takes a step back to see systemic connections and plan a few steps ahead while employing its material means as a strategic lever. It is about making the simplest thing to lever the intended results with foresight, to open the door at the right time, in the right context, to the right participants (and to my seventh-grade self; not too often, or teachers will be alarmed).

As we are surrounded by all kinds of matter, finding the right place is at the heart of strategic making. As mentioned before, the meta is not evenly dispersed but rendered denser in certain spots and situations. In the case above, we made a tool to move the latch bolt, not the handle, the door itself, or the hinges. Strategic making is manipulating matter to address the meta, and it can be practiced with primitive tools. Through the dark matter (the door, lock, latch bolt), meta (school culture of recess) becomes tangible in our everyday and thus accessible to the tools of the workshop (coat hanger turned into wire hook).

While getting into a classroom is a pretty straightforward task, designers often deal with more complicated and multifaceted issues. No matter what you create, it quickly gets entangled in tensions around distribution chains, social issues, labor practices, and much more. As is typical, the meta remains complex and intangible, and it seems intuitive to think of the meta as bigger than the manifestation of matter. The meta appears higher, as ideas are general and global, whereas matter, manifestations, and arrangements remain local and lowly. Finding a leverage point is hard enough, like balancing a pencil on one's finger, so it is undoubtedly puzzling with more complex and entangled concerns.

Environmental systems thinker Donella Meadows famously argues that to find leverage for change, one must think strategically about at what points to intervene in systems. Meadows stresses that "leverage points are points of power," and at these points, a shift can produce big ripples of change throughout a whole system.[1] For a designer, this is good news; as Flusser argues, making levers is the backbone of our trade. But what kind of levers should we make, and where should they be?

In Meadows's line of thought, intervening at the level of parameters (such as standards, taxes, materials) has a low impact factor. The more abstract levels of design (affecting incentives, values, and goals) produce deeper and more systemic change. For increasing effectiveness, one has to go for the "deeper" leverage points. To reform a system, one should modify rules and information flows, change the incentives and organizational form rather than the "shallow" points of products and objects that designers traditionally have worked on. It is a compelling and intuitive model; if you try to turn a system, tweaking form and materials only gets you so far, whereas if you change the intention and course of the system, the whole ship can turn around. When applying Meadows's advice to design practice, it guides any serious attempt of change toward the levels of meta, yet it leaves out the tangible matter of the lower world. The redesign of products, objects, or tools can only affect local parameters and instances. Thinking of Meadows's model as a seesaw makes the argument clearer: put your weight at the higher end of the lever, and your efforts can move the whole system.

It is easy to conclude that Meadows's model focuses on the far end of the lever. The seesaw is such a powerful mental model you can feel its power balance. Find ways to push the mental models, goals, incentives, and overall paradigm. As a designer, this means turning toward the meta. If you cannot go for policy papers, workflows, trade negotiations, committees, you must shape the mental tools that shape these in turn: you design new cultural concepts, speculate,

---

[1] Meadows (1999: 1).

PLACES TO INTERVENE IN SYSTEMS

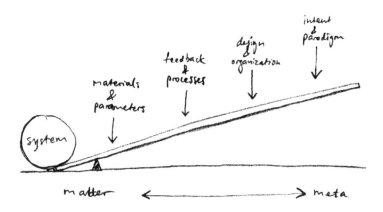

create visions and fantasies—make another future possible to imagine. And as Meadows's model makes clear, the best way to do so is to work on the meta. Yet, with this perspective, the shaping of matter seems insignificant and almost foolish. If goals, concepts, incentives, values, and visions must change, then the workshop is just very far removed from where the real action is.

Taking one example, thinking of trying to manage carbon capitalism and climate change through household composting is hopeless. To "be the change" on an individual level, as an atomized part of a system, can only create a very local impact on matter and parameters. Even if my action is spread across social media and thousands start modeling their behavior on this instance, the movement toward the goal is still only taking place in a multitude of dispersed local instances. Isolated, it fails to mobilize broader affect that challenges the meta issue (the complex knot of pollution, capitalism, colonialism, mass extinction, and so much more).

FINDING MATERIAL LEVERAGE

Even if intuitively powerful, I would argue this is a limited understanding of Meadows's model. I would suggest complementing it by addressing the forces between material, organizational, and cultural spheres—or that, in many instances, the different positions on the lever are interconnected to offer strategic points at which to intervene. Finding such strategic places affects how the leverage points are distributed and at what locale. Intervening into matter at a strategic point can add more weight to the lever.

Let's just think of an example: a treehouse. The kids may have a treehouse in the garden or the local woods, but there is a big difference between this one and the treehouse of an anti-logging campaign of environmentalist civil disobedience. Structurally they may look similar, but their framing, place, and intention differ vastly. The anti-logging activists make a treehouse with strategic intent: increasing the force of the action by using the activist's body as a tool (or the body's vulnerability as a "weight" on the lever). The protester's body is used to embody an argument, showing determination, while also being an obstacle for the loggers. With the treehouse, the body forms an assemblage together with other tools: tarps, harnesses, ropes, buckets, food, and a support network of fellow activists in affinity groups that support the protesters up in the treehouse.[2] But not least, the activists have not built their treehouse in just any tree. Their treehouse is probably built on a tree chosen from a strategic perspective—a tree that is occupied because the matter of the action is tightly bound

[2] Treesitting has a long history but became a much-publicized form of activism in "Timber Wars" of the 1980s and 1990s in the US Pacific Northwest, especially around the actions of Earth First! against large logging corporations, also creating rifts between proponents of ecosabotage and "monkeywrenching" (Abbey 1975; Foreman and Haywood 1987) versus other forms of activism (Bari 1994). As with other forms of civil disobedience, activists put their bodies on the line as a barrier against their opponent's agency, yet in 1998, David Chain, an Earth First! protester, was killed when loggers felled a tree on him.

to the meta: a highly visible tree or of considerable age? An endangered species? A tree at a topographic bottleneck that controls access to other groves?

The choice of which tree to occupy, the auxiliary materials, and the making practices of the action; they all become a series of strategic decisions made to shape the meta. The mobilization of matter is used as leverage to move the meta. One of the most famous tree-sitting actions in recent decades has been that of Julia Butterfly Hill, who maintained her vigil in a 55-meter-tall, roughly 1,500-year-old California redwood tree named Luna for 738 days, from December 10, 1997, to December 18, 1999.[3] In a case like this, the material tree platform in Luna is an epicenter for several layers of nonconformity and conflict as the affects of the protests engage with extractive economies, logging corporations, environmental regulations and laws, media broadcasts, and public opinion, and not least emotions and moods, as part of shaping what Noortje Marres calls "material publics."[4]

Mobilizing matter is central when it comes to *making that affects the meta*—that the manipulation of a seemingly minor component can ground and escalate emergent strategies. Whereas much design addressing the meta, in strategy, policy, and social projects, emphasizes coherent cooperation, organization, and impact, a focus on matter can reveal the infrapolitics of everyday rupture or boundary objects that help displace obedience. It is the "politics of small things."[5] Struggle that emerges in correspondence with the material protocols of local assemblages acts indirectly and looks very different than

---

[3] Hill (2000). Acts of environmental civil disobedience, such as treesitting against logging corporations, activate several ecological levels of meta and contradict capitalism, communism, patriarchy, and social hierarchies towards what environmental activist Judi Bari (1997) calls "revolutionary biocentrism."

[4] Marres (2012).

[5] Goldfarb (2006). For example, Latour (2005: 15) suggests:

> Each object gathers around itself a different assembly of relevant parties. Each object triggers new occasions to passionately differ and

one focusing on the organizational meta level. The perspectives are not exclusive but can certainly coexist; it is indeed possible to be writing papers and policies against logging while chained to a tree.

When it comes to everyday acts of resistance, less organized and unarticulated struggles are often dismissed as not political enough as they do not match academic frameworks of conflict. Sociologist Asef Bayat has examined how the urban poor in the global south use constructive forms of resistance to create a better life through quiet direct action, for example, by building illegally, tapping into the water pipes and power grids, or by establishing businesses on the pavement that in each case exist at the legal gray zones or explicitly challenge state regulations—survival that may appear apolitical but exists as acts of defiance.[6] In a similar vein, women's constructive resistance often acts in less explicit and violent forms, from historical examples of illegal tailoring made outside the guilds, to clandestine healing, reproduction, and abortion services.[7]

dispute. Each object may also offer new ways of achieving closure without having to agree on much else. In other words, objects—taken as so many issues—bind all of us in ways that map out a public space profoundly different from what is usually recognized under the label of "the political."

[6] Bayat (1997, 2010). As James Scott also points out, much academic analysis misses the everyday dynamics of resistance to domination because it focuses on explicit and organized protests, such as marches, petitions, and violent eruptions, stimulated by "left-wing academic romance with wars of national liberation" (1985: 28) and "based on an ironic combination of both Leninist and bourgeois assumption of what constitutes political action" (Scott 1986: 24). For more emergent and "bottom-up" perspectives on conflict, and the gritty and insubordinate localities that undermine strategic overview and analysis, see also Chia and Holt (2009) and, as used in armed conflict, see Kilcullen (2013).

[7] Ehrenreich and English (1973); Federici (2004). For a perspective on indigenous knowledge principles, using the making of boundary objects, see Casemajor et al. (2019).

THE CONTENTS OF POLITICAL MATTERS

While daily practices of people are only a minor part of the life of a society or state, we underestimate their potential if we imagine these "politics of small things" as insignificant compared to meta. With the global reach of mental models, it is easy to think of meta as emerging from ideas that are always larger than matter. For example, just take mental models of social hierarchizations, such as ableism, capitalism, patriarchy, or authoritarianism. These may all appear to us as intangible ideas that can only be touched by political deliberation and decisions, yet they are also expressed in physical arrangements that cause real social affects and behaviors. Ableism is present to various degrees in almost every object, capitalism in virtually any product, patriarchy in practically every garment, authoritarianism in nearly all public buildings. All these aspects can be manipulated and mitigated with hands-on interventions. If done strategically, this will affect arrangements beyond the discrete matter of the local situation. We will see more of this later.

The trouble in most cases is that designers fail to mobilize the connections between the local matter and the meta. Often, we think in the wrong scales, as the meta always appears larger than the matter we hold in our hands. As capitalism is present in almost all global trade, and ableism is demonstrated at so many places across society, this cup of coffee or these stairs right here in front of me are like small mirrors reflecting a much larger phenomenon. But it is possible to approach this scale in an inverted way, and this may just be very helpful when thinking of how to intervene with design in meta issues.

Let us look at an example to make it a bit clearer. Take the instance where the same matter is drawn into different meta. Consider for a moment four glass bottles: a bottle of Coke, a bottle with a message, a bottle of moonshine, a bottle of gasoline with a cloth wick.

These are all everyday used bottles, commonly dispersed across the world, often appearing in similar local contexts. The bottle emerges from the dark matter of global trade, a

meta made up of capitalism, ideology, culture, and lifestyle, and much more. The material content between bottles differs; from artificially flavored sugar water, a sheet of cellulose fibers with graphite markings, homemade ethyl alcohol, and clear petroleum-derived flammable liquid with a piece of cotton fabric. With its four different contents, the material capacities embrace different domains—corporate soft drinks, handwritten communication equipment, untaxed moonshine, and gasoline— to become a popular incendiary device. In each case, you can pour out both matter and meta, wash the bottle, and fill it with another content. In each case, the bottle, which may only be a container, is itself *larger* than the meta, which only fills the bottle to a certain degree: *there is also air inside.*

To give an example on the other end of the spectrum, similar matter may be of different sources and meta. The same heirloom tomato grown in grandmother's backyard is different from the greenhouse one, or the one picked by undocumented migrants, or the one grown on occupied land—and then of very different matter than the GMO version. They may also contain pesticides and pollution. Yet they all still hold more than 90 percent water. The meta is undoubtedly part of the matter, yet seldom bigger than it. The meta is dispersed, in different concentrations between contexts, yet everywhere, and all of these components can be manipulated. If done strategically, the mix of contents can be something much more than the tomato you hold in your hand.

Matter moves between contexts and through different intensities of meta; the tomato grows long without much interference, undisturbed but for the caress of wind and sun. But, then, in a short amount of time, it is picked, shipped, processed, and sold through many distributed steps that move matter through the meta of trade regulations, labor policies, supply chains, which all have their varying degrees of checkpoints, forms, taxes, and labels.

Unpacking how the meta is manifested in matter is a theme I always find rewarding to come back to and discuss with the students after a day in the workshop. What the practice with of primitive making makes concrete is that the world designers engage in is *as large as that we can change.* Your world changes just a little as you refill bottles or grow your tomatoes, but a little bit more when you pick locks and access service tunnels, hack into the power settings of your electric car to make it go further, or build a secret rooftop hideout to ferment alcohol for you and your neighbors. Sure, in each case, the issue at hand may be complex with many variables. Still, you also use making to trespass across meta boundaries (such as property, warranties, fire regulations, etc.). Even if our worlds are constituted and framed by abstract concepts, that does not mean the making that challenges such boundaries remains abstract or left to be addressed only on the level of representation, policy, or white papers. Strategic making is the challenge to find how matter and meta are bound together, how both can be manipulated together toward explicit goals, and how we can materially *hack into reality itself.* By choosing the instance and matter at points of leverage, we can manipulate the meta.

This means the modes by which matter is manipulated can be done in a way that acts locally and pins down and challenges the meta, intensifying or displacing aspects of it. The metal wire from a clothes hanger can manipulate the latch bolt of a classroom door. The same bottle that is an emblem for global capitalism can be refilled and used to challenge the same domains. A chair can be made in ways that make it embody either feudal values or democratic ideals. A piece of domestic knitwear can become an active instrument to displace or stop a war. Means and ends can meet in the process of making.

Yet, as Meadows notes, leverage points are points of power; to be effective, the material transformation needs to happen at a point of leverage. As will become clear further on, some matter is located at more critical positions and intersections in the distribution of the dark matter of meta. A guerilla-knitted cozy on a door handle is different when it spells out "love" on the school doors versus when it spells out "mercy" on the door handle to the supreme court. A forged membership card to Disneyland opens different doors than a forged passport. The leverage points differ radically, depending on their intersection with the meta, even when the same techniques are used.

Hacking into matter has different levels of impact, depending on how it is positioned in relation to the critical nodes or knots of meta, such as strategic points and bottlenecks—locks, alarms, bridges, gears, breaks, corridors, gates, distribution coils, or hinges. Small actions come to regulate more significant material flows and speeds at such locations. In these places, material activism intervenes to impede, repurpose, or repair, to slow down, displace, or redirect. Each site requires its own tools and techniques. Yet, the materiality of such spot makes it open to be manipulated by primitive making—even with the basic utensils of the average home toolbox. So let's take a look into the toolbox next.

"CHOOSE YOUR WEAPON!"

4   Making Agency

Art is not a mirror held up to reality but a hammer with which to shape it, Bertolt Brecht famously argues. What agency should we ascribe the process of making? There is undoubtedly agency in consumption, in the shaping of the self through products and experiences. Growing up, creating a mixed tape was a great source of pleasure for me, and it provided a sense of agency, even when just recoding and ordering popular (and some unpopular) songs with a particular intent. Drawing images and writing barely comprehensible titles on the sleeve could make every tape an art piece of sorts. Enough of effort, and you were almost a band member. In even simpler ways, users may become what cultural theorist Nicholas Bourriaud calls "semionauts," by remixing memes or flipping between TV stations.[1] While this is a suggestive form of easy breezy artistic creation, just make sure it's your finger on the control panel (or you may end up zero the hero).

Agency can appear before us in many ways. Even certain forms of inaction, slowdown, or refusal can be highly refined forms of agency, especially when mixed with ironic acts and

---

[1] Bourriaud (2002).

jokes that reshuffle concepts and unmask power.[2] There is certainly also the practical agency of sabotage and creative destruction: the same superglue you repair things with can be used to efficiently jam someone's lock.

Caught somewhere between the hammer and the mixed tape, the practice of design has over the past decades become ever more linked with the concept of "change."[3] Yet what is often connoted with the term is neither the individual change of perception or meaning nor the change typically suggested by parliamentary politics, bureaucratic processes, or long-term cultural evolutions. Also, this new change designers strive for is something different from what the paradigm of consumerism has offered over the past century, like changing cars, clothes, or furniture.

When designers talk about change, it signifies something more than what has traditionally been transposed through the profession of design. It is no longer the alteration of colors on a product, a new font on a poster, or even the invention of a new sleek gadget. Change for designers signifies a word of hope. It seems to imply that design itself may move beyond its prison in the market of consumer goods and no longer share its deeply intertwined fate with mass production and its entrenched economic injustices, sweatshops, unsustainable practices, and environmental degradation. The term change in design-speak escapes some of the dilemmas of consumerism: that it is essentially unfair, sustains an asymmetric division of power in society, upholds mechanisms of exclusion and discrimination, and keeps reproducing addiction, submission, and slavery. As author Ivan Illich argues, there are inevitably two kinds of slaves in a consumer society: the prisoners of addiction and the prisoners of envy.[4]

---

[2] As shown by Scott (1990), discursive resistance, in code, irony, and jokes, even if understood by few, is essential in opposition to domination: gossiping about and making a fool of a leader is a powerful method of dethronement.

[3] Defining titles in the popularity and change hybris of design has ranged from Bruce Mau's towering book *Massive Change* (2004) to Tim Brown and IDEO's influential overtures about *Change by Design* (2009).

[4] Illich (1973).

Design's emphasis on change suggests people in the profession are eager to deal with more significant problems than consumer objects, to engage with the meta. A sign of this may be how the term often comes with the word "social" attached to it: as in "social change," or "social innovation," or "social design." The social easily connotes meta. Even if much of our interactions happen on, through, and over matter, the complexity of togetherness draws sociality toward meta. Engaging with meta aims to change people's social behaviors, conditions, values, and organizations. This happens in the political realm, and changing the distribution of agency often stands in direct opposition to preserving the status quo. Thus, it is crucial to understand how design can change both matter and meta.

MAKING CHANGE, MAKING RESISTANCE

The artificial is as political as the actual, which is crucial to design as the "politics of the artificial" emerge from the industrial production of what is routinely defined as progress or social development, framed and facilitated by mass-produced objects. The introduction of many new designs has also transformed the political landscape: new technologies replacing previous types of labor, a new weapon or military technique shifting the balance of power, or innovations opening up for new structural organization of society.[5] Yet the intention of the designers as they shape social relations is seldom explicitly political, even in the design of passports, weapons, or camps, but covered up behind labels such as "beauty," "function," or "ergonomics." The claim of future betterment comes to designers by habit.

---

[5] There is a rich literature on the societal changes coming in conjunction with design and technologies, not least that of Margolin (2002). The books of Manuel DeLanda (1991, 1997, 2006, 2016) have been especially influential on my relationship to the power of making and matter.

When designers talk about change, it is more than just on the surface. Even if not always explicit, as used by designers, change suggests a social reorientation that challenges the conditions of domination generally encountered in the delegations of agency in consumer society. As a resistance that does not speak its name, "change" seems to promise something to the listener: it hints toward setting you free.

Change requires a transition from one mode to another. If such a process is "resistance" or not is of endless debate; at what scale, social or individual, does it require intent and impact, disruption or not, too romantic or not idealistic enough? What is the difference between a strike and calling in sick to work? Is listening to illegal radio channels enough, or does it require being the one broadcasting them? Can the choice of clothes or hairstyle count in the same category as an organized march on the capital? How about knitting a hat versus building a barricade? Does writing a pay-walled journal article from the comfort of your office correspond with prison notebooks? Does youth rebellion count as anti-government activity, and does reposting a meme?

If one puts change as a break with the status quo, it is not just an update of the current running of things. It signifies some form of conflict or at least competition between alternatives. But if the idea of change has some grounding in empowerment or liberation, it stands against a condition of disempowerment or oppression. But, can't change just be nonconfrontational? Even work toward peace challenges established structures and interests in whose interest the conflict has preserved. Only focusing on change as peacebuilding risks entrenching injustices, as conflict is supposed to be "solved" and thus buried. It is essential to see how even peace negotiations occur in power asymmetries. When it comes to peacebuilding,

> there is a deep structural symbiosis in the philosophy and methods of counterinsurgency and peacebuilding that lie in securing the population against unrest through the

implementation of governance, development and security strategies that instil acquiescence and ensure control.[6]

To challenge injustices, a change toward peace may require the paradoxical *promotion of conflict*. It puts contestation on the map in order to encourage listening to promote transformation, with the aim of renewed negotiations.

The recent hype around change in design also boosts a megalomania of meta. Designers can easily think they can do anything and solve any issue; just add some design thinking to the mix, and even social conflict will be fixed. With new thinking and new ideas, anything can change for the better. On the other hand, manipulating matter only seems to offer very little of such possibilities. In many ways, matter is precisely the stifling constraint designers work so hard to get away from.

Yet, the promise of matter is that one can see and touch the change one works toward. As Richard Sennett suggests, manipulating matter through crafts offers a practice "anchored in tangible reality," and with this comes a very defined pride and sense of accomplishment in tactile work.[7] The making of objects has always made social relationships permanent and tangible, bringing along political consequences. Yet, most

---

[6] Turner (2015: 97); see also Jackson (2015) for a discussion on the differences between peace and resistance studies.

[7] Sennett (2008: 21). Craft offers an interesting insight to the relationship between maker and the material at hand: whereas matter has the power to affect, with craftspeople the relationship between material and hands seems to move beyond *concern* toward *care*. As affective states, concern and care are related, but as noted by Puig de la Bellacasa (2017: 42), care has stronger affective and ethical connotations and also connects to agency:

We can think of the difference between affirming "I am concerned" and "I care." The first denotes worry and thoughtfulness about an issue as well as, though not necessarily, the fact of belonging to the connective of those concerned, "affected" by it; the second adds a strong sense of attachment and commitment to something. Moreover, the quality of "care" is to be more easily turned into a very: to care. One can make oneself concerned, but "to care" contains a notion of *doing* that concern lacks. (original emphasis)

often, this distribution of agency is submerged underneath the surface of the market. If one is to unpack the change that can be accomplished through making simple things, the question is how to understand the agency of design that is closer to the workshop or available to us when we engage in primitive making.

MAKING MATERIAL AGENCY

Let's take a step back and look at the agency designers use to shape matter according to their intentions. I suggest a simple diagram to map out the material agency making operates.

Along the X-axis, we put the *material agency* employed to push for the desired change. At 0 percent material agency, impact stays in the realm of representation, or the blueprints are left unrealized on the workshop desk. When it comes to social relations and politics, I follow the news, vote for a political party, and perhaps even discuss and raise opinion among my friends. Yet, I employ no material agency to physically affect the condition of my concern. At the other end, at 100 percent design agency, I use all assets I have got to affect this condition. I gather material, manipulate and build the change, using tools and local settings to maximize the impact of my efforts. I hear the faucet dripping; do I go and try to fix it or not? Simply thinking about it won't help much.[8]

To see what happens on a broader scale, let's add an *affect* Y-axis, stretching from "me" to "many."[9] Here I think of the term

[8] Thinking and defining a problem certainly helps addressing it, and similarly, speaking to inanimate objects can be an intrinsic part of interacting with them. A common Swedish example may be otherwise rational people speaking to their cars (not KITT) on cold winter mornings trying to convince them to start working: "come on, come on, start now" (for other types of interpassive relationships to objects, see Pfaller 2003).

[9] It could be "alone" to "together", or from individual to convivial, depending on how the material agency affects the relationships between people. Similarly, the axis could be stretched from "private" to "public," yet this runs into the complication of these definitions failing to ask what the values and purpose is behind such distinction. As Geuss (2001: 34–5) suggests, the

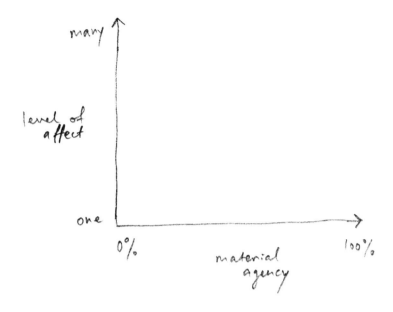

affect as something that connects infliction with impact—that the population affected means they get involved and have their agency shaped by the intervention. With affect, I want to stress the implications of agency and embodiment, from isolated action to vast reproduction and ripples of modified behaviors. An act may inform and help shape concepts and mental models, but it is the expansion of action spaces I am after here.[10] Thus,

notion of public stretches from the Greek notion of constituting oneself as a slave to the nation in order to live fully, to the Roman connotation of the public as belonging to the whole people, which practically meant being part of the men that made up the legions.

[10] To view action spaces through the lens of affects, materialist methodology primarily seeks the connections between assemblages of animate and inanimate affects, how forces are inflicting behavior onto a subject (DeLanda 2006, 2016). These alter the reproduction of social worlds with regard to desires, feelings, and meanings (see also Braidotti 2000).

along the Y-axis, we move from my own activity (e.g., at home), which affects only my life, toward the material changes that impact the lives of the many and possibly on a systemic scale. But it is not only a matter of numbers, from unique pieces to mass-produced bestsellers, or from a fire in my kitchen to a fire that burns down the whole block. Think of it as a qualitative axis; it measures the scale of participation, how it affects us together.

Both these axes have implications on the dissemination of agency among people: the X-axis goes from material inaction to complete action, the Y-axis from affecting an isolated individual to affecting many. These two dimensions map out a field of political effects. Material change in my home may cause or reduce trouble for me, but when it starts affecting the many, the scale impact as well as trouble starts multiplying. As design agency pushes outwards, collective material action starts to affect the meta, possibly challenging the status quo. Push action upwards toward the top right corner, and the boat may begin to rock.

Let's use an everyday example to map out this space of agency, one I encountered in January 2015 in Istanbul. People across the city were concerned about the freezing street cats this frigid winter. As a result, they made small improvised shelters for the street cats, popping up all across the city, both in private and public spaces. It ranged from cardboard boxes and cut-out plastic containers, small wooden chests on stoops and street corners, to elaborate structures containing ten to twenty improvised small shelters under one long tarp along a house facade. One can think of it like Aesop's fables to reference human relationships.[11]

Perhaps I do nothing, in which case my agency stays in the corner. Along the Y-axis, I may privately write a small note and set up in the building that we should do something! Or send

---

[11] Even if involving cats, I will stay with an anthropocentric perspective in this argument. While a more-than-human framework would open for many angles, the purpose of the argument is to address civic design agency in relation to making.

a letter to the local newspaper, or put out a post on social media about the freezing cats, hoping people will read it and get together to help the cats. But I would still only be using 0 percent of my potential material agency to keep the cats warm. If I follow the politically designated paths of public action, I may search for a political party with a clear plan to help the cats, and I can cast my vote for them. In this case, I use my political vote; it affects the many and public realm, and I move up along the Y-axis, but I still employ close to 0 percent of my own material agency to help the cats. The technology of the vote makes sure I stay inactive, as famously argued by Thoreau.[12] Once again, it is at the 0 percent of material agency most action is directed under the usual arrangement of politics, where citizens are left only a little space to fill, the room left empty by government designations. As I cast my vote in isolation, I hand over my claim to the agency to self-govern as I submit the act of governing to my elected official. I participate in my own subordination, and the cats are still freezing.

If I start moving along the X-axis, I begin to take action with matter around me; I employ *material agency*. As I build a cathouse on the street, I start using my agency as a maker: I use my skills and materials to change local conditions. I may start with just putting out a cardboard box, then cut out a sturdier shelter from a large plastic container. My second try becomes better, improving the design, utilizing materials and tools in my workshop, and so on. As the design improves, I use more of my material agency. As I put out my cathouse in my yard, one cat gets a bit cozier winter; I used my material agency toward a positive change in the world.

So far, I have still stayed at the bottom of the X-axis. Now I start disseminating design, using all my networks and tools to

---

[12] Thoreau ([1849] 2008) famously argues in his tract on civil disobedience that the purpose of voting is to keep the population away from dissenting and disobeying the decrees from the government they have nominally elected. One can draw parallels to how the typical division of agency in design processes similarly disempowers the stakeholders from the opportunity to dissent.

help the cats, and I do it together with others; we move upwards toward the many. As I move in the direction of the top right corner of the matrix, I spread the blueprints of the design. I negotiate with material suppliers to get a better price on what we need to build a thousand houses. I mobilize people to act in concert to help the cats. A design movement has taken off to help the cats on a broader scale. In Istanbul, in the winter of 2015, there were plenty of initiatives like this, and it was a beauty to behold. You could find improvised cathouses all over the city. But we could imagine, if taken further, all the way to the top right corner of the diagram, we could envision the cathouse movement to have mobilized a massive change with also structural affects, appearing in policy instruments, governance, and perhaps the very conditions of being a cat in the city. Direct action saves cats.

However, as you may have noticed, trouble starts to emerge when moving out from the safe spaces along the X and Y arms of the diagram. The meta of parliamentary politics allows my agency to move up along the Y-axis; I can write letters, sign petitions, and vote as long as I don't employ too much material agency. Staying close to the base of the X-axis, it is acceptable to use a more and more material agency, make a cardboard or more permanent shelters, as long as I house them in my backyard. I am allowed to use quite a bit of material agency if it stays private.

There is plenty of organizational meta you run into when out in the middle of the diagram. It is the meta of established regulations that need to be upheld, agreements that perhaps took years and long struggles to be made, and there are bureaucrats whose job it is to make sure these agreements are maintained. And there are invested interests, from landlords, police, and politicians; the fire department needs to come out to inspect, not to mention the allergic neighbor who perhaps complains to the mayor. There is also dark matter that manifests these positions: parking spots get occupied, streets get littered, and garbage trucks have trouble passing through the street because of all cathouses. Troubles emerge as soon as we move into action and step over the boundary from the private sphere.

The arrangements of agency under the state designate civic action along the edges of the diagram while putting various forms of obstacles in the way of concerted civic action. The state produces not a totality of domination; we are not programmed robots, but the government arranges consent production through what scholar of resistance Stellan Vinthagen calls the subject's "participatory subordination." Vinthagen posits:

> The social phenomenon of "power" is characterized by *one actor who subordinates him- or herself, partly or entirely, by relinquishing the practical responsibility of intention of their own behavior.* The actor behaves like a "non-actor," as an instrument to be used. The crucial point is that a transfer of behavioural control happens through the actor *relinquishing* control, whether they want it or not, consciously or not. What matters is the existence of obedience, or, rather, the active and participatory transfer of

responsibility, which produced subordination, *the de facto behaviour*, no matter what motive, reason or cause underlies the act of subordination.[13]

The meta offers a cultural and organizational framework to stabilize authority, punish dissent, and reward subordination, not least through legal authority and mutual contracts. But certainly, also material arrangements align behavior toward participatory subordination. In the end, we all too seldom take action to actually affect the suffering around us, even with the most primitive means.

Nevertheless, the boundaries of normative action serve social purposes and are not necessarily evil, or anti-cat (well especially not in Istanbul, where the pro-cat sentiment is very strong). Societal and historical negotiations between parties have encouraged citizens to avoid taking action without proper consultations with their community. The same material agency that saves cats can be used to further other means of power to coerce, enforce domination, and concentrate agency to those who have the means to occupy positions of power. Perhaps the street dogs do not want any change, simply because most of them are too big to fit in the small cathouses. Maybe other pet owners get jealous. There may be unrest and barking in the streets. In most places, there are vast interests invested in keeping us inactive and the cathouses off the streets before they turn into more permanent settlements.

If our "change" would really matter, if it would really unsettle the conditions of subordination, we could be sure it would be illegal. And curiously enough, when we start testing the boundaries of social relationships with the help of material agency, one quickly notices so much of making is illegal: the potentials of matter are circumscribed by meta in the form of morals, regulations, and laws. This becomes very apparent if we move the argument from cute street cats to pigeons and rats; the neighbor that starts making shelters for unwelcome

---

[13] Vinthagen (2015: 167f, 179, original emphases).

guests runs into contested domains. This certainly becomes apparent when we move to the realms of humans, such as the controversies around the poor, migrants, or homeless people. State representatives, or vigilantes, quickly show up when uninvited populations build their own shelters. Here, new political conflicts open up, entangled in layers of organizational and moralistic meta. The troubles become more manifest: the improvised shelter for homeless people is seldom met with the same civic generosity as cathouses.

MANIPULATING META

What I am after here is the contested dimensions of primitive making. Cathouses are cute, while shelters for the homeless quickly fall into the not-in-my-backyard discord. So let's examine an example with slightly less moralistic dimensions to emphasize the question of making and agency.

In this case, I would want the speeding cars to slow down on the street outside my house. The meta of traffic laws in the neighborhood allows 50 km/h. To change this meta, I can send a suggestion through the established political channels and raise the concern at a town hall meeting to address my local politicians and planners. I then wait for something to be done. If I get agitated, I send in articles to the local newspaper or start a petition. I can set the infrastructural interests of cold traffic flows against the safety of the children, as this usually mobilizes political affects. Nevertheless, I am using very little of my material agency.

If I gather people and we act together, perhaps we even create a street protest to raise attention to the concern. We can increase the affect of our protest with posters, flags, and megaphones. An example of this kind could be the 1967 Black Panthers action concerning a street intersection in Oakland, California, plagued by accidents among the local African-American population. Local politicians had long ignored their demands for installing traffic lights. To emphasize the issue, members of the Panthers came armed with weapons to escort pedestrians through the dangerous intersection. Very soon after the action, traffic lights were installed.[14]

If not engaging in this type of escalation, I can take more material action and set up various forms of permanent signs to remind cars to slow down. I can get friends together for participatory monuments for traffic safety, such as the white-painted "ghost bikes" that mark the site where a biker has been killed in traffic. These simultaneously commemorate, raise public awareness, and warn traffic of dangerous intersections.

To use more material agency, I could set out one night to dig and build a speed bump, a material obstacle Bruno Latour uses to show what he calls the material politics of "actants." Latour suggests the speed bump is a technical delegate that redistributes the various agents to materially interfere directly with the daily life of the driving car-human. As he suggests, the driver modifies their behavior through the mediation of the speed bump: they fall back from morality to encounter the material force of the bump. Even so, for the pedestrian, it does not matter through which channel the car's behavior is attained. Latour argues that the material impact of the speed bump creates an "actorial" shift as it translates meaning from a decree into a nonnegotiable material state. Discussing Latour's example, Peter-Paul Verbeek emphasizes how emotional, moral, and rational positions are also part of such translation of agency. The speed bump modifies a driver's intention from the "driving fast, because I'm in a hurry," over "driving slowly out of responsibility," to instead experience the speed through the materiality and technology of the vehicle, to instead become "driving slowly to save my shock absorbers."[15]

---

[14] As noted on the "Black Panther History Marker," a commemorative historical marker and collaboration between former chief-of-staff of the Black Panther Party David Hilliard, artist Jeremy Deller, and the Center for Tactical Magic.

[15] See Latour (1994) and Verbeek (2005) for more in-depth discussion on the entablement of human and nonhuman actants and the embodiment of intentions in this specific case.

But again, the political dimensions of the many also play a part in this case. When the participatory subordination in the delegation of these kinds of decisions is overridden, and I take action myself, we start running into trouble. If the road would be on my property and only affecting visitors to my house, I could go out and construct the obstacle myself, and there would be little concern. But if the purpose is to address the speeding cars on the shared city street, and we start to construct the speed bump ourselves, we may run into trouble with the law. Even more so, if we then start raising the speed bump to also slow down the SUVs. To slow down the SUVs, we may also block public service vehicles, and the controversies escalate. Slowly, after many nights' work, the bump gets higher and higher, bigger and bigger, to finally become something like a barricade. Government agents will be after us, and neighbors will be upset, and it will become evident; *the higher the speed bump, the further the agency of matter reaches into the troubles of meta.*

As the speed bump increases its material affect, it becomes the concern of more and more people, as well as formalized policies and political agreements; will the neighbors' cars pass without damage? Will the ambulance? Whereas the speed bump merely impedes traffic flows, the barricade explicitly stands in its way. Its purpose is to slow down to the degree it sorts who gets to pass. The barricade shapes access, helping to inspect and control logistic flows. An elevated speed bump is a matter that cements positions. When increasing its material impact, we get to the barricade, the wall, the bunker. It becomes a political speed bump with a goal to slow down a strategic progression of speed and time; one side wants to push and move on, while the opponent wants to hold back, regroup, and hold on to territory.[16]

---

[16] Paul Virilio (1995) elaborated on how obstacles slow down political time, such as in walls and bunkers. Political theorist Jane Bennett posits that objects are imbued with "thing power," and this can also work as obstacle, as a cultural form with capacities that "are themselves material assemblages that *resist*" (2004: 348, original emphasis). From this perspective, objects set up to undermine participatory subordination become truly "wild things" along Judy Attfield's (2000) ideas, objects refusing domestication, appropriated

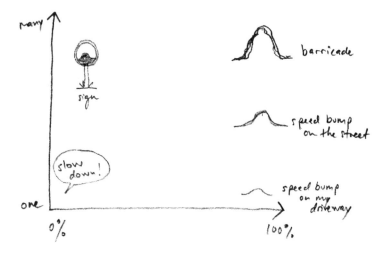

If put on a continuum, walls are matter, while political borders are meta.

But in its process of making, the barricade is typically different from a fence, wall, or bunker. The barricade can be seen as a *participatory technology*—its purpose is to engage and organize its makers toward its political goal, impeding logistic mobility, and communal defense, while simultaneously acting as a magnet for action and an affective monument for the community that builds it. With something like an ironic twist, the barricade works as a participatory "boundary object," around which communities of practice gather to form a nexus of perspectives that do not necessarily come into agreement. The configuration of the barricade underscores two opposing forces around which many views clash, yet primarily in two camps on the opposite sides of the barricade (for or against, civics or state, or, like the riot shield, between chaos and cosmos). This mobilizing and organizational quality of matter has driven

by the users to new modes of making sense of the world through physical artifacts.

the history of the barricade throughout its political history of opposing organizations of meta, anchoring them materially against each other.[17]

When we build the speed bump into a barricade, this process of primitive making provokes a special relationship to meta: it attracts systemic issues to itself like a magnet, making the meta tangible and open for material manipulation. The barricade makes the conflict tangible; the need for negotiation between two opposing meta camps becomes materially urgent. State organization is set against civic organization as participants are mobilized on each side of the conflict. Here, participatory affects become mobilized through matter, as matter becomes a trouble-making interface between social spheres, systems, regulations, and behaviors.

To return to our diagram, what we can notice is that as making mobilizes more material agency and engages the many, it unsettles more and more meta. Where it makes meta tangible, it also destabilizes the tacit agreements that uphold the participatory subordination that otherwise keeps meta in balance.

The door latch can be manipulated with primitive tools. We can build a cathouse, speed bump, or barricade on our street. Primitive making gets the goods.

---

[17] Arthur Pacey (1999) discusses a multitude of engagements with objects on a participatory level. See more of Wenger's (1998: 107) discussion on object as a "nexus of perspectives," whereas Traugott (2010) would stress the barricade's history as a nexus for political disagreement.

5   Doing and Sitting

Building models of bridges from simple materials is a classic assignment in architecture education. The challenge is often to make a sturdy structure that should hold a particular load. The materials are cheap and accessible and, on purpose, also weak, such as newspapers, sticks, straws, or dry spaghetti. A small competition is set up in the classroom of who can build the sturdiest structure from such ephemeral and flimsy materials. It is a fantastic introduction to structural engineering principles and to experience how a latticework of individually weak parts is assembled to form a resilient structural arrangement.

I see the construction of a simple justice machine as something similar to the bridge assignment. But instead of introducing structural engineering, it is an exploration into how simple designs sort and weigh people's behavior concerning the weights of ethical or legal arrangements. Take, for example, a justice machine for sitting—how would it work? How would it look? Are there seating arrangements that give shape to more or less just relations?

When I use this assignment in class, we start with a seesaw. Build a seesaw that manifests a principle of justice. What is the idea of justice you would like to make tangible, and how does this translate into the seesaw design? How would it operate?

Building a seesaw is a lesson in how design manipulates balance and fairness. The power of the seesaw is its rich sensory feedback. It makes relationships tangible; *you experience imbalance with your body*. It is a form of representation that is more than verbal, less abstract. While it connotes play, it facilitates inquiries into how equilibrium, or the lack thereof, is achieved.

The typical seesaw at the playground seems designed with the hope that the older (often heavier) sibling will have to compromise and help the younger (usually lighter). The one at our local playground seems to be made to enhance conflict between siblings, teaching an embodied lesson to the smaller one that life is never fair, or at least that society is ordered against the weak.

The seesaw can be a crude example of how social order is embodied in objects. We could imagine more just seesaws. Perhaps one with where one can adjust the pivot point? Madeleine Akrich points to how designed objects have intentions, or "scripts," and these impose behavior back onto humans by the object's "prescription."[1] Playing with the design of the seesaw not only gives a direct experience of how the scales of justice are tilted in favor of some and not others but also gives the act of sitting its moral and ethical dimension. Each seating device tells users the prescribed way to act. But perhaps more importantly, a simple thing like a seating device exposes how the designed world of objects is arranged to orient people's behavior toward particular ends. Objects are weighted and tilted in favor of a specific order.

SITTING IS NOT ONLY SITTING

Sitting is a negotiation between forces, the weight of flesh versus durability of materials, the consolation of tired legs meeting a

---

[1] Compared to Sara Ahmed's (2010) discussion on "orientations," Akrich's idea of "scripts" (1992) puts emphasis on the programming of intentions into objects that then inscribe users with behaviors.

surface made to address various cultural and functional demands. Yet sitting is an activity most of us seldom consider too much, and perhaps even less the objects that support our mass to relieve us temporarily from the burden of gravity with such great sense of graceful care.

If the everyday objects people interact with have "thing power," this emerges from their process of making, their manifestation, and how they arrange bodies and surrounding relationships. In alignment with Ahmed's material orientation of sitting, in a most fundamental sense, the chair is a machine for shaping the lives of its sitting citizens. This is also why sitting "right" on a chair appears to be such an essential part of upbringing—to sit upright at the table, to sit with the correct body language in the proper cultural context. The teacher helps correct the pupil's posture to assist in getting the writing to stay between the guidelines in the composition book. The chair orients the body and its possible actions, and the body's posture orients the attention of not only ourselves but also our spectators or conversation partners. The chair is thus of great interest in the *design of users*. The matter of a chair aligns a user's body to perform downstream from the "script" of intention. It inflicts the user with a specific force of use.

It becomes more apparent when a body is arranged with the purpose of afflicting pain, using the "hurtability" of the body, not least using the chair as an instrument to shape the sensory realm of the victim. The powerful affect of matter is at use in disciplining bodies, from sitting straight at school or the medical or dentist chairs to the more sinister instrumental use of the chair designed for discomfort. In such cases, the purpose is power and domination, and the chair's thing power is used as a physical force multiplier. At the interrogation room chair, sitting is used for state-administered fear and terror, designed for torment and the infliction of pain.[2] Examples can

---

[2] Elaine Scarry (1985: 44) elaborately᾽ frames design in relation to the "hurtability" of the body. Rejali (2007) argues that throughout the twentieth century it has been democracies that have set the international pace for torture and have pioneered, developed, and exported the current excess in techniques that leave no marks and thus escape much scrutiny. Parallel to the

be the Brazilian "dragon chair" or Chinese "tiger bench" used for interrogation in prisons, or the infamous electric chair, long known to be used for interrogation as well as execution. However, these kinds of modified torture chairs, especially combined with electrotorture, are troublesome for the torturers as judges and journalists can easily identify them as instruments of pain. Thus, stealthy torture requires anonymous devices that are not easily recognized as pain-inducing equipment. Instead, everyday objects are used to enhance positional torture, sometimes called "stress positions," forcing the victim to hold or bend limbs in unnatural or contorted positions. It is a form of pain infliction that leaves little, if any, visible evidence of injury yet could cause potential disability. One such position is the "banana," or "German chair," a posture where the victim is placed with his or her back bent over a standard chair, tying the victim's hands and feet to the chair's legs.[3]

Torture painfully exposes the thing power present in a chair, how it orients bodies to participate in their arrangement. Here, the victim's body is aligned along the trajectory of meta, the intentions, and organization of real state power. The matter of the chair places and directs the body to line up with its meta; in its thing power, meta and matter intersect. As Langdon Winner argues, artifacts enact particular forms of politics through their "arrangements of power and authority in human associations as well as the activities that take place within those arrangements."[4]

rhetoric of human rights across democracies, police, intelligence, and military forces in these countries have experimented profoundly in learning how to inflict pain leaving little scars on the victim (infamously waterboarding). Using "clean" techniques, especially prolonged stress positions, causing limbs to painfully swell, is the current go-to method.

[3] Rejali (2007: 128, 327); see also Amnesty International's (2012) reports on torture. One can note the use of music for psychological operations, sound torture, and sleep deprivation. In 2014 the Canadian industrial band Skinny Puppy demanded $666,000 from the US Department of Defense after it was revealed their music was used in Guantánamo torture. James Hetfield of Metallica, on the other hand, argued he was "honored my country is using [Metallica songs] to help us stay safe."

[4] Winner (1980: 123).

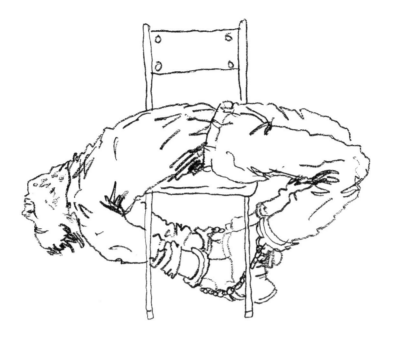

Stress positions such as the "banana" show again how the simple act of sitting manifests the making and unmaking of worlds, the making and unmaking of specific forms of civilization, and these are easily inverted, to use Scarry's vocabulary.

> As the torturer uses the immediate physical setting in a direct deconstruction of the smallest unit of civilization, and as his actions allude to and subvert larger units of civilization, two of its primary institutional forms, so his words reach out, body forth, and destroy more distant and more numerous manifestations of civilization.[5]

---

[5] Scarry (1985: 42).

The sadistic feast of torture can manifest in the average stool or chair; and even without physical marks on the body, an inner, as well as an outer, world is dismembered. The only way to exit is going piece by piece.

ROYAL CRAFTS AND CITIZEN CONSUMPTION

Torture is an extreme form of unmaking of an inner and outer world. But other acts of sitting also make and manifest worlds. By sitting down, we make a world of our own, even if it may be seen as a form of inactivity. In the perspective proposed by Stellan Vinthagen, power should not be seen as a totality of domination but always a form of consent production and participatory subordination. Yet, in the case of torture, the victim is more victim of violence than power. In its more everyday use, the chair is a device for orienting a sitter toward more subtle shaping of power in the form of *subordination to the designations made by its designer.*

> When we moderate our behavior to fit a routine or scheme of techniques, we become part of the shaping of power. It does not matter (for power production) if this happens to be what we want to do or if we do it without thinking. Power will be at work anyway, if our action produces subordination.[6]

Following Sara Ahmed's idea of how the orientation of objects also makes history "sediment" in certain patterns, many everyday objects sediment history toward state subordination. Design historian Victor Margolin traces the "politics of the artificial" back to Britain's Crystal Palace Exhibition of 1851, where he argues the politics of imperial state interests and design became inextricably bound to mass-produced consumer goods.[7]

---

[6] Vinthagen (2015: 177).
[7] At the Great Exhibition, design and the state politics merge with objects clearly made for the emerging consumer classes. Henry Cole, one of the promoters of the exhibition, attempted to improve the appearance of products

It followed directives to develop the processes of mass production to enhance manufacturing power. Still, the explicit goal of the Great Exhibition was also "the intention to improving public taste and educating artisans."[8] One of the chairs featured in the exhibition catalog was the throne-like "State chair." Carved and gilt framed, upholstered in ruby silk, it was designed and manufactured by M. Jancowski in York. According to the catalog of the exhibit, the State chair

> is embroidered on ruby-coloured silk velvet; on the back is the royal coat of arms, the lion raised in gold, the unicorn in silver, with a gold coronet; the crown worked in gold, silver, silks, and jewels. From the ribbon which shows the motto, a wreath of the rose, shamrock, and thistle, worked in silks, is suspended, and the roses are raised so that every leaf may be lifted up. The seat exhibits the plume of the Prince of Wales, worked in a new style of silk embroidery, having the appearance of silver; the coronet is in gold, silver and jewels; the motto in gold and silver.[9]

It is the chair for the head of the family, the sovereign; in this you can sit down with royal pretension.

The State chair manifests matter in ways that align with state decrees, and it does so by evoking historical grandeur, feudal order, and sovereign power. Its elaborate detailing suggests a direct relationship to making that aligns with historical materials, techniques, traditions, symbols, and crafts. These

---

by confronting the "confusion and profusion of historical styles that were being loaded onto Victorian objects" to instead promote a closer collaboration between artists and industry with the aim of developing how objects "should look" (Margolin 2002: 107). This authoritarian streak of design is later taken up by prominent figures in the modern history of design, not least Hermann Muthesius, Adolf Loos, Le Corbusier, and Walter Gropius where "function" became the mean evaluating feature for the social as well as aesthetic qualities of objects and how they fit into the organization of a modern society.

[8] Forty (1986: 58).

[9] *The Art Journal Illustrated Catalogue* (1851: 54).

STATE CHAIR

are shaped here according to the state's interests and meta of the Great Exhibit. In its manifestation, in matter, technique, and symbolism, the *State chair is a speed bump for meta*, built to slow down time, preserve hierarchies and values, and close down new forms and orientations of social mobility. In this way, the State chair also presents a particular form of making I call *royal crafts*, aligning practice, technique, and matter with meta in a historicizing way while also preserving existing hierarchies.

Royal crafts echo Deleuze and Guattari's concept of "royal science," techniques of inquiry that appropriate and contain the process of investigation into homogeneous and striated forms.

Royal science is inseparable from a "hylomorphic" model implying both a form that organizes matter, and a matter prepared for the form; it has often been shown that this schema derives less from technology or life than from a society divided into governors and governed, and later, intellectuals and manual laborers. What characterizes it is that all matter is assigned to content, while all form passes into expression.[10]

To Deleuze and Guattari, the royal science of *axiomatics* differs from the minor or nonlinear science of *problematics*. Axiomatics approaches matter through linear models and stratified forms of equilibrium with "molarizing" processes of normalization and standardization—axiomatics orders to facilitate predictions and production. Problematics, on the other hand, examines processes operating far from equilibrium, involving intensities and morphogenetic creation, processes that open a system's possibility of becoming something new. Royal craft not only endorses certain materials and techniques but also enforces what Deleuze and Guattari call an "epistemological violence" by ignoring and rejecting subaltern crafts that do not resemble acknowledged and curated crafts that fit the categories of academic disciplines, museum collections, craft associations, fairs, grant criteria, competitions, education systems, and so on. Royal crafts work to purposefully ignore craft beyond its parameters traditionally supported through institutional crafts. It is crucial to notice how crafts exist outside of the academy, outside of institutional control, as a feral and unclaimed practice of making: overlooked, unrecorded, and institutionally silenced.[11] One can think of royal crafts as a parallel to how the state relates to "controlled substances," whose manufacture, possession, or use is regulated by government agencies. Royal crafts are "controlled crafts," types of making that the state

---

[10] Deleuze and Guattari (1987: 369).
[11] For related discussions in the realm of Silicon Valley–centric making, see Denzin et al. (2008) and Wilkinson-Weber and DeNicola (2016).

modulates as they help reproduce and align behavior and practices across the population.[12]

But if royal crafts close down the possibilities of making in alignment with state reproduction, something more open does not necessarily escape state interference. The creation of a home is also a maze of the homesteader's political choices; in the acquisition, building, furnishing, decoration, and later in maintenance and repairs, the domestic articulates cultural ideals embodied into habits and political routine.[13] In this type of chair, the alignment of matter according to meta takes another form, not as petrifying as the State chair but in the dynamic openness of consumerism. The IKEA Poäng armchair manifests this relationship between the empire of things and its user: its matter speaks of progressive leisure: comfy, modular, and made for reclining while consuming media.[14]

---

[12] State regulation may include cultural institutions, education, museums and exhibition venues, grants and funding, stifling irregular behavior or innovation. Yet, simultaneously, the absence of state regulation (e.g., on nonethical agrobusiness using untested pesticides and GMOs) creates a response of civic innovation emerging from tradition, such as heirloom vegetables, ecological farming, urban agriculture, or guerilla gardens (see Söderberg 2010; Hren 2011; McCay 2011). It is important to notice there are forbidden knowledges that may undermine Royal directives, spanning from the dissemination of copyright-infringing software and illegal repairs to how copyright legislation has produced a need to exempt professional cryptologists so they can do their mathematical research without the fear of prosecution under copyright law (Shah 2004).

[13] The home goes beyond embodying social relations, as it is both a reflection of and a medium for the construction of a variety of social relations: marriage, child-rearing, representation, and so on. As Elizabeth Shove (1999: 138) points out, "IKEA appears to be selling a series of images and ideals, carefully disguised as chairs, tables, and lamp shades."

[14] The Swedish furniture maker has produced over 30 million Poäng chairs since it debuted in 1976, and it continues to sell about 1.5 million every year, making it among some of the most ubiquitous home furnishing products in the world (Budds 2016). The mass convenience and price can be set in relation to historian Frank Trentmann's (2016) consumption state ideologies in the "empire of things," how social-democratic governments or revolutionary states under modernism use material politics to create object-based relationships between the state and the subject.

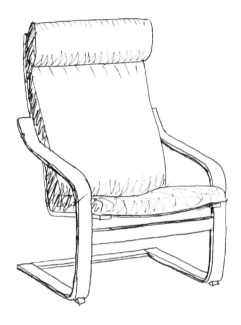

Resembling Alvar Aalto's Model 406 chair, an icon of Scandinavian design, Poäng embodies a particular form of consumer freedom, modularity, and "democratic design" to prices accessible to many consumers while still aligning bodies toward state directives of being a good consumer. In tracing the development of political consumerism, Lizabeth Cohen makes a distinction between two types of consumer engagement, what she calls *citizen consumers* and *customer consumers*—

the former being consumers who take on the political responsibility we usually associate with citizens to consider the general good of the nation through their consumption, and

the latter being consumers who seek primarily to maximize
their personal economic interests in the marketplace.[15]

However, even citizen consumers have their agency stuck
downstream from producers, however rich interface for
modification the matter of products allows. This is a good
reminder when it comes to experiments in "open source"
furniture, with freely distributed digital CAD files and other
open formats for physical reproduction. Even products made
for "hackability" are configured in ways that align the user
toward likely, often considered productive, outcomes. This can
be seen in many systems that are open for user configuration.
For example, a pile of Lego pieces gives a more structured
space of possibility than a pile of twigs, even if both may contain
very rich emergent properties to form all kinds of playable
configurations. Yet the Legos give easy access to assemble the
parts into objects that align with familiar tropes of play (houses,
vehicles, figures, etc.). The random twigs, on the other hand,
may require more skills and access to tools for aligning the
outcome in similar ways, to render the twigs recognizable and

---

[15] Cohen (2001: 204). Also Sandel (1996) sketches a similar position in the
struggle between these ideals in anti-trust laws, with one type of argument
promoting small independent and self-governing shops and industries
dedicated to a republican civic ideal, whereas the other lifts the concerns for
how increased competition can promote cheaper goods for consumers. But
as Cohen (2001: 220) highlights, the citizen consumer, aiming to promote an
enlightened and egalitarian form of civic engagement through consumption,
got the tables turned as government started treating citizens not as civic
members but as customers:

> Over the last half of the century, American confidence that an
> economy and culture of mass consumption could deliver democracy
> and equality—that it was in fact the best way to secure them—
> led from the *Consumers' Republic* to the consumerization of the
> republic, where politicians and their customer-voters would reject
> whatever did not pay. A century that began with *citizen consumers*
> inspiring the expansion of government for Progressive reform ended
> with consumers inspiring government's retrenchment to enhance
> their customer satisfaction as citizens. (Cohen 2001: 220, original
> emphasis)

playable as designed toys. The path of least resistance usually means it's hard to make any resistance at all. Most systems designed to be open still orient the user in a way he or she does not end up making any trouble.

RESISTANT SITTING

The very act of sitting down is inscribed by moral judgment (don't slouch!). The person sitting down on the terra firma may be grounded in nature, but also of lower rank than the person sitting on the throne or the high chair (like the chair of the umpire in tennis). Loitering is a form of waiting, which often involves sitting down, that in some places can be punished by law. It is common to see benches in public spaces prepared to make permitted forms of leisure possible, while others are impossible (sitting but not sleeping). But sitting can also become action, and when it comes to nonviolent forms of activism, the sit-in is the classic go-to method. Intensifying the act of the sit-in, a protester locks his or her body onto a piece of critical matter, such as infrastructure or a machine, often called a "lock-on." Using chains to lock one's arms together inside a PVC or metal pipe makes it even harder to remove the protester. Or simply anchor a bicycle U-lock to one's neck and around another object, using the body's vulnerability to increase the material friction, as well as vulnerability or risk, of the act.[16]

In the lock-on, the protester not only withdraws participatory subordination but also turns the body into an obstacle, merging the body with critical infrastructure, which means essentially to meld the matter of the body to the meta.

---

[16] Loitering is codified in the New York Penal Law under sections 240.35, 240.36, and 240.37. Queensland, Australia, has of 2019 banned various forms of protester lock-on devices, and their use can result in up to two years' jail. The ban concerns "dangerous attachment device" that can "unreasonably interfere with the ordinary operation of transport infrastructure." The ban illustrates the radical effect of matter in lock-on tactics.

LOCK-ON

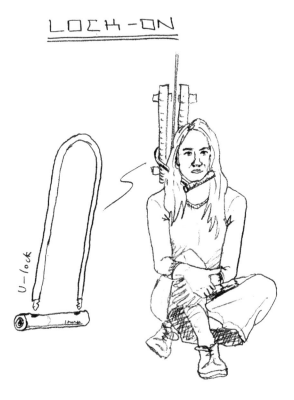

The lock turns the body into a speed bump, slowing down operations to leave time to enable other parts of a protest to emerge or address the meta (such as issuing proclamations, leaving statements with media, negotiating, or escalating). Locking down, hindering, opposing; this is resistance by inaction. It is a refusal to accept the premises of the current negotiation. It means *refusing to be "constructive" within parameters set by an opponent.* Yet the refusal to cooperate, the strike, offers few paths forward for allies. It takes effort to turn zero to the hero.

Without falling into the romantic settings of countercultures that have tried to build new futures, such as the Owenites, Shakers, and Fourierists, one can see materiality as a sturdy base for subjectivity and identity, but also for honest labor, reproduction, and healthy leisure.[17] I find the work of William Coperthwaite, an American craftsman and educator, very inspiring in this sense. Coperthwaite takes inspiration from Gandhi's practice to foster a civic relationship to craft and making. He suggests that craft can inspire living and encourage a more profound social and environmental engagement with society, thus making sure crafts play a social and civic role. Here, the expressive power of crafts lies, like democracy, in its utopian potential. It lies not in its executive power but in *limiting domination*. For Coperthwaite, the process of crafting, as an embodied form of nonviolent living, not only shapes materials but also arranges civic agency that can embody egalitarian and socially responsible values.[18]

To Coperthwaite, our living environment defines our social relations. For example, a house can be more or less honest or dishonest, more or less violent and exploitative. "The larger and more complicated the house we build, the more that house becomes a time-consuming luxury, requiring an effort that could be focused on areas of greater need and worth." Certain houses are in this way more violent than others, as they require experts and underlings for their mere sustenance. Using a chair as an example, Coperthwaite draws parallels to violence hidden in our everyday concepts of beauty:

[17] Reimagining society comes with reinventing the arrangements and distribution of tools and matter, perhaps most famously in the Shaker crafts (see also Bestor 1950; Jennings 2016). The ideal of homesteading is in itself situated at ideological crossroads, where values such as self-employment, frugality, and escape from society into nature overlap with a wide range of political perspectives. A hermit cabin in the backwoods can be a utopian outpost, spiritual retreat, meth-lab, or bomb-making facility, and all at once. In these ideological settings, "you're either buried with your crystals or your shotgun," as quoted in Strange (2020).

[18] Instead of demanding change as a form of resistance in a zero-sum game, constructing the alternative offers a niche of autonomy and "focuses on creating, building, carrying out and experimenting with what is considered desirable" (Sørensen 2016: 57).

If we are ever to develop a nonviolent society, we must eliminate violence on our concept of beauty. A Louis XIV chair and a Shaker chair are not equally beautiful. One was created by a violent, tyrannical way of life, the other by a peaceful and cooperative community that made fair treatment of all people a basic precept—so that the person making the Shaker chair and the one using it received equal respect. … Here's a yardstick: That which deprives another cannot be beautiful.[19]

Instead of celebrating the authoritative life of a Louis XIV chair, or a State chair, Coperthwaite promotes the civic making of "democratic furniture," pieces that require the least possible exotic materials, power tools, and expert labor, to instead seek perfection in simplicity and embodiment of egalitarian values and practices, much inspired by the more communal organization expressed in the furniture and simple tools of the Shakers. Reserving the process of making to either expert craftspeople or outsourcing it to exploited laborers undermines the possibility for a more practical civic community. A democratization of crafts means to foster abilities and enrich talents with encouragement and the rewards of everyday usage and technical as well as social functionality. In a "democratic" chair, matter and meta of democratic ideals and social organization are one, merged into a beautiful, simple, and useful design, and open for participation and change. Most importantly, it "will invite people to use their hands."[20]

SEATED DEMOCRACIES

Coperthwaite was part of a wave of postwar educators who saw homesteading as a way to challenge the dominant culture in society and also use the process of making as a practical journey for both social and inner change. Manuals took on the challenge to open up furniture-making to the extreme, such as

[19] Coperthwaite (2007: 70, 26–27).
[20] Coperthwaite (2007: 98).

COPEARTHWAITE'S

DEMOCRATIC CHAIR

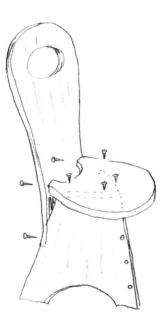

making nomadic cardboard furniture or constructing furniture without any tools.

With clear ideas of using the construction of furniture for changing the makers, Italian designer Enzo Mari published nineteen furniture designs that one could make by oneself. Mari called the process *autoprogettazione* (*auto* "self" and *progettazione* "design"), suggesting how building acts as a way to improve the understanding of the world beyond simply furnishing it.[21] Using rough boards and nails, the reader/builder

---

[21] Mari ([1974] 2002).

is guided through simple techniques intended to democratize design. The end product has an expanded function; "although usable, [the end product] is only important because of its educational value." The pieces produced through the methods were not intended to be the sole means for people's homes, yet Mari was accused of fascism by critics for making people have to add more labor to their lives. Mari instead tried to convey the use of design as self-development, furniture as didactic tools to see, touch, and build a place in the world.[22] In examples of such "democratic" chairs, matter and meta seem to be less about exquisite objects to instead be incarnations of punk furniture anarchism.

Another example of DIY furniture is the crowdsourced project and book *Hartz IV Moebel* by the designer Van Bo Le-Mentzel. Named after a controversial welfare system in Germany, Hartz IV, the DIY book features crowdsourced, simple, and cheap furniture designs that comment on modernist design classics. Making your own Bauhaus-inspired chair in twenty-four hours and with easily accessible material and tools (wood for around 24 euros), the result is something in between the design classics of Marcel Breuer's "Wassily B3 chair" (1925) and Gerrit Rietveld's "Crate chair" (1934). By making furniture in the simplest and cheapest way possible, Le-Mentzel aims to make the methods accessible not only to handy people but also to wider socioeconomic groups. Also, by naming the project after a part of the German welfare system, Le-Mentzel points out the socio-critical elements of DIY practice; using the workshop for making the furniture is a way to also address unemployment, burnout, and illnesses in the context of labor and consumerism.[23]

---

[22] Mari (1974: 5). Mari's designs have been used by CUCULA (the Refugees Company for Crafts and Design), an experimental design space addressing social challenges in Berlin. CUCULA is a design manufactory but also an educational program, where up to eight young refugees (in constant rotation) learn basic skills in design and craftsmanship to train toward permanent employment in the field (https://www.cucula.org).

[23] Le-Mentzel (2012: 12f).

In these examples, craft is part of activating the matter of the chair. Matter is closely interlinked with the making. As made explicit by Coperthwaite, craft should not be limited to a product, heritage, or expression, but seen as a *skill that opens up the world*. Refusing royal decrees and delineations of authenticity, hierarchies, and cultural alignments, Coperthwaite emphasizes making that homes in on the revolutionary proposition of democracy—that things can be radically different if we come together to build them. This is a civic craft of pragmatic possibilities, opening up new forms of practical and constructive togetherness—*by making civic capabilities concrete*—toward new prefigurations. Like barn-raising and a community soup kitchen, it addresses an issue, makes the proposed reality real, gathering participants to live the constructive program while opening up to new connections. While craft as a skill can be used in many ways, even corrupt ones, it opens a continuous room for the unexpected, for improvisation and radical new freedoms. It does not suggest a take-it-or-leave-it utopianism, but an unfinished program open for constant modification.[24]

If we set the sitting devices in relation to each other to compare their material agency, we can see how they all manifest different relationships to the alignment with social structure under state organization.

The seats differ in how they relate to state regulation; do they align with it, either by reproducing hierarchies and feudal posture or by enhancing consumer citizenship through DIY subordination, or do they suggest resisting it, as in hindering or slowing down things, or by opening up and encouraging civic engagements with matter and the crafting of a more democratic social validity of everyday things. As the diagram tries to make

---

[24] Here lies the promise in the process of making, where life possibilities are unbound. As Roberto Unger (2007: 236) has it, radical reimagination of life is the true promise of pragmatic democracy: "We do not live that we may become more godlike. We become more godlike that we may live. We turn to the future to live in the present."

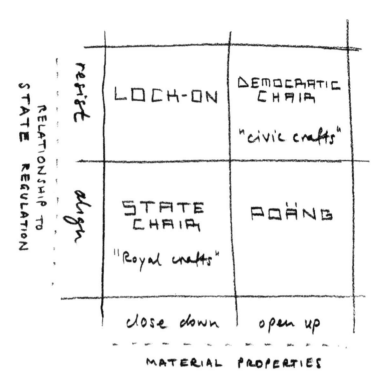

apparent, I propose these alignments are displayed in the material properties of the different devices.

While incomplete and tentative, the schematic representation draws out directions that primitive making can take in everyday settings, and how such ubiquitous home arrangements as chairs and sitting can manifest relationships to participatory subordination. Building democratic furniture may only address some minuscule facets of social ills. But, when applying a diagram like this to other designs and technologies, a broader landscape of possibilities may emerge, manipulating matter in ways that do not deprive but invite people to use their hands to build more equitable forms of togetherness. These ways of relating to making can be utilized in more strategic ways, in everyday primitive objects. But we can also think of ways to manipulate and repurpose simple domestic things for more provocative purposes, actually setting out to challenge the boundaries of meta in more tangible ways. Make sitting matter, and do something!

This is also where Coperthwaite's work shares an ascetic principle with primitive making. Coming back to the Greek meaning of ascetic, as a form of "exercise," making a simple chair is a training or exercise in applied civics. It is about minimizing representation or the need for externalization of agency. It is a chair that calls for finding the appropriate levels of effort, skill, and accessible materials to reach the intended goal to make the process of production as open and easily applicable as possible. It is "democratic" in the sense that it opens itself for direct participation as well as immediate pragmatic use, or, to put it differently, it works, it is good enough.

Things do not need to be as simple as those suggested by Coperthwaite to be democratic; the purpose is to open up for engagement and invite people to use their hands. Here we can once again see the primitive as appropriate as set against surplus, in the meaning that it uses minimal surplus technology, minimal surplus meta, minimal surplus subordination, and *minimal surplus alignment*. It promotes craft as a direct sensation of control—it aligns primarily with parameters set by the maker. It embodies democracy as *a design that limits domination*.

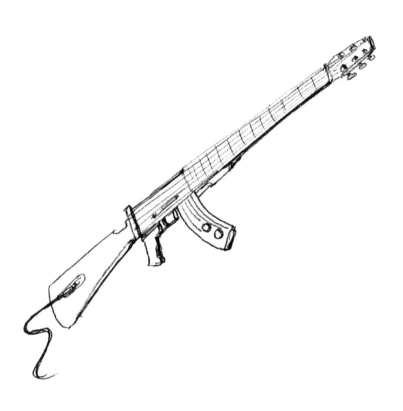

6 Recursive Matters

Having long had an interest in guitar-building, I was immediately captured when I first saw a guitar made from a decommissioned AK-47 by Colombian musician César López. The "Escopetarra" (a portmanteau of the Spanish words *escopeta*, meaning shotgun, and *guitarra*, meaning guitar) seems to play symbolically with a romantic symbol of revolution, merging it with the anti-violence of the troubadour, twisting the allure of weapons with the glamour of the guitar-hero. As a symbol, a machine gun guitar can be read in many ways, but on a material level, it actively strips guns, one at the time, of their power to take lives.[1]

López stresses how the transformation to a guitar suggests a more virtuous destination for the circulation of weapons.

---

[1] Exhibited at the UN building in New York, the Escopetarra joins the Soviet statue "Let Us Beat Swords into Plowshares," the sculpture by Evgeniy Vuchetich from 1959 (which stands outside the United Nations Headquarters in New York). Like reggae legend Peter Tosh's M16-shaped guitar, the use of symbols like the Escopetarra is fraught with troubles. In 2012, Guatemalan president, Otto Pérez Molina played an Escopetarra at a concert to celebrate nonviolence, yet he himself had been deeply implicated in the violence of the civil war (Neustadt 2014). A similar concern can emerge even from the material itself, such as the use of Humanium Metal, iron made by melting down firearms seized in conflict zones.

For example, one of López's Escopetarras began as an AK-47 in the German Democratic Republic, to later be airlifted to leftist guerillas in the Colombian jungle. The same rifle was later captured and used by right-wing paramilitaries. Finally, it was handed to government authorities, from where López had the luthier Alberto Paredes remake it into a guitar. Instead of continuing its cycle as a means for violence, it was ultimately transformed into a musical instrument. A design oriented toward death is transformed and tuned into an instrument for life.

Another artist working with this theme is Mexican Pedro Reyes. In one of his works, "Palas por Pistolas" (shovels from pistols), from 2008, weapons destroyed by the Mexican police were melted down and made into shovels. These shovels were later used to plant trees. In cases like these, the phrase of turning swords into plowshares (originating from the Bible) is taken literally to signify how weapons are remade into tools for promoting life, war into peace. In one act of remaking after another, the material circulation of weapons is displaced, and a world of violence unmade. A product, optimized for inflicting harm, is transformed to instead increase its usefulness for a more virtuous end.

The same action can have a different impact depending on the context. The treehouse in my backyard is not the same as that at an active logging site. The leverage created by matter differs in intensity depending on how and where it is set into action. Bending wire with pliers when building a model of a justice machine at a design academy stands in contrast to using the same pliers cutting down razor wire along a border fence. Here, the context and the material differ; one wire is purchased to make models with, whereas the other wire has been specifically engineered with a cruel material property in mind; razor wire is made for cutting up human flesh.

Facing the cruel reality and the massive scale of the state apparatus can be daunting and overwhelming. Attempting to remake the state with a plier or a hammer is a hopeless cause. A sense of proportion and scale is needed. It is essential to ask how small things can be made to matter. While a speed bump or barricade has an actual physical impact on the many, what can a metal wire, a bucket, or other such rudimentary material means accomplish? What politics can emerge from a small workshop equipped only with primitive tools? And what can making on this scale really change?

INTENSITY VERSUS SCALE

It is undoubtedly naïve to think small-scale material interventions can take on meta concerns head-on. However, even if small, there is a defined and undeniable realism in material action, which is its strength. Manipulate matter at a place with intense levels of meta and you can see a more significant impact. I will try to unpack how I see this.

A perspective on the world that I find helpful as a designer was introduced to me by nonviolence activist Per Herngren, a Swedish member of the plowshare movement.[2] I first read Herngren's work in my late teens and was inspired by his suggested perspective on action. According to Herngren, we tend to perceive concepts such as the state, capitalism, power, or nuclear armament as big abstract entities or containers (what I would say is the faciality of state meta). These concepts appear to us so large and complex a citizen cannot touch them. Thus, the only possible way to address them is to turn to politicians and petition *them* to act for us. Overwhelmed by the scale of troubles, people turn toward the government as the only means to govern, as society is arranged to make the population *ask to*

---

[2] Much of my approach is inspired by Per Herngren's work, in many cases developed together with Stellan Vinthagen, and the work we have done together in discussions and workshops. For an English introduction, see Herngren 1993, and Herngren's blog, https://ickevald.net/perherngren, and http://perherngren.blogspot.com. For a discussion on design, fashion and resistance see von Busch & Herngren (2016). Another important influence has been the resistance studies seminars at University of Gothenburg (and the network around *Journal of Resistance Studies*), and I owe them much gratitude.

be governed. While there may be many social and psychological reasons for voluntary servitude, the factor stressed here is arrangement and scale; we get overwhelmed by the size of the issue we want to address.

For example, to stop the nuclear arms race, the most apparent means to protest for a citizen would be writing petitions or going out on the street in a demonstration, carrying a sign saying "Don't start a nuclear war, Mr. President." Or wait for the next election and hope there is a party against nuclear war to vote for. In both cases, such action affirms the participatory subordination of the subject, who keeps on resigning agency to politicians. It also makes the activist feel they used the agency available to them in the best possible way while *not doing anything.* Instead, action must intervene to stop oppression while with the same action enacting the alternative.

We live in worlds shaped by meta, culture, language, concepts, ideology, and arrangements. These worlds are manifested in matter and shared behaviors that give permanence and stability to social relations. We subordinate under the meta, in the form of government, institutions, or arrangements of knowledge. While the meta-perspective may give overview and predictability, it is hard to know how to address these complex figures beyond the designated avenues for influence. Sending petitions and marching seems to be the most appropriate, if not the only way.

But material activism can offer another approach, emphasizing the sites where the meta becomes tangible and accessible with primitive tools. Material activism addresses and intervenes at these tangible expressions, manipulating them and using these physical examples as grounded experiments. It most effectively happens at the material interfaces of meta; gunmetal has a higher intensity of violence than that of cutlery, and a razor wire on the border more violent than the chain link fence in your backyard. Seeking the matter where meta is intensified, remaking such objects, people find themselves hands-on *governing* rather than orienting themselves toward the government while aligning to be governed. Tensions are grasped and handled, not delegated. The issue is addressed with the means at hand, realizing the ends through the action itself, using material means to realize the desired future, even if on a small scale. In the act of remaking a weapon, the action itself *takes place*. It expands from matter into meta; it pushes away or dissolves violence, even if only at this specific site. Violent meta-arrangements (the organization of armament) are made tangible and locally displaced.

But at what scale and through what kind of processes does this become feasible? Thinking of activism as "acupunctural" can be a helpful step. This means picking strategically important nodes or knots as spots for intervention, releasing energies throughout societal feedback loops. But the acupunctural metaphor also connotes a single silver bullet (or needle) to a problem after finding the knot, which risks exaggerating expectations on what is possible while confusing the scale of action. Is the knot big or small? How do I know if my tools are appropriate? How do I know means and ends coincide in the action taken?[3]

MAKING MEANS AND ENDS MEET

Thinking in scale can be confusing, not least since individual action seems hopelessly insignificant compared to the enormity of the world of artifice. To escape this inhibiting way of thinking, Herngren suggests practicing activism recursively. Recursion comes from the Latin *recurrere*, meaning "run back," and is commonly used in software programming. The term refers to a loop where one of the steps of the procedure invokes the

---

[3] Darren O'Donnel (2008) suggests artistic interventions as "social acupuncture," small actions that aim to redistribute the energies throughout the social whole. With reference to Eastern medicine, O'Donnel sees the social body as a continuous feedback process, where holistic problems in the social body affect its immune system. Local interventions can release healing energies through the body, and this could apply also to the social body: "small interventions at key junctures should affect larger organs, in turn contributing to feedback loops that can amplify and affect the distribution of energy resources." (2008: 49)

procedure itself, calling it back to reiterate the cycle of running the procedure. It can be a subroutine repeatedly reactivating the execution of a program procedure, creating a successive repetition toward the intended results. The important part is that it is a repeating process that keeps concentrating on a minor detail, continuously implementing itself.[4]

In recursive action, means and ends coincide within the act itself, a perspective from Gandhi that Herngren builds further on. The task is to avoid addressing a massively complex issue all at once, as this risks imprecise action or simply being overwhelmed by the scale of the challenge. Instead, recursiveness offers a method of shrinking an issue until it is small enough to address. Recursive action is performative in that it realizes its goal in the act of creation instead of pointing elsewhere or pushing its goal toward the future. Means and ends coincide as *the goal is the method*, and the goal is contained within the technique. In the recursive action, the whole is smaller than the parts, meaning the ultimate goal (the whole) of the action is implemented within each part of the action itself. In each instance, the whole stays realistic throughout and is never an abstract vision. As the goal is practiced in the action, it trains the participants in living the purpose. Thus, the action implements its program on *the scale it is effective on*. It does not wait around to scale up or to overorganize, which usually means delaying or avoiding action. Instead, the point is to stay nimble and always stay real. It can be idealistic while simultaneously realist.[5] By being iterative,

---

[4] Christopher Kelty (2005) suggests hacker communities often try to implement cohesive relationships between social as well as technical relationships what are recursive in nature. Kelty calls these communities "recursive publics," signifying a group constituted by a shared, profound concern for the technical and legal conditions of possibility for their own association (185). The recursive public is "a particular form of social imaginary through which this group imagines in common the means of their own association, the material forms this imagination takes" (186). Kelty uses the term to "comprehend something more tangible than ideology and less absolute than a technocracy" (187).

[5] While it is easy to think of Gandhi's political nonviolent action as an example of moral idealism in politics, he stressed it as being a "practical idealism," or even, as Mantena (2012) suggests, political realism (see also Naidu 2006, and Vinthagen 2015).

it multiplies through pulsations and imitations, rather than becoming large, abstract, and intangible: recursive material activism concentrates action at the point where the meta is most intense in matter. It intervenes with the meta *where it matters.*

But let's first look at the recursive loop to help identify the point and method of intervention. In recursive action, means and ends have to coincide. Set the scale accordingly or shrink if needed. In recursion, the function/action calls upon itself to iterate or shrink and reiterate. Herngren suggests recursive action as similar to a program executing itself while calling back upon itself in a cycle:

– The starting point: is action necessary here?
– If so, frame the issue needing action, check; is the context small enough to realize means/ends fully?
– If correct scale, start action,
– If the issue is too big for the action to realize means/ends fully, then shrink and reframe,
– If correct scale; start action,
– If the issue is still too big for the action to realize means/ ends fully, then shrink even more and reframe,
– If correct scale; start action,
– [repeat]
– If action is successful and means/ends are fully realized, then move on and multiply, and start again.

The cycle thus shrinks to a level where it is effective, where means and ends coincide within the scope of the action. If the issue remains too big, shrink and test again. To use one of Herngren's examples, if I am working towards nuclear disarmament, I focus on the critical material component or manifestation of the issue, the real problem: nuclear missiles. I need to turn the metal object designed to kill people into a tool designed to feed people. I must turn a missile into a plowshare. Use the means you have at your disposal, making sure means and ends coincide. I need to disarm not to sabotage but transform the act of disarmament into a constructive act. Use the primitive tools at hand. For the moment, stay at the scale you can handle. As Herngren suggests, if I cannot disarm a giant missile by my own physical capacities and start turning it into a plowshare, I need to go for a smaller part, such as the top lid of the silo. If this lid is still too big, I get to work on the hinges, and so on. Using an appropriate tool, a tool for metalwork such as a hammer, I start transforming the hinge from part of a weapon into part of a plowshare. Accomplish means and ends within the action, move on, and repeat.

A crucial component in recursive action is that it is proactive; while it opposes one thing, the same action proposes a way out of the dilemma. Rather than protesting against weapons or war in general, being stuck in a reactive position, the action is life-affirming, transformative, and utopian. By hammering on the hinge to the silo, I am actively working on disarmament on my way to create a plowshare. It is the opponent that is reactive (and pro-death), and the police will do the protesting, and who has to stop me from doing the right thing. But the important thing is that when I am done, I move on to the next silo. The action is small, but as means and ends meet, it realizes its goal in each action, and it is ready for multiplication and escalation.[6]

---

[6] Development practitioner Nabeel Hamdi (2004) suggests taking steps that could be affiliated with recursive action, in his "small change" approach;

> This philosophy of "acting in order to induce others to act," of offering impulses rather than instructions, and of cultivating an environment for change from within, starts on the ground and often with small beginnings which have "emergent" potential—a bus stop, a pickle jar, a composting bin, a standpipe. (Hamdi 2004: xx)

While Hamdi stresses the emergent properties of small action, it is always practical and offers empirical situations; the results can be immediately evaluated. Hamdi encourages small visioning because it is close to people and their participation for grounding and testing, but also as it allows room for uncertainty, while not falling into passivity. It "leaves space to think creatively, uncertainty gives room to think" (39). Work towards strategic smallness; "Start small and start where it counts" (139). The realization of local means and ends suggests a material form of political realism, an ideally grounded power politics (in actions and behaviors rather than motivations). This is reminiscent of Gandhi's claim of being a "practical idealist," in acknowledgment of the

RECURSIVE ACTION

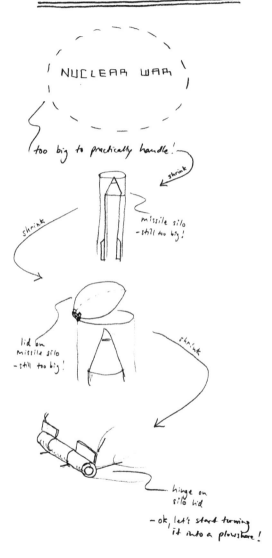

The recursive approach suggests that if you want to address an issue, shrink the size of your action to be at a level where means and ends meet and you have agency to affect a successful outcome. If you cannot reach a point where you control the outcome, you risk delegating or pushing the action away. To feel in control, you need to experience that not all possibilities are placed downstream, dependent on rivals, structures, or abstract forces, such as fate, the king, or the market. To "do the right thing" implies exercising control over ourselves and our environment; we must perceive that control is possible, even if at a minuscule scale.

To take direct action means to do it yourself (or together), with the idea that the individual takes control over their actions to influence others. But the focus on "doing" easily misses the issue of control: who *does* what versus who *controls* what? What action promotes is a shift of the "locus of control." With this concept, the personal conception of a *locus* (Latin "location") can be either *internal* or *external*. In the former, the person experiences being in control of his or her life. In the latter, on the other hand, the person experiences that life is controlled from the outside, by systemic, environmental, or political factors that cannot be influenced or changed, be they higher forces, fate or chance, or by power such as hierarchies, state, market, or culture. Action is a training of agency, practicing the possibility of control. Herngren often uses dance as an example; even if I *know* salsa, I must practice it *to do* salsa. Similarly, I may know nonviolence, but I may still have problems doing nonviolence.

This means that knowing is not enough to enhance control. The risk is always that the perspective on an issue grows or abstracts itself from reach. The chain of cause and effect pushes the scale of what matters away from your hands, away from your control, and the possibility to self-govern. Foucault

confrontation in Hobbesian realism. Here, the recursive material practice in plowshare actions reflect Ursula Le Guin's call for "realists of a larger reality" (Le Guin 2016: 113).

famously posits that governmentality repeats throughout the scales of social organization, echoing from bottom up and top down. "Whoever wants to be able to govern the state must first know how to govern himself, and then, at another level, his family, his goods, his lands, after which he will succeed in governing the state," and then in reverse, repeating the same diagram; "when a state is governed well, fathers will know how to govern their families, their wealth, their goods, and their property well, and individuals will also conduct themselves properly."[7] As Foucault alerts, the art of governance becomes an external science of population control, a meta-system of knowledge, or epistemes or discursive formations, working across all levels of governance, from larger administrative systems and mirrored into the smallest components. This perspective moves the locus of control even further away from the population into meta and leaves subjects with few interfaces toward affecting their living environment. The recursive perspective, on the other hand, highlights the material components and makes them accessible for hands-on manipulation, where subjects can interfere with the processes of governmentality. Recursion gives participants an iterative formula to aim and center agency toward self-governing action.

PULSATION

So scale down to the point where action matters. Focus on a part of the conflict, narrow the area of your intervention, or shrink the number of participants. Calibrate and iterate, adjust again and reiterate. However, don't narrow down too far, so you retreat into Lilliputian action and stay there. The method is about testing, training, and then repeating. Strive to multiply. As Herngren underlines, practice and repeat to make your actions start *pulsating*. The scale has to be on an appropriate

---

[7] Foucault (2007: 133).

level and within the reach of participants to easily be imitated and replicated. But as it is being repeated, means and ends have to coincide in each instance. Through pulsation, actions start affecting the larger whole, creating resonances throughout the surroundings.

Imitation and pulsation may give associations to emergent and self-organizing behaviors. While this offers helpful visions on how behaviors replicate and scale, it also comes with some risks. References to the phenomenon of emergence tend to strip away the importance and responsibility to *initiate and reproduce action*. Citing emergence, the hope among many designers seems to be to initiate a self-replicating process that does not require any more input. The designer starts a fire and then just leaves. Pulsation and imitation underscore the need for human agency to keep staying involved, and that support and energy are needed to sustain action. Even if minor, action requires commitment, courage, and stamina. While nonhuman actors and agency must be included in broader perspectives on nonhierarchical cohabitation and conviviality, it is also essential to acknowledge the importance and impact of human agency and sustained commitment to action.[8]

People can get inspired and start reproducing the action, and it replicates. The initiative is reproduced as the goals of the action become visible to others. In this way, the pulsating replication of action, each having means and ends coincide, becomes a more potent force for change than convincing people while they remain inactive.[9]

---

[8] In Eagleton's (2016: 12) words; "Men and women are indeed in some ways more creative than hedgehogs. They are also unspeakably more destructive, much for the same reasons. Those who deny the former are at risk of ignoring the latter."

[9] In many ways, the recursive perspective could be seen in correspondence with the Situationists' "revolution of everyday life" (Vaneigem 2012)—it is by multiplication of realized situations of liberation that general insurrection takes place.

A recursive approach helps make nonviolence more actionable as it also forces participants to turn abstract issues into something concrete. It suggests a scale and a place to intervene that is relatable to the individual and the tools at hand. This is why I find the method so suggestive for primitive making. It aims limited and practical action to the crucial points where meta and matter coincide.

As suggested in the example, nuclear war is not addressed on the meta level of geopolitical power struggle or trying to convince politicians that war is terrible. This stays too meta. Instead, the problem of nuclear war is framed as a particular number of physical missiles armed with nuclear warheads, made from matter in a multitude of small physical or mechanical parts. As long as one addresses issues on a large or aggregated level, the meta remains abstract and seemingly intangible, only approachable by governments. Instead, intervening with the matter that matters offers a possibility to take on the tangible manifestation of the meta.

Herngren suggests one can address other meta in a similar vein. As long as patriarchy is addressed as an intangible ideology, the instances remain out of reach. Instead, actions and manifestations of patriarchy can be challenged and displaced. A similar approach can be taken to capitalism: while it is a global and dispersed system, it can be addressed in scales where means and ends coincide through primitive action. Capitalism surely exists in small parts in every commodity, and it appears in the aggregations of everything around us. But it can be displaced from these incarnations. Merely protesting or staying meta concedes potential agency or pushes activity

$$\text{Recursion} =$$
$$(\text{resistance} + \overset{\text{material}}{\text{change}} + \text{prefiguration} + \overset{\text{small}}{\text{win}}) \bigg\} \overset{\text{means} +}{\underset{\text{merge}}{\text{ends}}}$$
$$\times \text{ repetition/multiplication}$$

ahead. A more action-based approach would be to ask how I can displace, push out, or minimalize capitalism. Can I push it out and displace it from my community? From my family? From my kitchen? From my lunch? Should I start from a minimally capitalist sandwich? If successful, repeat and move to the next target, keep escalating scale and impact. I start from my kitchen and move upwards, adapting to the challenge but making sure at every instance I simultaneously realize means and ends. I keep repeating the pulsation and multiplication.

This is where the impact of matter multiplies with human agency; power is broken, and participatory subordination is displaced. Such politics of small gestures bring people together to claim power. In his definition of such political power, Jeffrey Goldfarb suggests:

> When people freely meet and talk to each other as equals, reveal their differences, display their distinctions, and develop a capacity to act together, they create power. Hannah Arendt distinguishes this power from coercion. It is underappreciated, both in everyday life and on the larger political stage.[10]

It is the power in the small scale where governmental authority is unveiled and broken, the anti-elitist type of power that defined the feminist and civil rights movements and also contributed to the fall of communism in Central Europe. The togetherness that forms concerted power among people is brought together around small everyday objects, such as kitchen tables.

> During the Soviet period, small circles of intimate friends were able to talk to each other without concern for the present party line around the kitchen table. This free zone, where one

---

[10] Goldfarb (2006: 4); next quotes, pp. 10, 16, 68.

could speak one's mind without concern about the interaction between the official and unofficial, produced unusually warm and intense ties among family and friends. Here Communist Party members would complain about "them," meaning the party, without consciousness of contradiction. Here personal and collective memories were told and retold in opposition to official history.

Around the kitchen table, or in the exchange of controversial or forbidden books, people were not conspiring but acted as if they already lived in a free society, "creating a regularized pattern of social interaction, an institution in fact, which was a component part of a free civic society." In these small zones of independence and dignity, the politics of small things play out. "It's the independence that matters, not the size."[11]

A helpful framework to turn action more accurate and proportionate is the so-called SMART model, which I find helpful with recursive action. The acronym stands for Specific, Measurable, Achievable, Realistic, and Time-bound, parameters to check in order to increase the effectiveness of a campaign. The SMART model for activism, which comes out of marketing and management, makes a campaign more focused and tangible. Pinning down these parameters helps align expectations and efforts while also shrinking down unrealistic goals to what can

---

[11] Georgy Katsiaficas (2006: 84) captures the use of material objects in an experience in one of the anti-nuclear activist camps in Germany in 1980 in order to stop the construction of a nuclear waste site in Gorleben;

> A city was built from the already felled trees—a wonderfully diverse collection of houses—and dubbed the Free Republic of Wendland (a name taken from the region's traditional title). Local farmers, about 90 percent of whom were against the nuclear dump yard, provided the thousands of resident-activists with food and materials to help build their "republic." Passports were issued bearing the name of the new republic, imaginative illegal underground radio shows were broadcast, and newspapers were printed and distributed throughout the country. ... National identities were temporarily suspended, since we were all citizens of the Free Republic of Wendland and owed allegiance to no government.

be achieved and further built on. An essential aspect of the recursive approach is that it requires *engagement with power and resistance*. It does not merely create something (even if SMART) but actively *breaks power* by displacing the undesired element as it withdraws the user's participatory subordination. In that sense, it is not only protest (opposition) and not merely prefiguration of a more desirable situation (proposition). It acts into the conflict, reconfigures it, and realizes its whole goal through the method itself.

In this sense, it follows the "two hands approach" of queer feminist Barbara Deming and aligns with the constructive program of Gandhi. Arguably Gandhi's most widespread constructive campaign of material activism was taken in the 1930 Salt March. What made this campaign so powerful and open for participation was the practical manifestation of the resistance and the active confrontation with the legal boundaries of British colonialism. In the Salt March, Gandhi and the participants showed how each grain of salt contained British imperialism in the form of tax (the salt came from the Indian ocean). The only salt available was the British-taxed version. But the salt was also more than imperialism, as a necessity for human survival and a staple in cooking. The challenge was to take British imperialism out of each grain of salt and make sure people could do so themselves rather than asking a leader to do so for them. By explicitly challenging the salt tax and making one's own salt, each grain of salt was detoxified from the meta of British imperialism. It also became more; each grain became part of hands-on training in the displacement of domination and a tangible manifestation of independent India. As salt production is a constructive and life-affirming act, the opponent (the colonial British) had to be reactive to deny such action, thus effectively revealing the oppression. The strategic use of salt matter upsets and displaces the imperialist meta, simultaneously displacing participatory subordination. Multiply. Escalate. The British were forced to negotiate.

The ingenious technique employed in the Salt March is turning grains of salt into small justice machines that any participant can engage with. Turning an AK-47 into a guitar or a shovel requires much more effort, skill, and organization. Yet the method is the same; identify where a high-intensity meta is tangible in matter. Where violence, domination, or injustice is made explicit, start remaking at this point. Employ a recursive perspective. If you can't address the issue and simultaneously realize the aim at this location, shrink and test again. Repeat. Pulsate. If the result is beautiful and the refrain is catchy, even better.

Is action needed here? Is the scale appropriate? Transform the matter. Move on, keep going, and pulsate.

STRATEGIC MUG

7   Strategic Objectiles

In 2010, Nabeel Hamdi, an architect and a pioneer in participatory planning, made a presentation at the School of Design and Crafts in Gothenburg. He discussed using participation and thinking in self-organized systems in participatory development with the audience. Hamdi suggested using small-scale, incremental change in practices that have long cherished top-down planning executed through large-scale organizations. It seemed to all make sense from the perspective of architecture, but I struggled with what this would mean to craft practitioners and students. So, I asked Nabeel how we could think of textiles, jewelry, or ceramics from his suggested perspective. Nabeel answered that if I make mugs, I should try to make a more "strategic mug." This would mean a mug that is not only functional and aesthetically pleasing but that builds toward a goal and mobilizes assets in its production and life.

After the presentation, I could not get the strategic mug out of my head. I kept trying to formulate how a strategic mug could work, informed by Nabeel's ideas. As Nabeel has emphasized, first, the mug has to be practical as well as strategic. In its making and use, it has to be part in realizing its goal. It sounded familiar; means and ends are meeting in the same object. Second, it is also a thing that empowers and turns stakeholders toward taking ownership over their livelihoods. Its materiality is a common cause around which participants mobilize work around their vision. It gives tangible results. This creates small wins. Small wins build trust. It is a mug with an objective.

On a more practical level, it is a mug that mobilizes tangible and intangible assets. It is a mug that not only makes money circulate in the market economy but also builds skills and capabilities that in turn enhance societal flourishings. It helps bring about authority and control to its handler and responsibility in partnership with other stakeholders. It takes part in power sharing. It is a mug that helps participants govern their own lives.

Making this strategic mug would require a shift of perspective. The mug is functional and aesthetic, and it spends most of its time in the kitchen cupboard, like so many other of its siblings. But in its journey through the world, it also does more. It asserts itself as a material catalyst; it helps participants define what is desired and needed. It raises interest among partners that can take part in the mobilization of resources and creates partnerships.

It is not only a single thing but manifests visions and goals, and its material form and presence also helps provide continuity. If done right, a strategic mug not only sells and is used by many but also takes part in realizing its vision. It is a mug that plays an active role in organizing and arranging the sociopolitical realms around it and can significantly reduce dependency and bring about local authority and control.[1]

As we discussed, it sounded more and more as if our attention was drawn to the organization around production and distribution more than the material mug itself. But Nabeel emphasized the need for the practical example to bring people together in a shared effort. The mug must be the main character in the drama. Doing something hands-on, showing actual results, is central to overcome differences of opinion. The more

---

[1] Hamdi's books *Small Change* (2004) and *The Placemaker's Guide to Building Community* (2010) have been great influences to my own work. I often try to use his advice: scaling down to scale up and working backwards to move forward.

practical examples of betterment the mug could help realize, the better it would be to reach the vision set out. A mug can be a justice machine.

MATERIAL MOBILIZATION

Gandhi's campaign of distributed DIY salt production in the Salt March was masterfully planned and executed. What differentiates the march from other types of protest-driven activism is the strategic use of primitive making. By being so simple to engage in, direct in application, and tied to a kind of matter necessary for survival, the actions make their goals and methods inviting, visionary, real, and political at once. In this case, material activism comes to embody civic action and crafts. Participants simultaneously withdraw their subordination by engaging in them, with no advanced tools or organization used (and no revolutionary consciousness or schooling is a prerequisite). By taking aim at tangible mechanisms of exclusion, such as the salt's entanglement in colonial laws, the actions call the borders of meta into question. Using material manipulation, the issue at stake is made tangible. This is what strategic making can do: employ primitive manipulation of matter through small recursive actions that can pulsate to produce more extensive social affects, challenge meta boundaries while simultaneously realizing its means and ends.[2]

---

[2] To emphasize: boundaries are not automatically a problem. Any form of activism can be used for many types of purposes and aims. Meta boundaries are not unjust per se, and limitations in action spaces can be the result of fair negotiations and civic consensus. Limitations are essential for agency and power to be directed and useful. Restriction is not automatically negative. Eagleton (2016: 16) critiques blind followers of Deleuze's admiration for change and argues:

> Deleuze can see constraint only as negative, a view that faithfully reflects the marketplace ideology he otherwise finds objectionable … with a handful of qualifying clauses, we are offered a banal antithesis between the vital, creative, desirous, and dynamic (to be unequivocally endorsed) and the oppressive realm of stable material

Strategic making employs material manipulation to reach specific outcomes with critical effect. To better see this connection between matter and affective impact, it is helpful to see objects as interlinked chains of events, projected through space and time as a series of instants. Drawing from its Latin origin, the object or *obiectum* (literally "thrown against") is propelled through or against the world. As it moves through the world, it forms what Deleuze calls an "objectile," which, like the projectile, is traveling as an ongoing happening through time and space. I use objectile to think of how *matter is thrown against the metaxu* between worlds, against boundaries that separate, mechanisms of exclusion and demarcation. An objectile is made to provoke and raise a silenced (material) voice against a delimiting border. In the examples of Gandhi, the khadi and salt were objectiles launched into conflict with British imperialism, stirring things up while also recursively realizing their goals. The objectile is of matter, but is also a becoming, a verb, a project in space-time—meta entangled in matter, unfolding (ex-plicating) what was contained within or in-folded (im-plicated). Deleuze introduces the term objectile in his book *The Fold*, and I often think of Veronica Scott's Detroit-based project The Empowerment Plan as an example of this, an initiative that starts with a jacket that can also be a sleeping bag for homeless people, but unfolds to be a factory for life support, employment, job training, and education.[3]

The purpose and capacities to achieve the goal of the objectile are folded into the object. Through its journey, the strategic plan is realized through the way it interacts with its environment. To use objectiles strategically means to aim the process of making

forms (to be implicitly demonized). … What we offered, then, is a Romantic-libertarian philosophy of unbridled affirmation and incessant innovation, as though the creative and innovative were unambiguously on the side of angels.

[3] Deleuze (2006). For more about the Empowerment Plan, see https://www.empowermentplan.org—the use of a jacket in accordance with the idea of the objectile would also stress the expanded use and end-of-use phases of the product.

toward the strategic goal. The objectile emphasizes how matter keeps futuring. It develops and acts in ways that promote and manifest means and ends. Means and ends are im-plicated, or folded into the object itself: *the objectile is active matter set in motion*.[4]

The enfoldment of capacities is central to the objectile. Think of it as a Swiss knife, an inconspicuous object with tools ready to be extruded and used. But whereas the Swiss knife is multipurpose, the objectile has a target. As the concept plays with the word projectile, it is the more controversial objects that catch the imagination. Take, for example, Norwegian black metal band Burzum's iconic album *Aske* (Norwegian for Ashes) from 1993, famous for its cover image of a burned-down church where the record was sold together with a lighter. A more constructive example could be the community fridges that people set up around New York, where people donate fridges and electricity to keep them running, setting them up in the streets for food donations. With such primitive surplus infrastructure, mutual aid becomes a bit more practical and accessible; the arrangement is as functional as utopian; free food from a free fridge, free for anyone to give and take. However, just because the objectile is there does not mean its goal just happens. But its material capacities help arrange reality around it in a way that facilitates the purpose set out to be accomplished. There is still a need for agency, willpower, time, and organization to keep it sustained and real. Even the lighter needs to be lit, the fridge cleaned and kept stocked.

---

[4] MacAskill (2015) suggests a series of guiding questions to help develop and evaluate effective activism: How many people benefit, and by how much? Is this the most effective thing you can do? Is this area neglected? What would happen otherwise? What are the chances of success and how good would success be? An interesting example of a monetary objectile can be Peebles and Luzzatto's (2019) biochar-based currency—a currency that is bound to the sequestering of carbon (rather than "mining" gold or digital algorithms): just like gold has been dug out of the ground to be used as currency, this is a process where carbon is sequestered from the atmosphere and its tokens used for trade and speculation. The more it is traded, the higher the value, the more the incentives to sequester more carbon from the atmosphere.

So, to come back to the strategic mug, the mug is the active matter. Depending on what the vision is for what it should help accomplish, the making, dissemination, and use are all processes "scripted" into mobilizing and activating assets along its way. The collection of the clay, the making of the mug, the sale, use, reuse, and waste cycle; each interaction has a potential for activating and aligning assets to become allies. The aim is to make sure the mug's continuous becoming is designed to make means and ends meet.

But even if we could utilize recursive practices and mobilize lasting pulsations of resistance that could create local change while also launching strategic objectiles into political institutions, we should not expect primitive making to be a silver bullet to any injustice. Even the impact of thousands of people defying imperial laws and starting to live differently only changes the world to a certain degree; a wider political struggle is also necessary. But with its tangible results, the objectile forms the foundation for a lived practice with a permanence that promises increasing control and trust in the practical spirit of a shared commonality that animates civic imagination. With a strategic approach, an objectile can animate participants, unifying their efforts, building a shared experience of accomplishment while making civics contagious.

TACTICAL PRESENCE AND ITS LIMITATIONS

While the term strategic design appears in many places, the strategic element seems to mean many things, from undertakings being goal-oriented to simply design that is in alignment with the business plan. The term strategy has a baggage of warfare, elitism, exclusion, and hierarchical planning. It connotes a masculinism and warrior mentality and brings a zero sum and violent worldview. This is a world inhabited only by winners and losers. It limits visions, innovation, and a questioning of the rules. But without a strategy, the risk is always to play an illusionary, reactive or merely survivalist game rather than configure new futures and act on them. The objectile engages its environment.

It takes place. It has a presence. Strategy guides the objectile toward the target, even if the goal is still on the horizon.

In work with matter, a core element of strategic design may come forth; that strategy makes an uncompromising claim to achieve its goal. A strategic approach to a subject knows it entails struggle and competition. It is not enough to plan and envision. Using objectiles strategically forces the maker to look up from the sketch paper, workbench, or knitting needles. For a strategy to be implemented, even if it concerns a strike or sit-in, *action must be taken*. And I mean this in two senses: an undertaking is set in motion, and initiative is claimed, taken. Taking action asserts itself, making irrevocable claims onto contested reality.

While there is strategic rhetoric and use of speech acts, I want to stress the importance of material assertion, that is, the use of materiality to make strategy tangible and enforce it. It makes a more steadfast claim on the world than visions or speculations. Compare, for example, to management. Operational management within a company concerns primarily improving efficiency and controlling costs. On the other hand, strategic management is about overall direction, specifying the organization's objectives, developing policies and plans to achieve those objectives, and then allocating necessary resources as well as the authority to implement the plans.[5]

Strategy is thus not something we often connote with the workbench. Strategy is done on the map or in the headquarters, not on the workshop floor. It is about overview, not the nitty-gritty details or lived experience. In his famous book *The Practice of Everyday Life*, Michel de Certeau puts tactics in opposition to strategy.[6] Strategy presumes control and a chain of command; it is top-down. Strategy is the perspective of those in power. Tactics, on the other hand, adapts and bends the environment created by power. Whereas strategy is planned from the top

---

[5] There can certainly also be *strategic inaction*, not least in strikes or more local refusals to work or collaborate—and there should certainly be more strategic refusal to design unethical applications. See also the many successful examples of strategic ignorance (McGoey 2019).

[6] DeCerteau (1984).

and drawn on the map, tactics are lived from below and trace the terrain of experience. Tactics are the bricolage of getting through the day, of making-do. While strategy is stiff, tactics are adaptive, using the unpredictable to enhance its force. Tactics are present on the ground, responsive and iterative.

For de Certeau, users are not passive consumers. Users are bricoleurs; they fiddle with things, tweak their use, trespass on laws for their own interests, and make their own rules. The user is an amateur taking liberties the expert refutes. The bricoleurs use tactics, or "poaching," to improvise, tweak, reappropriate, and reinvent the functions of products, texts, and environments, where use becomes unauthorized reinvention.

While tactics are agile and adaptive, they often lack overview and planning. It lacks a unifying vision of where it leads and orients behavior. This is what makes it lean and playful, but it is also its weakness. Like other bottom-up becomings, tactics are easily manipulated, not so much by the state bureaucracy but by agile psy-ops, by misinformation, agent provocateurs, affects and feeding confusion, playing with tactical shortsightedness. With no overarching plan, negotiations and compromises become confusing. The short horizon of tactics does not prepare itself for the possibility of actually succeeding in claiming power. Like in chess, a master player thinks several steps ahead; the master has experience, strategic overview, and taps into a long history of thousands of games played. New players may have some intelligent moves up their sleeves, even tweak some rules, but without thinking several steps ahead, the chances of winning are negligible.

Environmental activist Larry Lohmann unpacks the negotiations of carbon trading in the Kyoto negotiations of 1997. In the analysis, Lohmann uses chess to illustrate the limits of influence made by environmental NGOs in the politics of global trade. In the world of chess, an insult is being a "patzer." It is the mark of an amateur who quickly falls into avoidable traps, going for the poisoned pawn, falling into fool's mate, or, overall, failing to work toward strategic development to favor quick gains instead. The better player gives away a piece, which the patzer hungrily takes, only to give up a strategic position and end up mate.

A strategic player uses what may appear as a significant sacrifice to open up the position for more extensive operations. The tactical player, failing to get a strategic overview to see the big picture, easily falls for the poisoned pawn while waiting for what looked like a foolish mistake from the strategic player. If one thinks of politics as the art of the possible, without a longer perspective, tactical gains can quickly end up constricting one's own strategic space for action, and short-term gains can make long-term political struggles end prematurely.

The critical lesson from patzers is that a strategic player plays the same game on a higher level because of the masterly use of already tested patterns. What may appear as conspiracies from the tacticians of the grassroots NGOs is more accurately described as strategic pattern recognition from master players of the technopolitical structures of global capitalism. Noble ideas get utilized in geopolitical games. It is easy to start imagining behind-the-scenes workings of malignant masterminds when one is simply outplayed on the board. The problem, according to Lohmann, is that "lazy, superficial, tactical theories [are] prevalent among even some of the most well-intentioned professionalised NGOs and academics." Strategy means calculating many steps ahead, preparing for the opponent's possible moves. It involves experience from playing the long game, using institutional knowledge, and a deeply ingrained sense of what pathways will be advantageous and what will not. "You know you've been snookered when a deal you yourself helped make turns out to undermine your deepest goals and allegiances at every turn."[7] This plays out in the way the patzer has to accept the strategic player's setting of terrain, limiting the room to maneuver to a few small wins and a bit of damage control.

The use of strategy here is to insist on mobilizing force behind broader visions, to build advantageous practical positions and advantage for more political space of action. Strategy means to play the long game, not merely "intervening" into systems. The goal may not be limited to winning but to set in motion collective questioning and mobilization, building alliances through practical and proactive resistance. A strategic game means acknowledging a need to understand the game, its players, context, and positions, well enough to know whether, when, and how to play and what rules to break.

It makes perfect sense to associate primitive making as a tactic in de Certeau's understanding—and this is how we most often encounter it. They are the minor practical tweaks of everyday life that give us a sense of control by short-circuiting larger systems and structures. Yes, primitive making seldom has a larger plan.

But this is where the strategic objectile comes in; it is *an object of primitive making with strategic ambitions*. Strategic making challenges control not by evading it but by confronting and provoking it. Strategic making sets out to break power within a larger plan of action. It is not merely the teenage rebellion of small devices. It emerges out of an awareness of the organization and arrangements of the ecology at hand. A strategic objectile requires a good understanding of the landscape it engages; it requires a cartography and a realistic trajectory.

Strategy is a concept that makers need to be more accustomed to. Strategy sets directions, focuses efforts, defines goals and operations of actors working in concert, mobilizing force to execute on the plan: *strategy sets out to take place*. Through this plan, the strategy provides guidance in response to the environment that develops with actions from competitors or adversaries that aspire for the same power to make itself real. It's not only a matter of envisioning or planning, but the deployment of means to fulfill the ends. It is an implementation that happens in competition with other actors, in a continuous struggle over the terrain, whether market shares and increased sales or territory and domination. Strategy is realist, as it counts on an opponent, an actor that is never static but always moves to strengthen its position, always about to outmaneuver you at every turn. You have to take for granted that your antagonist will act to continuously undermine and fight back against your plan.

Strategic objectiles are explicitly made from matter and thrown against the metaxu of state space in incessant and dynamic trajectories, even though they may result from primitive making. They may be simple things: a chair, a lock, a cookie box, or a bucket, but their strategic impetus make a claim to power, or to break power, even if only to displace or withdraw participatory subordination.

Strategic making asserts means and ends. It goes beyond sketching and dreaming up scenarios, yet, as suggested earlier, even making is utopian. Primitive making of strategic objectiles summons "thing power" that escalates material activism toward its aims. It can be in the form of simple everyday things, such as DIY salt, but it is through the strategic trajectory and recursive practice the stage is set for how successfully it can be used.

STITCH FOR SENATE

Let us look at what I think is a powerful example of strategic making. Stitch for Senate is a project by textile artist Cat Mazza that took place in the United States in 2007–8 that uses craft as a tool to push into politics, connecting civic engagement with knitting, to *take place in state space*. In a time of continuous US wars, the project uses an explicit anti-war tone yet takes on a recursive strategy to shrink down the conflicting concerns around the wars into tangible material things and addressing these between individuals: citizens, soldiers, and elected politicians.

The project mobilizes knit hobbyists to make simple helmet liners or balaclavas, building on the history of wartime knitting to keep soldiers warm, a practice dating back to the American Revolution. During the Second World War in particular, women, men, and school-age children were invited to "Knit for Defense," a home-front campaign for knitters to keep troops warm. Tapping into this long tradition of patriotic organizing, discussion, and care work within knitting circles, the helmet liners to the soldiers this time take a detour over each state's senator in the lead up to the 2008 election. All hundred US senators get a helmet liner

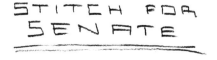

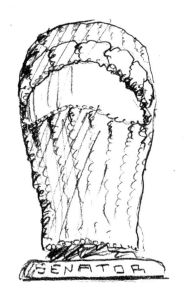

from hobbyists in their state, knitted to persuade the elected officials to care for and support the troops by bringing them home to safety. Through the organization of the project, every senator receives their own helmet liner and a letter encouraging them to forward it to a soldier.[8]

Mazza conceives ingeniously in the project how to use the knitted balaclava as a gift and objectile to be thrown against senators who decide on war and peace and stir up the meta. The same design that historically has unquestioningly supported

---

[8]　More thorough information and documentation of Cat Mazza's project can be found at http://www.stitchforsenate.us.

the war effort on the premise of political decrees is entangled anew in rerouting the gift's journey over the senators. As with the gift, it is the same matter that travels socially, creating relationships in each transition, where a micro-society emerges in every exchange. But here, it employs what bell hooks may call a "critical form of love," embodied in the objectiles; it is a love that does not distract from the moral orders it is embedded in; it is not passive but asserts what is right.[9] It is a love that sets out to stop war and bring soldiers home. The balaclava is sent from one individual maker to one individual senator and may or may not go on to a soldier, but the affective investment in the matter is made so that the objectile maximizes its level of care; it asks who really cares and stands to reveal hypocrisy. The care embodied in the balaclavas is as provocative as it is healing. It is a homemade mask that creates a new faciality for both a caring, knitting citizen and an anonymous soldier. The making process of the balaclavas is an interweaving—stretching across states and home-front knitters to soldiers while ensnaring senators in the dance.[10]

The knitted balaclavas in Stitch for Senate become examples of how *means and ends coincide* in recursive action. The knitters and soldiers connect, where people on the home front contribute to their community, both materially and discursively, and the soldiers get warm gifts. The making process produces highly affective matter through direct action. But most crucially, the journey of the balaclavas ensnares the senators in ethical meta. They are forced to ask how to actually best support their troops. Means and ends are tied up, with the senator between.

What Mazza does so successfully in Stitch for Senate is to intensify the meta within the home-knitted helmet liner (war versus care for soldiers) by redirecting this meta into a matter that reveals hypocrisy. Instead of knitting a quilt with a message

[9] hooks (2000).
[10] The work resonates with Tronto's (1993: 103) notion of care, as "everything that we do to maintain, continue and repair 'our world' ... which we seek to interweave on a complex, life sustaining web." Here, the role of the knitter is that of the goddess: using fiber to fight, embracing with textile to care while also ensnaring the opponent in a spiritual dance of creation (Starhawk 1979).

for a protest, or even making a sentimental object such as a flag, the engagement with home-front knitters ties communities that genuinely care about the safety of their "boys" to take anti-war action. Knitting and craftivism, as with other forms of primitive making, is here used strategically as objectiles when intensifying the meta within the matter beyond representation or rhetoric. The strategy uses *matter for tightening connection*, *drawing into proximity*, rather than speculating, lecturing, or raising awareness.

Many other activism campaigns use craft as a bearing element to embrace affect and care. Greenham commons actions, mentioned earlier, used textile craft to manifest protest by emphasizing motherly care. Or the Women's Pentagon Action in November 1981, where women wove a web of strings between themselves to close down an entrance to the Pentagon building. Other forms of primitive making attuning to care could be the creation of cardboard tombstones for each protester participating in die-ins by ACT UP in the 1980s, such as the die-in at the entrance of the FDA headquarters in Rockville, Maryland, in October 1988. And not least the powerful actions with the AIDS memorial quilt, a patchwork made in memory of friends and family lost to AIDS. The ever-growing quilt, begun in 1987, which in 2020 comprises nearly 48,000 three-foot by six-foot fabric tributes to more than 100,000 loved ones lost to AIDS, currently measures five railway cars containing fifty-four tons of quilt sections and related material. On several occasions over the past decades, the enormous quilt has been laid out to display across the Ellipse and the National Mall in Washington, DC. At each instant, the quilt literally *takes place* at the heart of state space.

With the threads of both knitting and the journeys of the balaclavas, the politics of objects signify as much a tool for passion in construction as well as connection—a multiplication of relationships rather than a taxonomy. It is a campaign of connecting; the strategy is in every stitch, which resonates with Aidan Ricketts's idea of activism, where "strategy is a key consideration in all campaign work; it is the golden thread that can stitch together the elements of a public interest issue into an effective and successful campaign."[11] In Stitch for Senate, the connection becomes the bearing element of the campaign. However, it also becomes its weak point: if the senators don't attune to the affective investment in the objects and fail to care for the soldiers, the affective force of the campaign becomes less successful, even if it reveals the lack of empathy or care for the soldiers of the local senator. Most of the responses from the senators exposed patriotic jargon more than affinity with the knitters and soldiers.

Where Hamdi's strategic mug mobilizes assets, Mazza's balaclava mobilizes affective resistance through the act of care. Both activate participants to break participatory subordination to instead stress the civic and democratic purpose of primitive making. In both cases, the strategic and recursive use of objectiles can mobilize material agency and increase the affective level of civic participation. The mug aims to maximize its tangential assets. The balaclava mobilizes the affects of craft and care to clash with state metaxu into a political manifestation for peace. Using matter strategically, they both go further than mere reimagination and prefiguration to displace state space. As objectiles, their trajectories aim for strategic nodal points, dispersed leverage points, manifestations at the intersection of power and resistance. They can be starting points for hacking into state designations.

[11] Ricketts (2012: 54).

BASIC LOCK-PICKS

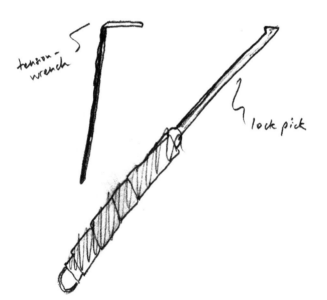

tension-
wrench

lock pick

8 Material Counterintelligence

I made my first set of lock-picks with a tangible sense of excitement during a nightly workshop at the Chaos Communication Congress in Berlin in 2006. Since manipulating the locks of classroom doors in my early teens, my fascination with hidden mechanics was again set alight. Around a table, a mixed group of visitors tested simple handmade picks on a series of padlocks. Following the facilitator's instructions, I filed down a piece of metal, a thin bristle from a brush that the street-cleaning trucks leave in the gutters, to make my first pick. I used two flat lollipop sticks wrapped with electrical tape as a handle.

After some practice with a basic padlock, it clicked open. The experience of picking open a padlock with such a simple device was exhilarating. Compared with my earlier experiences with the latch bolt, this was something else. When overcoming the latch bolt, I had just utilized an obvious limitation in an indoor setting (the school's locks to the outside were more protected). Now, I had managed to outsmart a device that had been explicitly designed to lock me out. I felt a bit like an agent in a movie using only a hairpin to open a door. It was also a very different feeling than the sense of accomplishment one gets from finishing constructing something. I had outsmarted and manipulated a piece of equipment—it was my hands and primitive tools against the engineered system designed to keep me out of it.

Returning home, with my fresh picks in my pocket, I started seeing locks everywhere: in childproof pillboxes, designed to be complicated to open, in security screws with odd heads, made inaccessible for standard tools, surveillance cameras, and alarm circuits, the spiky additions to the balustrades to keep people from leaning or sitting down on them. All these things were dark matter designed to make the meta of property and borders into tangible boundaries and done so in ways that they should not be tampered with. Surfaces that should be inaccessible, inhospitable, or even hostile. Intentions manifested to correct undesired behaviors, to nudge people to "do the right thing" by slapping them on the fingers. In such instances, antagonistic meta takes material shape to become a combative front, as for each new lock a new pick will undoubtedly be made.

Material is matter infused with intention and thus only waiting to be manipulated. The history of craft and making is a history of manipulations, and Glenn Adamson argues for this clearly, using the picking of a lock during the 1851 Great Exhibition in London. Present at the exhibit as a wonder of British engineering, the ingeniously conceived Bramah patent lock could only be opened with a unique key aligning a combination of pins (allowing for seven million trillion variations). It was considered impossible to pick. The makers proudly challenged the whole world on a material duel with a note on the lock claiming, "The artist who can make an instrument that will pick or open this lock shall receive 200 guineas the moment it is produced." Such a challenge could not go unanswered. When the American locksmith Alfred C. Hobbs managed the feat, he was considered an upstart manipulator by the fuming British press, as he had made the "prodigies of modern workmanship look foolish."[1]

---

[1] Adamson (2013: 2). Churchill (2015) draws attention to the interplay between securitization of property under early mass production, while simultaneously competitions in lock-picking exposed how insecure most tools for protection were. This interplay spurred the emergence of a new security industry.

Lock-picking offers a fascinating example of how the manipulation of matter intersects with meta. The lock is the material manifestation of property, sitting at a barrier of contestation between, for example, what one part considers part of the commons and the other part considers private. The status of the lock is anchored in contracts and law. Even owning the picks is regarded as a crime in many countries, as their very being suggests a possibility of unauthorized access that challenges boundaries upheld by the state. Picking a lock becomes a hands-on trespassing on the foundations of state legitimacy as the upholder of property. The act of picking a lock challenges what is accessible to whom and taps directly into conflicts between ideological interests and institutions.[2]

The boundary the lock protects is also deeply emotional, spanning from the heart-shaped lock on a diary to that of the prison cell. Yet, the locksmith is also a practical therapist, saving us from the immense stress that comes from losing one's keys. The locksmith—"whose calm is contagious as he restores your home ownership—is psychologically potent as a restoration of identity."[3] How are we to unpack the skill the locksmith possesses?

MATERIAL INTELLIGENCE

Adamson suggests we can understand craft in relation to what he calls "material intelligence." This type of intelligence is "the deep understanding of the material world around us, an ability

[2] Traditionally, the domesticity of women's craft has disqualified it from the higher arts (Korsmeyer 2002). A feminist perspective on crafts thus reexamines the hierarchical distinction between the making process in arts versus crafts in the aesthetics of objects historically made by women (Hein and Korsmeyer 1993). The gendering distinctions of making practice keeps being reproduced through educational structures (Kokko 2009) but also is sustained through more progressive and ironic gestures of craft, such as "Stich'nBitch" knitting circles (Minahan and Cox 2007). A similar feminist and colonial critique of "making" is crucial (see Vossoughi et al 2016).

[3] Shales (2017: 31).

to read that material environment, and the know-how required to give it new form." While a general material intelligence was universal knowledge not too long ago, it has suffered under specialization and new complex technologies and materials. Material intelligence is not merely about material properties, but the practical knowledge of how materials and tools work together in everyday situations. "Material intelligence in making is not just a matter of manual dexterity, but extends to the total productive situation."[4] While we may think it is a "hands-on" skill, it is almost always mediated through tools—we manipulate very few materials directly with only our fingers (except finger knitting, clay pinch pots, and building drystone walls). Like any other skill, material intelligence quickly fades without being practiced and nurtured.

Compared to the many other forms of intelligence promoted throughout society, not least standardized tests or social and emotional intelligence, material intelligence relates to the material world around us, everyday objects, and primitive gadgets. It means being clever with our hands, understanding the qualities of basic materials, and how things are made. Adamson's hypothesis is that people who have cultivated their material intelligence, with basic techniques and skills, *inhabit* the material world differently. Whereas other forms of intelligence value logical propositions and arguments, critical thinking, social dynamics, and emotional environments, material intelligence unpacks and understands the things around us. It is the practical reasoning we do in relation to matter, the hands-on perception of meanings imbued in the form of things or in-forming matter with our intentions. As Adamson highlights, material intelligence plays an essential role in sensing and appreciating material things, a sensitivity to the work, care, and traditions embedded into material culture.

Material intelligence has implications also with how we interact with designed objects. All design is a form of

---

[4] Adamson (2018: 4, 27).

designation—it advises, aligns, devises, arranges the capacities and frictions of the world to suggest, allow, and hinder behaviors. Designs are plans, materialized intentions, as Vilem Flusser famously argues.[5] Designs nudge users by making specific paths of action easier while others become less accessible—and as with all plans, to get people where you want them, you convince, coerce, or trick them there. Thus, the maker also puts intelligence into the design of an object. This shows itself in how it aligns users to behave in ways the designers want them to, such as pressing the right buttons, obeying property lines, or having people move in specific ways.

We could thus imagine two material intelligences in opposition. One is that of the designer, who tries to make people behave in specific ways, using material intelligence to align behaviors. This is the intelligence work of the designer: to make sure the user does what they are "supposed" to do. A designer using his or her material intelligence successfully utilizes the product's material properties to predict and shape the user's behavior. If the designer can do so without the user noticing, the better; then the product has become so user-friendly that it works "intuitively."

There is also an opposing material intelligence, or what I would like to call *material counterintelligence*. This is the material knowledge that seeks to outsmart the intentions of the designer's material intelligence. It hacks into reality, opens black boxes, but uses the same tools and pieces of knowledge as those of the designer. Also, here, these are knowledges and skills that allow the maker to inhabit the world differently. Material counterintelligence is the work of reverse engineering and repurposing, the craft and cunning we perhaps typically connote to burglars. Indeed, this is also the argument of Geoff Manaugh in *A Burglar's Guide to the City*, where he follows how burglars have an intricate knowledge of buildings, but it is at odds with the architect's knowledge. Understanding architecture through the lens of the heist

---

[5] Flusser (1999).

means seeing a building anew, beyond the designated uses of corridors and doors. The burglar instead moves through windows and drywalls, gaps and passages, structural joints and inverted spaces. These passages through a building Manaugh calls "Nakatomi space" with reference to the classic action movie *Die Hard*, where the main protagonist traverses a building through a variety of nonarchitectural means, in elevator shafts, air ducts, through walls and windows, with a significant degree of topological cunning. Nakatomi space unlocks new geometries and passages through state space. Trespassers make themselves new transversal openings, at odds with the designated use of walls, shafts, and ducts; this is the cunning of matter taken to the height of the arts, short-circuiting the meta of space organization. "Burglars are the M.C. Eschers of the built environment, approaching every wall and ceiling as a door-to-be, a connection waiting to happen, then making their vision real with the help of burning bars and Sawzalls."[6]

Lock-picking is not used as often in burglaries as in movies though. The burglar will use quicker means of entry, such as windows or breaching the porch door quickly with a classic crowbar. But what the lockpicker makes apparent is that material intelligence easily clashes with the alignments inscribed in designed objects. Cunning is a design skill, a key capability to open material possibilities. Intentions are usurped, the meta is manipulated, and making runs into trouble. As the facilitator at the lock-picking workshops told of the multiple occasions airport security guards were suspicious about his picks they saw in his bags: "They don't understand that I am interested in locks, not doors."

---

[6] Manaugh (2016: 185). "Disguised as an action film, [Die Hard] is actually architectural moviemaking at its best and most spatially invested, turning walls, floors, and ceilings—rooms, corridors, and stairwells—into the unacknowledged costars of the picture, demonstrating that heist films are the most architectural genre of all" (228).

ARTUS AND MÊTIS

Material intelligence is at the heart of the trickery that is the arts. When discussing the arts of trickery, Lewis Hyde points out how etymologically many of the words around making and creation still come from the Latin *ars* and *artus*, and the *articulus*, which can mean both "knee joint" and "summer solstice." These are words that come with meanings such as "to join," "to fit," and "to make." The solstice is when the realms of heaven and earth are the closest joined together, and the joints are where things come together or are easily broken apart. It is the place where the artisan or "joiner" applies the skills of "artifice," or the "articulate" wordsmith puts expressions together for leverage. These are the arts acting in the in-between, playing at the boundaries, in translation, divination, sacrifice, theft, and artifice, all working in "the *artus* that is a flexible joint on the boundary that is a permeable membrane."[7]

Using competent hands, making practices apply varying degrees of material intelligence. Lock-picking, however, approaches the material environment in a slightly different way, using material counterintelligence, putting the material manipulation in focus in the cunning practices the Greek called *mêtis*.

To the Greeks, *mêtis* is a form of cunning or trickery, the crafty intelligence of the artisans, creating ingenious new things, not least traps. It is the practice of Hermes, Loki, and Prometheus, embodied in both Odyssey ("polymetis") and in his crafty wife Penelope—who cunningly uses weaving as a material practice to speedbump the (meta) protocols of her 108 suitors. Mêtis means

> a type of intelligence and of thought, a way of knowing; it implies a complex but very coherent body of mental attitudes and intellectual behaviour which combine flair, wisdom, forethought, subtlety of mind, deception, resourcefulness,

[7] Hyde (1998: 264).

vigilance, opportunism, various skills, and experience over the years. It is applied to situations which are transient, shifting, disconcerting and ambiguous, situations which do not lend themselves to precise measurement, exact calculation or rigorous logic.[8]

It may be tempting to think of this cunning as the practice of the underdog, but it is not necessarily so. As with hacking, it is also a state-run venture. This practice of mêtis becomes clear when we look at how design is used today to explicitly affect behavior, not least in the embrace of design and "choice architecture" in behavioral economics. In these cases, the tactical mêtis is not used by usurping tricksters but by clients aiming to manipulate user-friendliness to make users do what they are supposed to. One of the explicit successes with design thinking is the use of design to affect behaviors, or "nudges," which have become more common in business and government, from the design of retirement plans to slot machines or internet gambling. Whereas most examples of nudging today may appear primitive (designs to encourage taking the stairs, throw the garbage in the right bin, etc.), we can only expect these methods to become more sophisticated as power brokers turn their attention to the power of behavior change, not least using interaction and service design, choice architecture, mathematical models, and big data under what some have referred to as *neuroliberalism*. Here, design shifts from being *for* people to instead indicate the precise shaping *of* people's behavior on larger societal scales.[9]

Under these circumstances, material counterintelligence can be an essential part of *taking back power* from nudging designers, service designers, user engineers, and choice architects. Set against the governmentality of neuroliberalism, material counterintelligence is a training in self-defense mêtis, the aikido of making: a safeguarding skillset against the

---

[8] Detienne and Vernant (1991: 3–4).
[9] This is an expanding field (Schüll 2012; Nodder 2013; Whitehead 2018; Zuboff 2019).

escalating influence of manipulative nudges and designations. However, it is not new per se, as cunning and trickery are an escalation across history: "Nothing counters cunning but more cunning."[10]

Material counterintelligence explicitly challenges alignments and designations, and it is a design dissent that executes a form of contrary reality testing. With the materiality of making practices, it does so beyond the constraints of the meta of laws, copyrights, and organizational delineations. Working in this manner, the designer is a cunning plotter laying his traps, as Vilem Flusser observes, where making explicitly manipulates everyday arrangements. Such cunning is traditionally moralized not only because it is trickery but also for how it is connected to laying traps as a mode of hunting. Such "lazy" contrivances do not promote the heroic virtues of the hunter and warrior, such as strength, agility, and endurance. There is only little bravery in the deeds of the artisan. But let's keep the focus here; material counterintelligence is a form of mêtis or design dissent, messing with intentions and arrangements. With every new invention comes new crimes, new traps laid, new tricks played.[11]

The legal as well as moral contestations around such practices are abundant. But as noted by Christopher Kelty about the politics of hacking, anything that is made is based on the worldview of its maker, and a hack challenges this worldview, making a conflict apparent, a conflict that was before unseen or ignored. New entities can overturn existing concepts and modes

---

[10] Hyde (1998: 20). For more about state-run hacking and misuse, see Follis and Fish (2020).

[11] With the invention of book printing came the wider spread of texts such as the Bible, but also of usurping texts, as the press allowed for sidestepping censorship, resulting in a rise in clandestine trade in blasphemous teachings and prohibited texts by anonymous printers. For example, by putting the whole book in lower-case letters, a printer could avoid the detection that could come from the more easily recognizable decorative initials and distinctively styled upper-case letters that might identify the workshop (Creasman 2004: 218). Similar tactics were used by Samizdat publications in the Soviet Union. For a historical perspective on usurping media practices, and *Homo Hacker*, see Kennedy (2015).

of representation, thus challenging current power dynamics. Behaviors change, maps are redrawn, software hacked, and the methods are shared, escalating the challenge. These types of constructive practices are "involved in the creation of new things that change the meaning of our constituted political categories."[12]

Once again, one can think of magic. A typical way to distinguish magic from the cause-and-effect relationship of natural science is that the former is contingent on human consciousness, whereas the latter is not. From the natural sciences, magic is considered superstition because it operates in the realm of mind rather than matter. This builds on the distinction between the material causality of Nature and the cultural and psychological causality produced by Society. The first is untouched by magic, while the second is open to manipulation and modification by the mental games of its inhabitants. Whereas Latour would dismiss such distinction between these categories, Alf Hornborg points to the usefulness of these analytical separations (even if they do not necessitate ontological dualism). Hornborg exemplifies this in the difference between keys and coins. Both are small pieces of metal, attributed with agency, and they operate doors. Keys do so because of their physical shape, whereas coins do so while contingent on human consciousness. Money requires the beliefs of the doorman about their value. In conventional modern thought, then, keys could be classified as technological artifacts, while coins could be classified as magic. But the magic of money has real physical consequences and substantial implications on cause and effect, ranging from starvation to climate change caused by global trade and carbon industrialization. Masquerading as reciprocity, Hornborg points out, the magic of money operates to globally appropriate human time and natural space and resources as if they were not contingent on unequal exchange.[13]

---

[12] Kelty (2008: 94).
[13] Hornborg (2016).

But if you have neither money nor keys, material cunning can be the next way to go.

THE COOKIES OF CUNNING

In Greek religion, Mêtis was a goddess of cunning intelligence, and her fate was to be eaten by Zeus.[14] As a form of replacement, Zeus later gives birth to Hermes, a god more open to interpretation, as a messenger, translator, tradesman, and thief, still a cunning trickster with the ability to move quickly and freely between the realms of the mortal and the divine. The function of cunning continues in the trades of Hermes, not least in his own mythical deeds. The purpose of such liminal practices is to cross boundaries without tearing them down; trade, translation, exchange, and movement between realms are the skills of the trickster. The character appears in the shape of Prometheus, Coyote, Loki, Raven, and not least Hermes himself. The trickster steals from the gods to give to their lesser creations while making sure the act preserves a clear distinction between these worlds; the high remains high, the low remains low. But the deed usurps the status quo. The trickster shows how such connections are needed for the guidance of the soul. The task is always to find a hole in the membrane between realities and use it for passage: a shrewd deed, a riddle, or utilizing a keyhole, such as when Hermes sneaks into his mother Maia's cave after stealing Apollo's cattle.[15]

In our more profane world, the works of the lockpicker and hacker offer a chance to question and reevaluate social

---

[14] According to Hesiod's *Theogony*, Zeus ate his consort Titaness Metis as she was about to give birth to Athena. Metis, with her magical cunning, was considered a threat to the "royal metis" of Zeus himself (compare to the "royal crafts" suggested in Chapter 5).

[15] As Hyde (1998: 263) points out, "with trickster in play, heaven and earth may touch without touching." Yet, as Hyde warns, the trickster is only temporarily domesticated; even a small kindling of fire may set off a blaze when humans try to wield the goods of the gods.

arrangements and the distribution of goods by forcing boundaries to open, almost as through magic. A playful and cunning group of activists working across these boundaries is the (now hibernated) collective Yomango from Spain. Through prank-like spectacles, the group enacts carnivalesque actions centering around habitual consumerism. In their work, they distribute methods and manuals to encourage shoplifting. One of their devices is a cookie-box shoulder bag that is a basic and clever manifestation of the everyday hide and seek of cunning design. Its simple construction and slight hipster look offer a portable, intimate, and surveillance-safe space in the shape of a handbag.

Yomango's handbag is a simple DIY project made from a classic Danish metal cookie box. Attach a strap and possibly embellish the cookie box with markers or stickers; and voilà, you are the owner of a trickster/hipster handbag. The trick is that the metal box produces an elemental Faraday cage, an enclosure that blocks electromagnetic fields. In our everyday lives, such electromagnetic fields come in retail alarms. Cleverly using the laws of physics to turn an ordinary object into a magical artifact, the cookie-box bag conceals its content from standard retail alarm systems. The name Yomango is a fusion of the clothing company Mango and the Spanish slang "mangar" (to steal), but they also argue for a practice of consumer magic:

> We did not talk about mangar, but yomangar, in order to differentiate it from the simple act of "stealing" or "shoplifting"… The spirit of Yomango is not a consumerist one, and the act of magic that takes place in a Yomango moment of liberation (the magic of making things disappear and reappear) escapes the legal-illegal dichotomy.[16]

---

[16] Yomango (2008). In its everyday use, magic is the art of illusion, of tricking the audience's perception. A famous example can be the "seven principles of magic" used by stage magicians Penn and Teller (Penn Jillette and Raymond Teller), where a trick is broken down into (1) palm—to hold an object in apparently empty hand; (2) ditch—to secretly dispose of an unneeded object; (3) steal—the opposite of ditch, to secretly obtain a

COOKIE BOX BAG

The meta that Yomango manipulates is how desire and the distribution of agency and creativity are organized under consumerism. Under this meta, subjects are aligned toward a limited scope of action; "creativity may be expensive when we buy it, but it is actually quite cheap when we sell it to big business! ... it reduces 'creativity' to the use of the credit card." As they

needed object; (4) load—to secretly move the needed object to where it is needed; (5) simulation—to give the impression that something that hasn't happened has; (6) misdirection—to lead attention away from a secret move; (7) switch—to secretly exchange one object to another.

have it, the box is a manifestation of critical thought, but it is "also a practical way of thinking; creative, disrespectful, with a taste for rupture." The handbag realizes Yomango's ideas through its matter, the metal Faraday box, but also in its simplicity, repurposing a commonly used consumer object and retooling it for radical critique. But it is also a space of ethical possibility; to shoplift, but also to not shoplift. To be a trickster, or simply have the space of opportunity to be that trickster, is Promethean enough to challenge the meta. In a time when alarm systems are ubiquitous in every store, the very act of carrying an unsurveilled space to enact theft (or not) becomes a provocation.[17] Will the guards now have to open my bag every time I pass through the doors? Only my bag or all bags? The meta of the expensively alarmed boundary is upset by the matter of the cookie box. Here we have the true cunning of the material trickster at work: what looks like a cookie box is an authentic handbag of Hermes.

To return to the difference between money and keys, the Yomango bag plays with the magic of both matter and desire. The metal box's material properties keep the alarm systems at bay. The space inside offers a room that can open for the social magic of desire.

But most importantly, the bag does not signify as much as act. The metal repels the electromagnetic alarm. It does not raise awareness in a traditional political sense, but modulates and sets several polyphonic layers of awareness against each other. The bag escapes electronic surveillance while revealing the processes that capture and exploit our desires. Through its

---

[17] Similar struggles to make oneself invisible to the state apparatus can be in challenging military action and the draft (Lynn 1967; Suttler 1970), not only listing medical or psychiatric reasons but also highlighting the irony that a conscientious objector has to go through many hoops and may end up in prison for objecting to organized killing, while a convicted person is unacceptable for the military. That is, a person convicted for murder is not allowed to kill for the state, and similarly, a person convicted for arson is also considered "morally unfit" and not allowed to burn enemy villages in the name of the state (Suttler 1970: 87). Literature around how to avoid the draft was widely disseminated across the United States during the Vietnam war (see also Berrigan 1970).

workings on a material level and by being such an everyday object, it questions the quotidian distributions of desire and agency in our lives. It reveals inwards, while it hides outwards. In this sense, the Yomango bag works as a tangible artifact of cunning, such as the Trojan horse.[18]

Neither a mere provocation for breaking the law nor a silent scream for vengeance against the electric eye of surveillance, one should perhaps see Yomango's cookie box more as a clever painkiller. The matter of the box, the DIY Faraday cage, makes itself *inaccessible to meta* in the form of ubiquitous and invisible surveillance. The material activism suggested by the Yomango handbag does not try to break down the boundaries, abolish all private property, oppose consumerism, or raise awareness to "reveal" the system as corrupt. Instead, it opens a "Nakatomi space" between realms, and it sneaks back into the cave through the keyhole. Through material counterintelligence, it opens a(n) (unsurveilled) space to manipulate the meta of consumerism by trespassing the invisible boundaries of alarms. With the primitive possibility of bypassing alarm systems, it offers the user to touch and intervene into the meta of consumerism itself.

We could also imagine a strategic use of Yomango's trickery, more in the classic style of the trickster hero Robin Hood. For example, if we think of the act of shoplifting also as a means for stealing back what rightfully belongs to some people, the method could be utilized for reclaiming that which has been commoditized through cultural appropriation. One could employ "strategic shoplifting" around extractive practices, shoplifting products from a corporation to channel funds to support court cases against the corporation's practices. Not unlike the work of the locksmith, the purpose is to restore your home ownership, but now with a twist. But this time, the locksmith is Prometheus, Loki, or Hermes. They are heroes of material counterintelligence, employing the use of minor justice machines. Trickery is at the heart of the arts—of creation, cunning intelligence, and the *attitude of artus*. It is spaces inverted and folded into each other, like in some M. C. Escher art of justice.

---

[18] For a longer discussion on the case, see von Busch (2017).

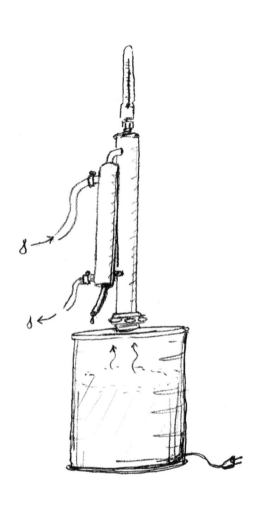

9 Brewing Dissent

After some very rudimentary attempts at making my own wine in my late teens, I finally got some practical fieldwork done on moonshining some years ago. A friend had inherited an old still from a distant relative in rural south Sweden. It was a beautiful old machine, made from what appeared to be various spare parts from milking machines and heating elements from household electric water boilers. I went to the local supermarket and got us kilos of sugar and then over to the local brewing supplier to get some Russian turbo yeast, and we set up the mash in a bucket with an airlock. After a few days of brewing, the bubbling in the airlock (a sign of fermentation in action) had ceased, and we poured the ready mash into the machine. Connecting the electricity and then cooling water from the garden hose, the machine started heating up, and soon enough, the first drops of distilled action research began trickling from the small outlet into our glass carafe.

My friend told me many stories about the culture of homebrewing where he grew up and how the landscape of moonshining had changed over the years. With cheap imports of spirits from the continent and rising prices of sugar, we were now actually practicing a dying heritage craft. There were long discussions online in the brewing forums mourning the lost skills of distilling quality bootleg liquor. It was a local tradition being displaced by globalization. However, on the positive side, the police made less fuss about it, looking for the more prominent offenders, and there was not too much trouble to be had as long as you did not advertise your work or sell it to minors. According to my friend, it was mainly the taxes on liquor the police were after, not necessarily the practice itself.

What a magical machine the still is: a simple empty chamber, a hollow space for letting nature do its work, fermenting sugar into alcohol. Not necessarily a justice machine per se, but just set it and forget it, and soon enough, what was before emptiness is full of high-value content. Fermented sugar turned into essential drops of life, or water into wine if you put it another way. This simple machine was a historical artifact, and I participated in an ancient tradition.

It got me thinking about the saying of Lao Tze, where the essence of the wheel is in the emptiness between the spokes, the essence of the pot is in the emptiness within, and the essence of the house is the emptiness inside the windows and walls. Here, we were not trespassing into someone's property or doing some cunning trickery. Yet, we were still making something transgressive in doing our own homebrew. We were allowing an emptiness to fill and *take place*, turning peaceful sugar into something that has been, and still is, controversial enough to be forbidden. With fermentation, we were negotiating with and occupying a void to have *presence be made*, and this presence was anchored to a long history of independence, autonomy, and resistance.

The still is a device that processes matter (sugar/mash) into sociopolitical material (alcohol) and the stuff of meta (taxes). So there's a lot going on here. But let's start at the beginning: how does a still work? The still operates on two general principles. First, that fermented mash contains alcohol and, second, that alcohol evaporates at a lower temperature than water. Heating the mash, the distiller processes alcoholic steam into condensation, leaving the nonalcoholic waste in the still bowl. Starting with fermented matter (the mash), placed in a closed container (the still bowl) and heated until alcoholic steam is produced. The steam is let out at the top of the container, passing through a pipe (the worm) that is cooled either by air, or let through tubs of cold water. This leaves the steam being recaptured as a liquid in a second closed container (the condenser). Each session of mash turned into alcohol is a batch, with a series being called a run. The highest quality of distilled spirits comes from the middle of the batch and from the middle of a run. The first drops coming out of the condenser are usually discarded. A stovetop still is quickly built from a large pot (for heating the mash) and then a pipe through a bucket of water for cooling/condensation. There are simpler versions where condensation occurs inside the still bowl, but it generally makes for tiny batches.

The making of self-sufficiency through the means of alcohol has a long-contested history. Yet distilling serves a local need for farmers: to turn harvest, which quickly goes to waste, into a more lasting and valuable product. The distillation process

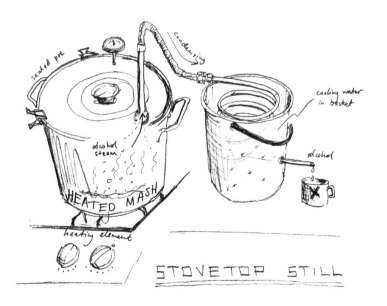

STOVETOP STILL

performed a vital economic function by transforming fragile, perishable, bulky, surplus fruit and grain into nonperishable spirits that could be easily stored, shipped, or sold. Unlike other commodities, spirituous liquor could be shipped at a profit, even when shipping required the payment of high overland transportation costs.[1]

But with its high demand, alcohol production is a tool in power plays, and state regulation of alcohol production and use has a long history within religion and law. It has also been a tool for imperial power. Like so many inventions, especially when it comes to intoxicants, someone's misuse is useful to another.[2] For example, alcohol production was an essential tool in the struggle for independence from the British in North America. The early colonies depended on Europe for their livelihoods by importing seeds, cattle, settlers, tools, and equipment. With this flow of goods, there was also a continuous stream of currency flowing to Europe, producing a lack of money in the colonies. This made the colonies dependent on various forms of barter, also to run the slave trade.[3] Barter was the primary form of exchange both on a local level among the settlers, especially with native populations, but it was also essential in the more extensive dealings between merchants in the colonial territories. However, not all goods serve well for universal payment, making trade values and exchange rates hard to translate. However, alcohol, especially rum and whiskey,

[1] Rorabaugh (1979: 74).
[2] Alcohol use has long been surveilled, moralized, and controlled in communities and societies. Johnson (2006) highlights also its instrumental use in imperial industrialization; as a common purification of water, alcohol affected the work quality of (often tipsy) laborers. To challenge this, the British empire could use the products of its global empire to fuel its industrialization: imported tea made boiling drinking water popular and adding sugar gave extra calories for long days of labor. Simultaneously, rum and molasses from the colonies added to more expensive alcoholic drinks, pushing alcohol revenues toward recreational use.
[3] Rorabaugh (1979: 62f).

turned out to be a preferred store for value and continuously in demand:

> Unlike other goods, including molasses, rum shipped easily, could be warehoused easily, withstood any climate and improper handling, and increased in value as it aged. Rum was the currency of the age.[4]

Distilling was a form of local banking, and alcohol was matter, meta, and money in one. It was money you could literally get intoxicated from. The still, which could easily be set up in most settlements, was independent of the powerful colonial creditors in London who controlled the flow of monetary currency and loans. The material intelligence of making one's own alcohol, and thus money, turned to support a countersystem to British colonial rule. Alcohol production in the colonies became a material form of independence struggle across the emerging nation, a high-proof predecessor to Gandhi's khadi, but also a powerful colonial tool to make native populations continuously dependent on trade with the settlers. The blockade of molasses and rum imports by the British during the Revolutionary War put pressure on the local economies, affecting the independent production of alcohol too, turning distillers toward homebrewing of substitutes from spruce, pumpkin, or persimmon beers and liquors, which in turn also affected the soldier rations of the Continental Army. Or, to put it differently, to pay for the independence struggle, a local insurgent army has to be sustained not only with local weapons and ammunition but also with local insurgent alcohol. The home still became an emblem for independence and a necessary tool for homesteading. Later, with established state control, industrialism, and the birth of the modern state, such autonomy needed to be legislated, controlled, and policed.

---

[4] Ibid., 64.

CONTROLLED SUBSTANCES, CONTROLLED CRAFTS

As state space gets more firmly established, alcohol becomes a state matter and is today, together with other forms of drug production, an emblem of the ties between *controlled substances* and *controlled crafts*. Together with explosives, weapons, and other drugs, alcohol is a state matter that is commonly policed. Like the other controlled matters, it is thus part of the continuous cat-and-mouse play between those who seek to control the production, flow, and use of such goods.

This type of hide and seek is a ceaseless dynamic. The state creates practices of making (regulating the process of materialization through laws and taxes, distribution, and definitions of labor and material practices), and simultaneously these makings, in turn, reproduce the state as a material manifestation that guides the everyday life of its subjects. At the same time, both parts play cunning games with each other. One of the many ways this manifests is in the many types of quasi-regulated markets in the legal grey zones with highly malleable and context-dependent enforcement, not least in the contested exchanges of weapons, human blood, organs, eggs, sperm, reproductive and erotic services, and many types of labor.[5]

But just like subjects hide from the eyes of the state, the state conceals the same practices from its subjects. Even if controlled by the state, it often requires some digging to find where legal weapons export really ends up, and in what contexts. Similarly, smuggling contributes to the dynamic reproduction of state boundaries, where agents of the state often break state-sanctioned rules, for example, in supporting practices that undermine their enemies or violate embargos. Heroes celebrated as "freedom fighters" are often such ambiguous figures. They fight against the taxman as much as illegitimate rules, making their suggested patriotism a matter of self-service or enrichment. The heroes fighting for the "people" may just as

---

[5] For an overview of these legal grey zones, see Krawiec (2009).

often be egotistic free runners, narrating their deviance, vice, and mafia business to sound like a struggle for independence. Many forms of illicit and illegal practices are central to liberation and resistance as much as imperialism and capitalism. For example, the notion of free trade often acts as a cover for a wide plethora of smuggling and trafficking practices, where celebrated legal production and consumption all too often blend into their illicit counterparts. States and corporations certainly black-box and shoplift too.[6]

The distinction between illicit smuggling versus sanctioned trade is also in flux and in continuous negotiation between merchants, states, and international laws, as states use trade to destabilize their competitors. Examples range from piracy to opium trade and wars, the support and arming of rebels and guerillas, and trafficking of humans and escaped criminals.[7]

---

[6] Disappearing can also be a libertarian tactic, as how Jameson Lopp, a Bitcoin engineer, decided to mask his presence and escape the all-seeing eyes of internet tracking and corporate America to his best ability, yet without giving up on social life and move to dark depths of the forests. Lopp suggests a fifteen-step process for masking one's physical and electronic presence (Popper 2019):

> 1. Create a new corporate identity, 2. Set up new bank accounts and payment cards, 3. Carry cash, 4. Get a new phone number, 5. Stop using the phone for directions, 6. Move, 7. Make up a fake name for casual interactions, 8. Create a V.P.N. for home internet use, 9. Buy a boring car, 10. Buy a decoy house to fool the D.M.V, 11. Set up a private mailbox and remailing service, 12. Master the art of disguise, 13. Work remotely, 14. Encrypt devices when traveling remotely, 15. Hire private investigators to check your work.

[7] Smuggling networks exist as a parallel and invisible infrastructure across borders. The same networks used for illicit trade of goods and money are used for moving people as goods in trafficking, as well as trade of kidnapping hostages. This informal infrastructure is also used by operators such as hitmen and escapees, with the knowledge of such persons only appearing in the exchange of spies and prisoners between countries, if at all (Harvey 2016). Such practices have a long history, as states use the grey zones around trade to seize goods, and persecute the people engaged in the trade, in order to hold hostages used in political bargains and exchanges, from pirates, drug lords, and spies to larger border populations (Karras 2010).

It has been pointed out how the rise of American capitalism is simultaneously the story of contraband capitalism, where the emergence of consumer society goes hand in hand with illicit mass consumption, innovations and copies, recreational drugs, and medicine. Consumerism in general, dependent on the perpetuation of consumer desire for new products, legal or illegal, is inherently based on copying, smuggling, and continuous testing of extralegal boundaries.[8]

Deception, fakes, and smuggling are central features in consumerism, especially in fashion, and are not limited to the goods themselves. The context of the purchase of counterfeits affects the status of the goods as much as the quality of the counterfeit itself: the flagship location differs from the outlet, which differs from the street market and eBay, and "fakes" may include goods, merchants, but also whole stores and supply chains. It has been hard drawing the distinction on what side of legality trade and production stands throughout history. Under globalization, it is almost impossible to recognize the different sides along these boundaries. Trade and production networks intermingle, payments and bribes are hard to distinguish, labor is exploited, and taxes dodged on systemic levels while respectable corporations lock up workers in Asian sweatshops and stow away profits in tax havens, often with the tacit approval from inspecting institutions. For serious competition, all means remain on the table. Religious organizations launder money for criminal networks; fake terror groups take responsibility for the latest bombing; and most free-market pioneers move in legal grey zones to find their innovative edge while exploiting laws to externalize costs and take down rivals.[9]

Being the god of both merchants and thieves, Hermes would not find this intermingling strange. The demarcation between

---

[8] The clandestine trade practices of states and merchants are covered by Andreas (2013).

[9] See Large (2019) for longer discussion on consumerism and deception. For a discussion on the deliberate confusion, hypocrisy, and the use of the distinction of crime to gain power and profits across state and legal boundaries, see Naylor (2014).

use and misuse is only a misty veil in the same landscape of practices.

MISUSE AND MISCHIEF

Using the everyday pots and pans to make one's own stovetop moonshine is not necessarily a misuse of the kitchen. Like so much other making, it means putting a new material alignment in the world and, in this case, also experimenting in tradition, independence, and autonomy, as well as liquor. As pointed out before, material manipulation is a central characteristic in material intelligence and is often commonly tied to mechanical contraptions. Simple machines get the curiosity started; they invite tinkering hands.

For as long as they have been in existence, motorcycles have been pushed by their users to excel in speed. The mechanic's skill is celebrated among the motorcycle communities, with tuning and repairs as a romantic, masculine, and meaningful craft. The mechanic sees the world as a craftsman, engages with the matter, taking things apart, becoming one with them.[10] But with motorcycles, such a potent symbol of freedom, there is always a meta rendering the potential of freedom inoperable: speed limits. Tinkering or modding the vehicle to challenge speed limitations is an inherent part of the culture. Markets are full of tools and gadgets that help users evade the law, from reflective paint that can be sprayed on license plates to overexpose the speed cameras to radar-warning equipment.

---

[10] See Crawford (2009) for a popular celebration of motorcycle craft, also present in the famous *Zen and the Art of Motorcycle Maintenance*, where Robert Pirsig (2006: 33f) makes a distinction between the worldview among the "spectators" versus the "mechanics" of reality. Spectators are involved in reality, but not in such way as to care; they take reality for granted and are not concerned about its workings. The mechanics, on the other hand, have an attitude of attentive examination and carefulness, the curiosity of the inner workings of the everyday.

But such outlaws are also the celebrated innovators within their fields. Few disruptive innovations obey the law. They bend the law their way as they prove their case. The misuse of hackers, crackers, file-sharers, and such troublemakers is located at the cutting edge of technological innovation and change. From the perspective of these makers, the politics of design is willingly blind to zero-sum games (such as labor laws or property), as it is inherently creative and constructive; it "does politics" differently, where incoherence makes room for promiscuous flexibility. Here, hacking and innovation overlap with criminology, where misuse is defined as a criminalized craft. Yet, misuse is inherent to use, always its adversarial shadow, or vice versa.[11]

The way I think of misuse here is not merely utilizing something in an unexpected way, such as hammering with the handle of the screwdriver. Misuse challenges the state-affirmed distribution of agency across state space. It goes against the designated arrangements that were intended and are upheld by state decrees. The misuser is out in contested space, often breaking the law.

Makers improvise, adapt, overcome. It is hard to get by without misuse. What is really the correct tool for opening a can of paint? Can I use the screwdriver as an icepick, hammer, or doorstop? Of course you can. Speed limits are just recommendations, aren't they? Shortcuts are necessary for the practice of life. Parking and where to throw out the trash is a negotiation primarily done with the neighbors, not necessarily the bureaucrats. Counterfeit or copied files or software reside in most computers, not merely for pleasure but also to get essential work done. Most people practically live inside misuse, in various degrees of irregular housing. The "papers" are not in order, the building material not according to code. Perhaps electricity is hijacked from the power grid, or at least much of

---

[11] Söderberg (2010: 161–5). Just like lawmakers must, by necessity, consider how every new law can be misused, designers should better take into account that any material practice is always already having an illicit sibling, a mischievous use.

the wiring is done by the neighbor or local handyman, rather than a licensed craftsman. Car modders take it seriously, and teens tune their mopeds to go faster. The X-box needs some tweaks and modifications, and while we're at it, the electric car may need some too, as a car today is basically a multi-ton, high-speed computer on wheels. It gets even more interesting when it comes to makers' inventions, when misuse triggers innovation of new substances, programs, routines, and open new worlds—worlds in tension with the so-far-negotiated arrangements that the state upholds.

Think of it like this; if user studies are the intelligence work of design, misuse is material counterintelligence making new worlds. This type of misuse is a crucial practice for autonomy as well as innovation. Misuse is a type of feral use. It engages "wild things" without the intention of domesticating it under state arrangements.

However, misuse is an understudied topic in design. Johan Söderberg argues for expanded studies of the structured misuse developed as "counterexpertise." He exemplifies this in the illegal work of drug manufacturing among psychonauts, for example, in the practices around LSD, dimethyltryptamine (DMT), and psilocybin (i.e., "magic mushrooms"). Innovation in this field is at breakneck speed. The European Monitoring Centre for Drugs and Drug Addiction (EMCDDA) identified seventy-three novel psychoactive substances in 2012 alone, with a continuous upward trend of innovation. The development of drugs among the psychonaut communities, whose intake of drugs they frame as intellectual and/or spiritual pursuit, differs from the "recreational" users who use drugs primarily at festivals and parties.

> The stress on informed drug use reallocates responsibility, as the uninformed drug users not only put themselves at risk, but jeopardizes the psychonaut community as a whole. Emergencies attract the attention of the media and politicians, accelerating the rate at which a novel substance is scheduled and thus imposing restrictions on the whole psychonaut subculture. There is consequently an esoteric and elitist strain in the psychonaut community—bordering

on the paternalistic—alongside the exoteric, libertarian
outlook, according to which psychedelic drugs should be kept
out of the hands of ordinary partygoers. ... Unsurprisingly,
psychonauts are as anxious as are the DIY biologists to
disassociate themselves from the methamphetamine cook.[12]

Like many other DIY communities, the psychonauts contest
the epistemological authority claimed by government agencies,
in their case the medical profession, and pharmaceutical
companies. As when a doctor, a holder of state-sanctioned
education, is assigned, the patient is deprived of the authority
to self-diagnose and claim ownership of their agency to self-
medicate. This epistemological challenge becomes even more
explicit when it comes to spiritual practices or practices
aimed to alter the state of consciousness to open the doors of
perception (e.g., to meditate while on drugs).

On another note, and as pointed out above, the state-driven
"wars on drugs" are often a misnomer as states have been the
biggest beneficiaries of drug production and wars throughout
history.[13] The narrative most frequently accessed by the public
tells the story of gang criminality and smugglers, while the
state's role is ignored, rather than the more nuanced version
where the civic realm has a say. Yet again, the psychonaut is a
maker, creating something novel to fill a void of psychoactive
substances. Compared to the primitive still, this may include
more complicated technologies, yet the direction is the same: a
counterexpertise at work to carve out a room of one's own with
autonomous crafts and fill the void with magic.

BUCKETS OF EVIDENCE

Whereas the smuggler uses a container as matter that conceals,
we can also think of a void filled with something to be rendered

---

[12] Söderberg (2016: 301f).
[13] See Andreas (2020) for an overview of state involvement in drug production.

visible. Like the microscope slides that put a specimen into position to be viewed, the void within a container also captures and holds in place that which needs to be examined. A contrasting container to that of the smuggler is the Summa canister, a standardized device used for grabbing air samples, capturing air to be analyzed by scientists in a lab. Such a device catches something unseen to the eye, such as air pollution, and "packages" it to be analyzed with lab equipment to check particles and present air quality data. As a scientific measurement tool, it can be used to challenge toxic industries and hold corporations accountable for the environmental contamination they hide and deny. It is a simple device of matter that makes organizational meta answerable for its "dark matter" of externalized toxic pollution. However, a Summa canister is an expensive gadget, which makes air sampling inaccessible to the impoverished communities that often come to inhabit land just outside refineries and chemical industries.

In the mid-1990s, communities in Crockett and Rodeo, California, set out to challenge the Unocal refinery, which had over time been releasing a toxic catalyst that had poisoned thousands of local residents. However, the residents had no proof that Unocal was responsible and so could be held liable. Air sampling with Summa canisters would be too expensive for the communities living around the refinery, so another system needs to be invented: a cheap plastic bucket. The DIY air sampling bucket is a conventional plastic bucket holding a standard Tedlar sample bag inside. This simple design is a tool for grassroots air-quality monitoring: a primitive, affordable, and accurate monitoring technique. Rather than the expensive Summa canister, the bucket is a sampler that community members could use, based on a standard sampling device initially set up by personal injury lawyer Edward Masry.[14] The equipment for a bucket can be acquired at a hardware store, with an ordinary five-gallon plastic bucket (to hold and protect the Tedlar air sample bag) and plumbing hardware to connect the inlet and outlet, through which air is drawn with a small vacuum pump.

---

[14] Most commonly known for work with Erin Brockovich.

BUCKET DIAGRAM

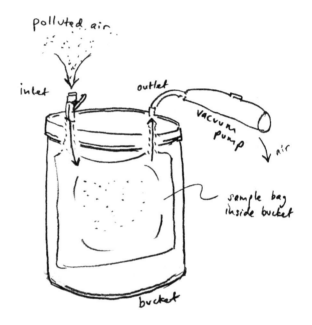

    The bucket is used among fence-line communities, around which they organize themselves into "Bucket Brigades." The brigade is an organizational model emerging since the 1990s, used to distribute roles across the community, from scouting and documentation of the pollution, air sampling and organization to legal advice and communications. With three main roles, the brigade is organized to make the most of the bucket air sampling device. The *sniffer* sounds the alert when an air sample needs to be taken. A *sampler* operates the bucket to take the actual air sample. The *coordinator* is in charge of the sampler bags inside the bucket, packaging and sending them with their air sample to the lab to acquire the data. The bucket is complemented by other supporting activities, such as (1) a log book: participants write down what they see, hear, and smell; (2) complaint to public officials: a written request for action by state officials; (3) a camera: pictures or video that are evidence of what happened; (4) bucket air sampling device: the collecting device to sample air for laboratory testing, making the community's claims harder to ignore.[15]

Without the material evidence, the captured polluting particles, the struggle in court is fruitless. Thus, at the center of the campaign is the DIY air sampling bucket that collects an air sample in the Tedlar bag, which is sent to a lab for testing. The data from the air sample is then used to advocate for stricter environmental protections or legal struggles against polluting corporations.[16]

Emerging from a local urgency as a resistance to an environmental injustice, the bucket emerged as emancipatory technology used to challenge the corporate polluters that poisoned the community. At about a tenth of the price compared to a Summa canister, the design of the buckets started as a community reaction to an increasingly toxic environment. With the bucket at the center, a system of measurements evolved that were accurate and systematic enough to be presented and published as "proper science," which could become material evidence in court as a central strategy in a political struggle:

> When the Louisiana Bucket Brigade contests the claims by Shell Norco about there being no chemical releases in their local community, they do so by displaying air sampling results. ... The results are territorial, metric and civil, against the secretive behaviour of Shell Norco, which

---

[15] For more about the activation of the bucket and its content, see Ottinger (2010) and Kullenberg (2015).

[16] In 1997, around thirty DIY buckets helped six thousand citizens or Rodeo in a lawsuit against Unocal to receive $80 million in compensation for their injuries (Nijuhuis 2003).

prefers working with 'public relations' rather than scientific methods.[17]

As the buckets became approved by the US Environmental Protection Agency, acknowledging them as legitimate instruments for environmental monitoring, the method of Bucket Brigades increased the legitimacy of the procedure. The organizational model of the Bucket Brigades spread to other communities, with the tools and techniques used as a case of citizen science.

> Citizen science as a form of resistance utilises a contradiction in modern sciences, in which science is regarded as neutral and free from politics while simultaneously being the driving force in the constitution of the societies we live in. By turning to scientific methods in their political struggles, citizen scientists are able to "short-circuit" the conventional modes of seeking political representation and use reference as a mediator in re-presenting the state of affairs that have come under controversy.[18]

The DIY bucket captures invisible pollution to package it to work in a litigation process, which translates it into a format to be read back and processed by the state against the corporation poisoning the community. Here, the DIY air sampling bucket is an instrument that makes the "dark matter" of pollution and environmental legislation readable by the instruments of science and law and data that can be shown, read, and interpreted in court.

As we have encountered in the cases above, there is a particular form of material intelligence in the process of making and misuse. Even with primitive tools and materials, in stovetop stills and plastic buckets, it is a form of *métis*, a cunning that uses matter to hack into meta, a type of mischief while also

---

[17] Kullenberg (2015: 65).
[18] Ibid., 67.

suggesting new, sometimes even utopian, practices, sometimes bypassing the state, while at other times leveraging state systems against corporate interests. It is a continuous game of cat and mouse, taking place in the workshop and across borders, but its source is the void within the container where dissent brews. While glitzy technologies can be seductive, simple domestic objects are perfect for cooking up some trouble.

HARRIET TUBMAN STAMP

10 Designing Back

In 2016 then treasury secretary Jack Lew announced a new design for the US twenty-dollar bill. The controversial president, Andrew Jackson, on the front face of the bill, would in the new design be moved to the back of the bill, replacing the White House, and his presence on the front would be ousted with that of abolitionist and political activist Harriet Tubman. However, after the election of President Donald Trump, the decision was reversed, and no new imagery was discussed.

The figures representing society, on stamps, bills, and street names, and not least monuments, are under constant debate. Their presence announces their statute as public figureheads, presenting deeds worthy of recollection and inspiration. As much as they come to represent values lauded during their erection, the monuments stay on to become the face of the state: emperors, kings, generals, senators, explorers, and, now and then, a scientist or artist. As they sit enthroned on their pillars, looking down on us, or peek out from their gilded frames, they come to represent the virtues cherished by the state, such as patriotism, heroism, industriousness, and service. In many ways, they also come to embody the meta: they are the faces of the intentions, goals, and paradigm of the state, and even if citizens are not necessarily looking up to them, the celebrated

figures come to be the expression of state organization with this
dark matter. Their deeds enshrined in the nation's heart, these
figures also have their creations residing in the state capital,
their institutions, and tombs. They are public figures as much
as statements and essential in forming the mythical container
legitimizing the state.

If the faces of the palace or parliament show the center of
the state, from which executive power emanates, the faces
on bills display another mode of representation, or "faciality,"
of the state.[1] The palace, supreme court, parliament, national
bank, cathedral, opera, indeed every institution, has a faciality
that most often is immediately recognizable; you see it and
know you look toward the center of authority (and such faces
often have high tourist value, making them also recognizable
to foreigners).[2] In the faces on banknotes, the design of state
faciality is dispersed to appear in almost every legal means of
transaction. It sets its own imprint on everyday life, yet with
different intensity. It is a state-sanctioned tool and is the primary

---

[1] The perception of the state overlaps with what Deleuze and Guattari (1987)
call the "faciality" of governance. People see and recognize faces everywhere,
overcoding recognition, constantly overdetermining relationships and
identities—between people, but also toward institutions, up and down social
hierarchies, creating recognition in the familiar as much as in othering. The
face is an imperial machine, as "all landscapes are populated by a loved or
dreamed-of face" (1987: 173). Deleuze and Guattari (1987: 178) posit:

> Racism operates by the determination of degrees of deviance to
> the White man's face, which endeavors to integrate nonconforming
> traits into increasingly eccentric and backward waves, sometimes
> tolerating them at given place under given conditions, in a ghetto, or
> sometimes erasing them from the wall, which never abides alterity.
> … From the viewpoint of racism, there is no exterior, there are no
> people on the outside. There are only people who should be like us
> and whose crime it is not to be.

[2] The reign of Louis XIV has been studied as a prime example of the process of
state centralization around the faciality in the figure of the sovereign. Peter
Burke's (1992) *The Fabrication of Louis XIV* explains how the French state
strategically deployed *state* organization and hierarchies through material
culture, art, and design to order population and territories around the
sovereign.

means the state accepts for paying its fees or taxes. The national bank or central reserve may be a prominent structure, often located in the capital, but the power of its bills is everywhere.[3]

Influencing the central bank to replace the face on the bill is an uphill struggle and may involve organizing campaigns and signing petitions. As much as such efforts make demands, they simultaneously orient participants' attention toward the central power, reinforcing the dominance of the capital's faciality. Subjects turn toward the capital to appeal for change, reinforcing their participatory subordination.

Direct action implies denying subordination. Taking action means to turn away from the capital, not seeking permission, to instead harness capacities within oneself or one's community to affect the situation. Instead of asking the central bank, it means using the bills as a canvas for "designing back" against state representation, defacing, or refacing, the currency.

As a response to the federal bank's refusal to redesign the twenty-dollar bill and the very explicit *inaction* of President Trump, New York–based designer Dano Wall initiated a process to make stamps available for people to take action. These stamps gave users the ability to replace Jackson's face on their twenty-dollar notes with Tubman's. Wall produces and shares online DIY methods and digital files to 3D-print the stamp and sells readymade stamps on Etsy and in stores. Wall's work can

---

[3] Governments have historically been issuing currency as a means to legitimize and facilitate trade, taxation, and extraction of labor from state subjects to pay for state-run services and mechanisms, and binding the citizens to the nation-state (or the colonial state, as shown by Roitman 2005). The economic foundations of modern nation-states is in "public credit" and national debt circulated as paper money (Brantlinger 1996). This in turn accentuates and reproduces a mutual dependency between the state and subjects, but also results in the centralization of power to the state and its banks (Davies 1997; Ingham 2004). Sometimes people set out to make their own currencies and create complex barter systems that may challenge state control over trade (Lietaer 2001). With subjects governing themselves while escaping the mechanisms of the state, such initiatives often run into problems with the tax office or police. We may witness this today in the controversies around online cryptocurrencies (Ingham 2020).

be seen as a method of publicly taking back the bills to honor a hero of the people and thus challenging the state through primitive making.

Appealing to the government and federal treasury to change the face on the bill could, if successful, modify the printing presses. While not as effective in terms of quantity (even thousands of participants can only stamp so many bills), the stamp alters the relationship between state faciality and the stamp-wielding subject. As a form of civic correction of the state narrative, the process is changing the *material faciality* of the state through the public circulation of bills, but not the currency itself. By making the instrument for taxation their canvas, people touch the material manifestations of the state. In the matter of each bill, the current political controversy of the meta has been defaced.[4]

In the breaking of state power, Vinthagen emphasizes the simultaneous entanglement of *subversion* and *construction*. Using noncooperation as well as role innovation, developing knowledge, skills, and behaviors for future society requires *functional demonstration*. It means showing the positive things that can replace what is considered unjust. This kind of civil usurpation escalates nonviolent action that displaces the hitherto dominant social arrangements.[5]

Such constructive subversion requires a questioning irreverence. An insurgent inquisitiveness, such as a stamp replacing the face of a ruler, resonates with the advice the Oracle at Delphi gave Diogenes to "deface the currency" (or "adulterating the coinage"). Following an earlier debacle in Sinope, where Diogenes had been expelled for counterfeiting currency, he interpreted the advice to mean defacing the "coins of custom" or the implicit value people tie to money, exposing their greed and vanity, thereby changing what people value. He

---

[4] Defacing and playing with representation has also been a prominent approach within "subvertizing," or speaking back through advertising channels (Lasn 1999) or "brandalism" (AdHack Manifesto 2017).
[5] Vinthagen (2015: 257ff).

did this not least by himself living a life of radical poverty and material renunciation.

I think of the stamps as another form of primitive justice machine, a device to deface, alter, and reface the currency, taking on the faciality of the state. As with Diogenes, this is nothing new, but it inserts itself into the means we use for valuation, trade, and interaction with the state. Even if stamping new faces onto banknotes does not challenge taxation or state control, it breaks with participatory subordination, and it makes the ubiquitous distribution of state power apparent and tangible. And it does so in a subversive yet constructive manner. The stamps provide users with the agency to write over the state narrative and challenge the seeming untouchable abstractness of its directives. It is a form of direct governing in its minuscule way, questioning who should be the heroic face on an everyday state tool such as money. If the toppling of a statue challenges the pedestal power of who we should look up to in our daily lives, the defacing of currency can be an example of making that confronts the dispersed mode more of state faciality.

MAKING CIVICS TANGIBLE

The Tubman stamp can also exemplify a "thing with attitude," as it shows how making can question and *design back* against the dictates of the state. This means employing the agency of design to challenge boundaries (of law and customs, as Diogenes would have it) while also breaking into and modifying the physical tools that align life under the state. This becomes very visible in the alteration of money as it is the interface between market and state, under which almost everyone is subjected. Printed currency acts as the merger of state and market.[6]

---

[6] As noted by Bollier and Helfrich (2019), whereas market and state appear as ideological adversaries ("private sector" as the opposite of the "public sector"), they are symbiotic to the degree they often appear as merged market/ state systems. The market offers growth, taxes, and social mobility, whereas the state offers legal order and mitigation of abuses or disruptions while also

I would suggest that designing back does not mean erasing or destroying state design, but manipulating, displacing, and writing over it, modifying it to align better with the values and wishes of the civic population or the state subjects. Designing back means practicing a civil right in a hands-on manner, in a specific context. It does so while breaking convention to make visible the power dynamics that deny or suppress rights or the agency of people to self-govern. Through provocation, making a silenced voice heard, the aim is to reveal the components of conflict. It is a tricky balance along the boundaries of civics, customs, and the law. If confrontation is amplified without enough constructive elements or alternatives made suggestive, conflict risks strengthening polemic and binary systems (legal–illegal, good–bad, etc.), mobilizing the opponent while alienating allies. A hands-on manipulation, creating and mobilizing civic realms, can divert state orders while also helping allies visualize the alternative to the status quo in productive ways. I think of this as *civic craft*, or making practices that animate while also manifesting civic life.

I see civic crafts as a material engagement in civic practice— it is a making that trains participants to embody the civic in more generous ways, in open negotiation rather than clinging to rights or entitlements, for example. When working, the civic realm simultaneously decentralizes both the government and the individual subject, producing the sphere where groups experience a sense of mutuality in engagement, recognition, praxis, and coproduction. However, for the civic ideals to be put into practice, they are dependent on a participation-friendly public realm, a vibrant public life, and open areas where the individual can develop and practice the habits of good citizenship; in ethicist Ann Mongoven's words, "True civic virtue must fortify civil society, while healthy civil society must facilitate the development of civic virtue." Mongoven

---

executing their shared directives. Both stand in contrast to both civics and commons. Local governance tries to limit state power; co-ops strive to limit market-driven injustices.

further argues for a humility of self-restraint and a redefinition of courage as "disciplined vulnerability." This courage is the maturation of character from an atomized individual to an invitation for overcoming boundaries and erstwhile disjuncture, being part of a reflection and continuous conversation in a spirit of self-restraint. This must be seen as the fostering of a healthy relationship between love and justice, "challenging virtuous citizens to cultivate just love for their political community."[7]

Small disseminated material actions like using the Tubman stamp highlight a specific power accessible through making in that *your world is as large as that you can change.* As you take on to manipulate your surroundings, you inhabit and partake in that world. This does not mean ignoring the underlying conditions and distributions encroaching on this world. But by making the civic and the issue at hand tangible and addressed locally, it shortens the imaginative gap between a problem and the means for addressing this issue. The world is undeniably much more extensive than what one has the agency to take on, yet civic agency opens it up also for critical unmaking and intervention. Civics are shared experiences, practical and ethical guidelines that concern the actions of human togetherness. We know they are civic virtues, as political philosopher Michael Sandel notes, because "when politics goes well, we can know a good in common that we cannot know alone."[8] A soup kitchen gathers a civic around the issue of hunger, and from there, the civic changes needed are less abstract, even if not less controversial. I think Brazilian Archbishop Helder Camara's experience is illustrative of the limits of local action: "When

---

[7] Mongoven (2009: 13, 16, 18). Sustained civic activism is however not merely material and often meets fierce reactions. It thus also requires collective organization, from in(formation gathering and distribution to more hands-on suggestions on printing and distributing leaflets, dealing with infiltrators and agents provocateurs, as well as legal as well as medical self-defense, and much more (see Alinsky 1971; O. M. Collective 1971; The Berkeley International Liberation School 1972). Examples of how to prepare for police confrontations range from practical examples of how to deal with being arrested and sent to prison (Boudin et al. 1969).

[8] Sandel (1998: 183).

I feed the hungry, they call me a saint. When I ask why they have no food, they call me a Communist."

To inhabit and change our worlds, we can use design, making, and manipulation. A primitive method, easily accessible, shared, and used, helps build a joint project. The task at hand is tangible and quickly evaluated: you see immediate results of civic action. The face of a genocidal president has been replaced with that of a Black activist and abolitionist. Starting with the twenty-dollar bills you can access and reface, you can disseminate your alteration throughout your immediate surroundings and then the world.

DESIGN AND ACTIVISM

We impose our will on these worlds by various means—and this is where we get to what is usually called "activism." Employing agitation, making, and manipulation, *activism challenges the official designations of power*.

This leads us to a question simmering under much of this book: how do I approach activism in making and design? A common understanding of design is that it relates to artificial or "what if" worlds that manifest ideas of progression and emancipatory directions. Famously, Herbert Simon made a distinction between design sciences and the natural sciences: Whereas the "natural sciences are concerned with how things are," design "is concerned with how things ought to be." This take on the artificial realm of design resonates with Simon's oft-cited line that a designer is someone who "devises courses of action aimed at changing existing situations into preferred ones."[9] That is, design is about making things more desirable and preferred (but all too often leaving out the question *who/ whom?*). A similar generous take on design activism is taken by Alastair Fuad-Luke, where almost any type of design becomes activism, as the practice addresses betterment by the intent of

[9] Simon (1996: 114, 111).

the designers, beyond politically designated avenues for public decisions or the market alone. Fuad-Luke suggests a broad (or meta) definition of design activism:

Design activism is "design thinking, imagination and practice applied knowingly or unknowingly to create a counter-narrative aimed at generating and balancing positive social, institutional, environmental and/or economic change."[10]

This definition opens many design practices and projects to be defined as activism, yet it gives no clear hint on what differentiates the activism part from just any other design. Sarah Corbett, who works in the intersection between craft and activism, posits how a too broad definition of activism, for example, including charity, can be counterproductive:

If we call actions of fundraising, donation or awareness-raising "activism" then we are diluting the potential of the word activism and confusing people about what activism is and can be. Worse, we are stopping people from having the courage to stand up, protest against injustice and demand change by offering them more comfortable actions to take instead. Activism can be difficult to plan, create and continue to do. It can be uncomfortable to stand above the parapet at times. It's not often glamorous. But it is vital.[11]

Just putting a spotlight on an issue or throwing ideas out there does not qualify as activism from this perspective. Something needs to be at stake, and action pushes a controversy into the public realm with the purpose of rocking the boat. Inspired by the agonistic politics of Carl Schmitt, some scholars suggest conflict as the center of analysis of how decisions and disagreements become political. Along these lines, a type of *adversarial* design sets out to challenge a given power

[10] Fuad-Luke (2009: 27).
[11] Corbett (2017: 15).

arrangement, which "manifests itself as a struggle between two or more groups that has as its goal a reordering of the relation of power between the existing groups."[12]

In this popular theory for understanding the political, conflict takes the front seat for understanding political contestation. While it clearly delineates between conflicting parties, it risks diminishing the possibility of constructing alternatives and proactive resistance. Nonconflict easily becomes the same as compromise. As much as it is a fruitful lens for seeing underlying tensions throughout society, when trying to untangle the chain of events (or who/whom), conflicts have a tendency to continuously drift toward higher meta. Blame for a local conflict is pushed upwards. The more significant and more abstract the meta conflict appears (*Capitalism! Globalization! Imperialism!*), the harder it is to find interfaces to engage politically with design in a way that goes beyond representation and awareness-raising. The more "critical" or "interrogative" the design, the more meta speculation and artistic interventions appear as the most suitable option for addressing the wrong. Design activism gets entangled by meta to the degree most cases become gallery or museum pieces. In such settings, design may get uncomfortable by its own instrumentality, and activism gets reduced to continuous questioning or problematizing, that is, it loses its material edge to take place in the everyday.

On the other hand, social theorists would argue the drift toward meta is not unique to a design with political intentions. Almost all forms of activism are in continuous compromise with organizational structures, such as state or corporations, to achieve acceptable agreements that have a significant impact. Setting out to change things almost always includes accommodating some level of concession. This is not least apparent in the corporatization of activism, as provocative organizations turn into NGOs and show up in the corridors of power.[13] Non-profits have their own C-suites. In a similar vein,

---

[12] Markussen (2013: 45) here discusses the framework of *Adversarial Design* by DiSalvo (2012).
[13] For a longer discussion on this tendency, see Dauvergne and LeBaron (2014).

a cynic would point out how most of what is labeled design activism still serves a paying client, gallery, or museum, and not least the CV of the designer (not to mention academic publications).

An attractive compromise seems to be that designers can pull on the artificial possibilities of design while acknowledging the proposal's adversarial contestation of sociopolitical relationships. At this intersection, a form of *prefigurative politics* emerges. The term *prefiguration* suggests "the attempted construction of alternative or utopian social relations in the present, either in parallel with, or in the course of, adversarial social movement protest."[14] Social scholar Marianne Maeckelbergh uses the term prefiguration to signify a development strategy with self-organizing purposes, especially within alterglobalization movements, beyond hierarchical decisions on goals. With prefiguration, the primary goal is not to confront and capture the state but to open up a multitude of possibilities for people to pursue many goals simultaneously. In Maeckelbergh's use of the term, prefiguration simultaneously combines both a challenge to established structures as well as the practical construction of a lived alternative.[15] Yet, once again, a critic might reply that all design prefigurates; and without explicit defiance, is it not just another aesthetic product on the market of ideas? Is there any difference here?

The definition of *material activism* I work with emphasizes *material involvement* in political contestation. It breaks open and hacks into the political alignments and orientations that matter makes tangible and solid. This activism manifests in matter. In a confrontation with state alignments, this affects more than representation; it works on bodies and other matter. In its challenge, this activism breaks participatory subordination and trespasses into contested realms across moral or legal

---

[14] Yates (2014: 1). The popular term *prefiguration* is commonly attributed to social activist Carl Boggs (1977).

[15] Maeckelbergh (2011: 14). For a powerful approach on emergent activism through embodiment, see brown (2017).

boundaries. To be activism, it leaves the designated paths of deliberation; it employs "stronger" affects than discussing, voicing, or voting. However, there is a design element in there too; it is constructive or creative and engages a process of making that engages participants in a manifestation that drives ideas and makes deliberation tangible. It is a mobilization through material means beyond the designated avenues for citizen's political influence. Material activism dissents beyond agitating, voting, and consuming; it breaks the reproduction of power, displaces material alignments; it pushes away and minimizes obedience and subordination, a process in line with what Vinthagen calls "power-breaking."[16]

Material activism is a form of making that *provokes* (to "call forth"), in that it materializes a silenced voice or perspective and thus challenges boundaries: cultural, social, institutional, and/or legal. It uses the process of primitive making to change things materially, making them unruly. As with the Tubman stamp, this is where primitive making can become the tool that makes the confrontation more evident. It allows the maker to challenge material designations of authority. In line with Attfield's "things with attitude," it is a production that stands in contrast to the limited room for maneuver within mass production and consumerism. Yet Attfield points this out, almost in a by-sentence:

> In craft practice the artisan is in touch with the material object and in control of the design, even when carrying out another designer's concept. Contrary to Giedion's [1948] 'mechanization takes command', ultimately it is the expectation that the *maker* can "take command." And it is only through knowledge of their craft that they are able to do so.[17]

---

[16] Vinthagen (2015: 165) underlines how a successful nonviolent campaign escalates power-breaking in order to increase the displacement of subordination.

[17] Attfield (2000: 70, original emphasis).

This sense of material command is what primitive making is after: the rearrangement of the physical world to break power while simultaneously prefigurating the alternative, making the contestation of visions tangible. On an everyday scale, material activism aligns with William Riker's theory of "heresthetics" or political manipulation, pointing to how the world can be structured in favor of a political strategy (from Latin *haeresis* "choice").[18] Riker suggests how powerful agents manipulate the political landscape under zero-sum conditions and with rational decision-makers to favor their view as a form of choice architecture of power. Riker gives examples of how this is done by rearranging and reordering the options available, thus orienting the alternatives toward preferable outcomes. Heresthetics is a helpful lens through which to also examine material forms of activism, much in line with Foucault's notion of the "dispositive." Our designated options as citizens are oriented in alignment with state intentions. Only designated paths of action are "user-friendly." Go against these arrangements, and you run into frictions.

Material activism hacks into state heresthetics to change the physical landscapes of choice: it makes contested activities more user-friendly, inviting participants to challenge state arrangements. And it does so with an explicit activist agenda to help the participant take command over their political agency in a physical sense. The state has chosen what face there is on the state-sanctioned currency, and the activist bypasses the formal channels for decision-making through material action. It exhibits alternative ways of political operation but, in the case of the bills, also disseminates the dissent across everyday

[18] Riker (1986) sorts the primary strategies for political manipulation as: A: agenda control: manipulating the agenda for favorable voting outcomes; B: strategic voting: using voting procedures to control outcomes; C: manipulation of dimensions, redefining the situation to create a stronger coalition. It may be worth noting that Latour suggests a Hobbesian and Machiavellian perspective on power in the realm of actants: the harsh realities of material power need to be understood in order to support a stable democracy (Latour 1988).

transactions. It makes the debate real and the refaced currency used as a physical reminder to better activate and practice self-governance.

MATERIAL CIVIC DISSIDENCE

If we see the making, dissemination, and use of the Tubman stamp as a form of design activism, or material dissent, we have to ask on what level it works more than materially. The question is not about what is and what isn't design activism or how much dissent is required to be activist enough to count. The issue at hand is how we refine the practice of material dissent to find the best interfaces with state matter to manipulate and find places where primitive making can break power. How can we understand material dissent that can displace and break power and also be disseminated across the social field to mobilize alternative social practices and futures?

I try to bring light to design disobedience practiced as "civic dissidence," as Frederic Gros articulates it. In these actions, even obedience can be turned into acts of dissent. A classic example can be The Good Soldier Švejk, in the novel by Czech writer Jaroslav Hašek, who follows his orders to the degree their execution undermines the intent. Gros gives another example in Socrates's refusal to escape his death sentence, to which Merleau-Ponty poignantly says, "Socrates has a way of obeying that is a way of resisting."[19] It is a way of acting where conscientious objection is merged with partial obedience and public action that still resists to exhibit a more *truthful* life practice. To Gros, civic dissidence means

> a disobedience that is not necessarily supported by a clear awareness of transcendent values, a conviction enlightened by a superior moral sense of laws governing humanity and time. Above all, what the dissident experiences is an ethical

---

[19] Merleau-Ponty cited in Gros (2020: 141).

impossibility. He disobeys because he can no longer continue to obey.[20]

But not every aspect of life is reformed. Not every cue is disobeyed, as this might turn into a life without any order. Some conditions still instruct behavior, but which? The paradox here is how the conscientious objector still obeys, yet it is disobedience in the name of a higher obedience. The point is to step beyond the passive disobedience that merely strives to change master, toward a more active disobedience, ranging from collective civil disobedience and individual insubordination or conscientious objection. It does not only protest, waiting for change, but this kind of action points to inner and societal reform.

This type of dissidence is the practical and ethical work of social and spiritual refinement, a development of conscience, individual as well as collective. Where the conscientious objector makes his or her ethics *present* through life practice, material civic dissidence *manifests* it in matter. As with other civil disobedience, injustice is denounced in a way that brings both attention to injustice as well as encouragement for others to take part. "Obeying and disobeying means giving form to one's freedom," as Gros has it.[21]

But not all actions have the same intensity of opposition, but there are degrees of dissent. I find it helpful to build on the diagram that German historian Detlev Peukert uses to visualize levels of resistance against state domination (in Peukert's case, the Nazi state).[22] Exposing many levels of nonsubordination, Peukert's analysis stretches from lifestyle choices to the explicit undermining of state authority, from dressing and dancing to outright state sabotage. We can think of material dissidence

---

[20] Gros (2020: 141).

[21] Ibid., 26.

[22] Peukert (1987: 83–4). Diagrams can expose proportions and relationships, yet one must be careful with ratios set in comparison to totalitarian regimes: dissent in Sweden today is obviously not the same as dissent under the Nazi regime.

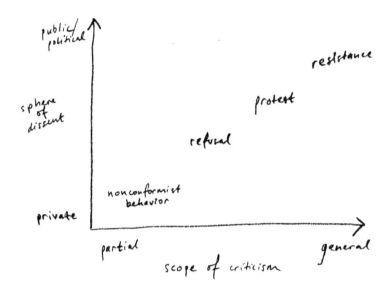

in a similar topology, or as a third, complementary, axis of the model presented in Chapter 4 on the agency of design, but here representing a level of opposition, from partial to general state critique.

Peukert's diagram traces the intensity of opposition, to what degree everyday action defies state alignment. The two axes in Peukert's model are the spheres of dissent (private to public) and the level of system critique (partial to general).[23] Starting with "nonconformity" (behavior in private with a partial rejection of the regime), a more expansive "refusal of co-operation" (Verweigerung) to "protest", and finally to active

---

[23] I have in this illustration switched the axes of Peukert's diagram to match the earlier diagram in Chapter 4.

resistance (Widerstand), which involved explicit rejection with active and organized opposition to the regime. These forms of resistance all still refuse alignment but increase the intensity of their stance. The spheres move from the four walls of the home outwards, from appearance and friend groups, from individual life practices to explicit mobilization in popular movements. The level of systemic critique stretches from a partial rejection of alignments and commands, "forgetting" to follow orders or not showing up for service, to an outright undermining of general decrees.

The basis for the diagram is still obedience, people being "useful" enough to uphold the current order. Why do most of us simply obey? One reason is that obedience translates to community. Obedience brings people together. We feel at home in compliance. Conformity makes for a good night's sleep. There is safety, comfort, and satisfaction in servitude. The default setting across society is obedience.

Dissidence, on the other hand, divides. Disagreement drives us apart. With sanction being uncomfortable and unbearable, disobedience simply does not appear on the horizon of possibility. Especially when taken out into the public, dissent requires a lot of courage.

This is where material dissent comes into the picture. It can be constructed in the privacy of the home but activated in public. The workshop is a place to manifest dissent, while also training for breaking power in public. The point is to use primitive making to displace surplus obedience. It is maximal dissent with minimal public discomfort. To use primitive tools means coming closer to control with less resignation and less self-imprisonment under tacit consent. It is not open mutiny but desertion. It is the small coins of political conflict, what James Scott calls "infrapolitics," a politics removed from executive power or protest marches, careful and evasive, purposefully avoiding dangerous risks. It is a politics of everyday cunning that does not want to make it to the news but circulates among the people like gossip, slandering, character assassination of people claiming authority. Infrapolitics is the politics of the night and anonymity, from poaching and gleaning to guerrilla gardening and graffiti. Concealment and anonymity allow the voice to be bold, the message clear. A fearful messenger needs to have the message hedged, but the statement can be sharp when concealed, the resistance more manifest.[24]

The Tubman stamp is a material manifestation of such infrapolitical dissent. Between the safe walls of my home, I turn to action, defacing currency in private, then sneak the banknotes out into circulation as a public renouncement of state faciality. The action is material and permanent, but the result is sneaked into larger political life. A user may not even notice the new face, and the circulation of the bills can happen almost by accident. Even so, each bill contributes to the whole, as cunning material activism from the private to the public, from the partial toward the general.

In this way, material dissent can be a submission that contains the seeds for future rebellion. It manifests resistance and opposition while correcting a public wrong. Even modest action puts dissent firmly on the horizon of possibility. The kitchen table and the workshop are training sites for public action, while each stamped bill is a seed for spreading the dissenting stance. Simple craft skills can serve obedience but also be employed against the master's house. Subjected skills can be skills for rebellion, a *re-bellum*, a war that again resumes.

---

[24] For more articulate examples of infrapolitics, see Scott (1990, 2012a).

THE FREEDOM FIGHTER'S MANUAL

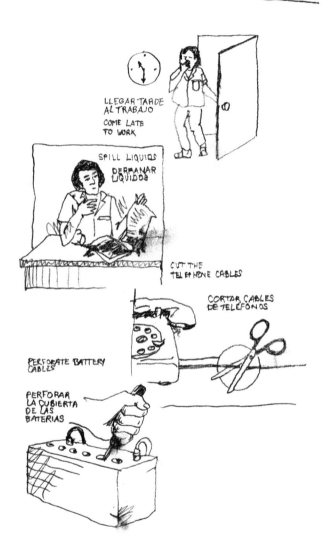

11 Trouble Making and Counter-Crafts

In 1983, the CIA distributed a sixteen-page *Freedom Fighter's Manual* in Nicaragua, encouraging people to use simple means to sabotage the operations of the Nicaraguan state. Airdropped over Nicaragua in spring 1983 and distributed through anti-Sandinista guerrillas, the Contras, the manual encourages Nicaraguans to "sabotage the Marxist tyranny" through simple means. It is a "practical guide to liberating Nicaragua from oppression and misery by paralyzing the military–industrial complex of the traitorous marxist state without having to use special tools and with minimal risk for the combatant." It continues:

> The following pages present a series of useful sabotage techniques, the majority of which can be done with simple household tools such as scissors, empty bottles, screwdrivers, matches, etc. These measures are extremely safe and without risk for those who use them, as they do not require equipment, skill or specialized activities that can draw attention to the doer.[1]

---

[1] *Freedom Fighter's Manual* (1984: 2).

Perhaps this is what is striking with the manual at the first look; how quotidian and straightforward the steps of sabotage are. The methods presented begin with what appears as simple laziness: "don't do maintenance work," showing a man taking a break while his truck remains broken behind him, or "come late to work," depicting a man yawning coming into the office at half-past-ten. Perhaps even better, "call in sick to work" is drawn with a man relaxing in a cozy armchair, telephoning work with a cocktail in his other hand. Resistance against the "military–industrial complex of the traitorous marxist state" appears as something most of us would not have much trouble doing. And now, as the manual is widely available online, with its own Wikipedia page, I guess the CIA would support that we all do our part. Which cocktail would you prefer?

These first steps of the manual illustrate how the workings of servitude are so deeply ingrained in everyday life that simply making room for oneself outside of labor becomes a form of resistance. Simply *not doing* undermines the state: "Leave lights on," or "Leave water taps on." Inaction undermines the imperative to do one's part. Being a bit lazy and relaxing at work is the birth of treachery. Don't be a good worker, stop being useful. But also, notice how hard it is to differentiate between explicit resistance and simply being self-serving.

Except for being a tool of subversion, I would say the manual is a work of art. Depicted in illustrations reminiscent of comics, the methods used for paralyzing the state range from laziness, refusal to work and passive obstruction ("hide and damage tools"), small unruliness ("spill liquids"), to more persuasive manners ("threaten the boss by telephone") and material means ("perforate battery cables" and "put dirt into gasoline tanks"). The methods get more elaborate and finish with fleshing out descriptions on how to plant nails on roads, sabotage toilets, start delayed fires using cigarettes, and how to make Molotov cocktails. Quoted in the *New York Times*, Edgar Chamorro, an officer in the Honduras-based Nicaraguan Democratic Force (part of the Contras) that distributed the manual, points out that the first comic book the CIA wanted to spread "didn't look very Nicaraguan." To solve this, a Nicaraguan artist in Honduras was assigned to redraw the cartoons "to give a Nicaraguan face to the manual."[2] Republished by Grove Press in 1984 for $2, the sixteen-page comic book guide got an English translation and broader distribution and can now be accessed online.

There are no weapons in the manual, no fighting, or explicit conflict in the way one may think of rebellion. The choice of simple household tools is explicitly to reduce the political signature of the objects used for sabotage; or as the manual states, it is about avoiding to "draw attention to the doer." These tools play out a clandestine form of Latour's *dingpolitik*, or politics of things: everyday objects that *should not raise concern*, not become "issues," but only act temporarily and then return to the kitchen drawers and cupboards. Domestic utensils are activated to affect the material politics discussed around the kitchen table. On this scale, there is a long history of the "little tradition" of peasant rebellions, where small acts of resistance are almost indistinguishable from immediate self-interested behavior and where such acts take place "off-stage." In small rural communities dependent on face-to-face loyalties and the landlord's personality, open resistance and dissent come with a high price of exclusion. As these communities are highly reliant on the social relationships between members, explicit conflict is subdued in the everyday to maintain social bonds and security.[3]

When I first encountered the manual, I was struck by how practical and simple it was and how it followed an intuitive progression of techniques. The clear and practical advice of the actions in the booklet has a designerly approach to sabotaging and paralyzing the state apparatus. Except for the ideological tone in the introduction, the methods are all hands-on and down to earth. Interestingly enough, almost all

---

[2] *New York Times* (1984: 8); see also Brinkley (1984).

[3] In rural and agrarian settings, more abstract class relations that primarily relate to "a struggle over the appropriation of work, production, property and taxes" are not so apparent as in the little traditions where opposition appears more in evasion, pilfering, profanation, gossiping than in more open confrontation (Scott 2013: 94).

the practical advice of the CIA signifies a materiality-based perspective on state power while simultaneously calling upon the population to care enough to take action.[4] The CIA seems to advise a reactionary countermaterialism against the Sandinistas' Marxist materialism: inactivism against labor, domestic rebellion against the reproduction of the state. And the counterrevolutionary instruments for this job are the everyday instruments of the household toolbox, or what most design students can find at the school workshop.

The *Freedom Fighter's Manual* is certainly not the first handbook of mischief. What I find most fascinating is how its pedagogical approach reads almost like a Bauhaus-like foundation course in craft and design, starting from the simplest forms and going more abstract toward more radical and encompassing practices. In its didactic simplicity, the manual develops almost like the palpable and educational "gifts" of Friedrich Fröbel, the founder of the Kindergarten movement. It follows a clear path in increasing complexity, effort, and impact and does so in a playful way. In its almost naïve expression, the illustrations reduce the hostility and violent effects of the acts portrayed. The only enemy depicted in the manual is a boss who falls victim to being threatened over the phone. Instead, it is the infrastructure of power that is attacked or sabotaged, mostly in ways that could disguise as angsty teenage vandalism rather than state subversion if it was not for its systemic and strategic approach.[5] And as the manual states, the whole idea is

---

[4] The material concrete doing of care is always specific and emerges in conflict between relational arrangements: Who cares? For what? Why do "we" care? and mostly *How* do we care? (Puig de la Bellacasa 2017: 61). To care opens to take action, to intervene (more than using "thoughts and prayers" to affect political injustices). In this sense, to care is to interfere in-between, break into mediation, into the *inter-esse*, the relation between the human and the material operation of the state.

[5] Not only rebels commit sabotage against the state, but also the other way around, in various forms of policing actions and state-sponsored counterintelligence, provocation, and destruction. One infamous example being the 1985 French sinking of the Greenpeace ship *Rainbow Warrior* in Auckland harbor.

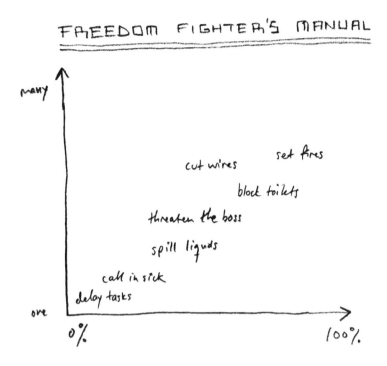

FREEDOM FIGHTER'S MANUAL

many

one

0%   100%

set fires
cut wires
block toilets
threaten the boss
spill liquids
call in sick
delay tasks

that it should be used by lay practitioners utilizing only simple household tools.

The manual suggests how to make trouble and not just any trouble. This trouble is explicitly subversive against the "traitorous marxist state," executed strategically and escalated to increase the impact of small local interventions. With every page of the manual, the force of the action is increased, from simple inaction to clear destruction. This is troublemaking explicitly aimed at challenging state space by subverting its boundaries, infrastructure, and functions. To the CIA, every person can be a designer of a post-Sandinista future, even if only sabotaging the current traitorous state. With small, local, and highly material manipulations, the manual suggests ways troublemaking works in clear resonance with Vaclav Havel's classic discussion on the power of the powerless, yet here with an emphasis on utilizing an escalation of material affect and for a more destructive purpose.[6]

These types of everyday resistance, what Scott famously calls "weapons of the weak," are ubiquitous in the lives of most societies where people try to avoid the attention and extractive mechanisms of the state. They range from the simple omission of maintenance, dodging a call of duty, or "forgetting" to pay taxes, instances and cultural practices Scott suggests as "infrapolitics." These include elaborate forms of creative misuse and challenging boundaries, explicit and detailed schemes, and strategic campaigns of disobedience. Slowness is a mild strike, a withdrawal of collaboration, and, similarly, design inactivism is making things *not work* and refusing to cooperate and design to fix a "problem."[7] Inactivism, or simple refusal to adapt, is not uncommon when introducing newly developed systems, not least of the technological and organizational sort. In such cases, troublemakers may range from conservative nonconsumers and late adapters to more explicit resistance and fervent Luddites.[8]

The manual primarily stresses primitive forms of manipulating matter to challenge the state. In a practical sense, the manual

---

[6] Havel (1985). This increase of force can be used in resistance or decolonization, as well as terror and destruction for their own ends. I am not trying to answer the question if making can be "progressive" or "emancipatory" in the sense of revolutionary politics, but for a fruitful discussion on a similar topic, see Lahiji (2016).

[7] These types of behavior come to test the boundaries of what Herbert Marcuse called the "repressive tolerance" of the state, using a grey zone of acceptance to conceal and restrain potential uprisings against appalling political realities.

[8] The term Luddite is often used broadly as someone who is against new technologies (twisting the mythical resistance of Ned Ludd). But in this case it is important to notice that technologies are often used against technologies, clogs against cogs, computer viruses against nuclear research, homemade bombs against corporations (as in the case of the Unabomber, Ted Kaczynski, who attacked the "industrial–technological system" with homemade yet sophisticated mail bombs). For a discussion on everyday Luddite practices of nonadaptation as a form of resistance to technologies and control, see Kline (2000, 2003).

presents techniques that make disruption to the flow of the everyday, or what one could perhaps call a "countermaking" or "countercrafts" (as a practical implementation of a counterculture). They strive to make an impact, from low-intensity inaction, such as leaving the lights on or calling in sick to work, to more aggressive means, like cutting wires and making tools to destroy other forms of infrastructure. But just like a counterculture, such disruptions are caught downstream and are defined by what they oppose.[9] And they are easily corrupted from their original intent or drawn into escalating cycles of countermeasures or violence responding to violence. It is a type of resistance that risks backfiring as it increases the techniques of domination by the state to trigger an escalation of repression and violence.[10]

However, it is not sabotage that interests me in the *Freedom Fighter's Manual*. Those aspects are abundant in other manuals of destruction, perhaps most (in)famously in William Powell's *The Anarchist Cookbook* and all its siblings, at least since the *Book of Fires for the Burning of Enemies*, the twelfth-century recipe book of incendiary weapons by Marcus Grecus. The printed sources for destruction are abundant, not only online. US Army manuals are in the public domain, such as *Special Forces Handbook* (ST131-80), and as Larabee notices, this handbook "includes a section on improvised devices such as soap and gasoline napalm, a Molotov cocktail, thermite in a can, a time bomb made with peas or beans, a pipe bomb, and a pocket watch detonator."[11] To state narrative, the power to cause damage and violence is safe only in some hands, and society is at risk if the tools with such concentration of agency "falls into

---

[9] This is also the problem the objects of protest often remain held back by their situation, suggesting little of futures beyond the protest; see discussion on obedient versus disobedient objects in Flood and Grindon (2014), as well as Traganou (2021).

[10] For a longer description on how the dynamics of resistance and increased repression and how nonviolent noncooperation can reduce such tensions, see Chenoweth and Stephan (2011).

[11] Larabee's (2015: 70) study contains an extensive list of controversial manuals and also how such texts have been used in court against defendants.

the wrong hands." As this statement makes clear, gatekeepers must guard such devices. This is highlighted with the danger of people with the "wrong hands" getting the knowledge of how to manufacture their own power tools, such as through popular weapon manuals, which have a long history tied to persecuting owners of such dangerous texts, from Johann Most's *Revolutionäre Kriegswissenshaft* from 1885 to romanticized manuals like Che Guevara's *Guerrilla Warfare* from 1961, to more current manuals distributed online, where persecutors continuously use their presence in trials to show the antisocial intent of its owner. These pieces of knowledge in society play almost mythical roles, and parallels can be drawn not only to the trickster like Prometheus but also to the Aesop's fable of "The Eagle and the Fox" with its violent course of revenge.

As is evident in the manual, the purpose is not to build a post-Sandinista world but to undermine and sabotage the current state of affairs. It is a form of resistance that lacks a constructive program or a direction out of destruction. The methods of the manual only oppose; they do not propose. It leaves a designer asking: What if you actually manage to overthrow the traitorous state, then what?

Still, it is the method of practical escalation and the building from inactivism toward activism that is useful for mapping out the potential of making practices. From a perspective of primitive making, the exciting part of the manual is how it helps draw a diagram of the intensification of resistance. When we put our attention to how the CIA maps a practice of resistance across the pages of the booklet, from inaction to full-on sabotage, we can trace an *escalation of material agency and affect*, much in alignment with the example of the speed bump growing in height and size to become a barricade.

As the manual suggests, the effort is sequestered and local, yet it strives to afflict systemic impact. And it can be effective, even if the individual perpetrators remain isolated and unorganized, to minimize the risk of getting caught. From doing things that are not illegal, such as not doing maintenance to leaving the lights on and leaving gates open, to more straightforward sabotage, like cutting wires and destroying truck batteries and engines, the methods are hands-on and primitive. As is explicitly said in the booklet's introduction, the manual shows how ordinary people can use everyday objects and minimal skills to mobilize increasing pressure on social systems and infrastructure. They increase the pressure by *making* more trouble, increasing intensity of impact on state matter through material interfaces and infrastructure, into state meta. Or, to put it differently, the manual exposes how the manipulation of matter is used for systemic *unmaking of dark matter*. By messing with state matter, the more abstract meta of the state apparatus can be touched and manipulated.

DANGEROUS MAKINGS

Designers can have a lot to learn from the CIA, and it may be a good reminder to students at the workbench that what they do there can be a craft with political impact. The escalation apparent in the *Freedom Fighter's Manual* is an invitation to think of making in the context of political and state-related action, what actions uphold and reproduce state space, and how they can be tweaked to turn making toward the engineering of primitive justice machines. As shown throughout the previous chapters, making is not disconnected from state matter but in continuous proximity to it. The CIA manual makes this explicit, as its purpose is to teach citizens how to undermine state space and sabotage state matter. But, as mentioned before, it is not sabotage we are after but how making in proximity to state space can help designers to turn their making into a material practice in their struggles for justice. As the history of labor and gender rights, independence, and decolonization shows, even when working toward peace, we have a lot to learn from more dangerous forms of making.

Why go close to danger? When we encounter friction in the proximity of state space, we know we have moved away from the designated paths. Again, one must notice that state space is not evenly upheld and enforced and affects populations differently. As with owning dangerous manuals that can bring you to jail, just being at a controversial place is for some considered a crime. Some bodies are allowed to be inactive, while other bodies doing the same get labeled as loitering and considered a crime. But overall, when we run into trouble with the state, we know we have run into something that matters, a status quo some invested interests need to defend, as it concerns the distribution of agency across the social realm.

If we add some more forms of material practices to the matrix, we can see a pattern where many types of making start to get into trouble, a boundary zone where legal concerns quickly emerge. One can utilize a lot of material agency as long as one stays comfortably within the private realm when the level of affect remains low. Again, the speed bump or barricade can be built on your property to not much fuzz, but it becomes real trouble when erected in public. In a similar vein, you may get away with moonshining as long as you don't sell it (depending on where you are in the world), and you can pick your own locks for fun (again, depending on state legislation—even owning picks can be a crime). On the other hand, along the other axis, you can engage a high degree of affective dissemination, as long as you keep it to media (spreading memes or fake news is most often not a crime). At the same time, problematic practices with a bit more material agency run into trouble, especially when they are made to be as accessible and user-friendly as possible (such as filesharing platforms).

While the gray zone between legal and illegal has been heavily debated over the past decades, when it comes to digital technologies such as filesharing, it is also present in many other making practices. Common among them is that the troubles increase when it comes to an increased material agency that can affect the many. This can range from simple and playful practices. In New York, an example may be the everyday conflicts around the utilization of the fire escapes as improvised balconies; how many plants am I allowed to have placed there outside my window before the complaints come that I am obstructing the passage and thus undermine the reason the fire escape is there in the first place. Or take the example of skateboarding, where just playing around in the built environment may not cause much trouble. Still, when we start to leave marks on the physical infrastructure, or modify the parking lot where we practice with more permanent and obtrusive obstacles, it may cause conflict with authorities. An everyday example I ran into myself was when I not long ago threw a rope across a branch in the local park and set up a swing in a tree for my children, creating an improvised playground. It seemed to work just fine until a park ranger came by and reminded us that we could be fined for damaging the tree. It might be acceptable as my children were young, but if the swing was left hanging, older and heavier kids would soon start using it, and the tree would thus surely be damaged. The heavier the affect of body weight, the more real trouble I would find myself in.

The friction gets more tangible and troublesome when making comes to involve, for example, biohacking, DIY clinics, and CRISPR experiments with possibly contagious or hazardous substances. More people may get affected and the consequences indeterminable. The "dangerous" aspect of making may also include services of care that run into trouble as they become practical, from illegal reproduction clinics to other medical services that require licenses and state approval. Thus, many such services move into legal gray zones to get done, spanning from alternative treatments to cancer and abortions, to trade in blood and markets for organs. Care is thus not uncontroversial but runs into all kinds of trouble, not least with state meta in the form of institutions, certifications, and patents. An example can be the OpenSurgery project by designer Frank Kolkman, where he explored and designed DIY surgical robots outside the scope of healthcare regulations. His aim was to promote accessible healthcare services to underserved populations by creating simple and open-source machines for robotic surgery, but Kolkman quickly ran into trouble with patents owned by big pharma, holding back efforts to make healthcare more open for innovation less expensive.[12]

---

[12] See http://www.opensurgery.net for more information about Kolkman's project.

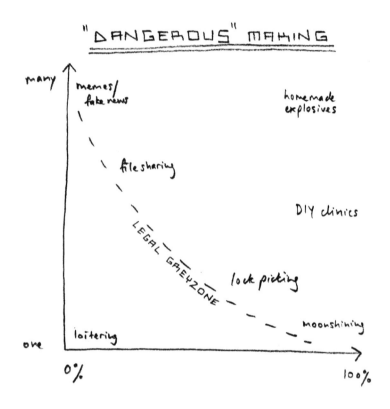

When it comes to explicit destruction, the state is extra watchful as violence directly interferes with the upholding of state space. With high material agency and impact affecting many people, the state is doing its best to keep homemade explosives and 3D-printed weapons away from people.[13] Explosives and guns have a long history of being considered dangerous forms of making (infringing on the state monopoly of violence). It is

[13] There is a growing literature on the contested interests around design and violence. For the morals of design see Verbeek (2011); for the morals of weapons see Dant (2019), Fisher (2019); for 3D printed guns and its connection to violence promoting ideologies, see Fordyce (2015), Record et al. (2015).

their lethality within state space that is controversial. Exporting weapons seems ok, while arming one's own population, especially the marginalized, can be more troublesome. The contentious and reoccurring issues around automatic rifles in the United States can be an all-too-obvious example of this. A barricade can be undone, but there is no ctrl-Z on explosives and weapons.[14]

Another example of dangerous making could be the young man in southern Sweden who in 2011 was arrested for violation of public safety laws for trying to build a small fission reactor in his kitchen from materials he had bought online. In interviews, the man mentioned he was "curious" and wanted to see if he would be able to split an atom at home.[15] Many would agree that nuclear experiments' material agency and affective level are to be considered a public hazard.

---

[14] Just like we have seen the rise of outsourced and state-sponsored hacking and mercenary warfare, we may soon see similar ransomware attacks using biohacking and fabricated hazardous substances. Think of it as the hacking of the internet meme "rule 34" (anything you can imagine is already turned into porn); anything you can imagine being hacked is already, or will soon be, used in power struggles.

[15] The young man, Richard Handl, documented his atomic experiments on his reactor-making blog. On May 21, 2011, he had a "meltdown" on his stovetop as he did some work, published photos of his soiled cooking equipment, and writes, "A meltdown on my cooker!!! No, it not so dangerous. But I tried to cook Americium, Radium and Beryllium in 96% sulphuric-acid, to easier get them blended. But the whole thing exploded upp [*sic*] in the air." Not long after, Handl was arrested and charged for trying to build a fission reactor in his kitchen with materials gleaned from clocks and smoke detectors he had bought over the internet. Handl was charged for violation of the Swedish radiation protection and Swedish Environmental Code. (Documentation of the experiments as well as the police inquiry are available on Handl's detailed blog as of May 2021.) Handl is not alone in his fascination with splitting atoms; perhaps the most famous was David Hahn, a.k.a. "The Radioactive Boy Scout," who in 1994 built a neutron source in his mother's backyard. Larabee (2015: 134) underscores how in the 1950s the explosive "pranks" made by (white, male) youth, using chemistry kits, were often dismissed or tolerated in court as "an unfortunate side effect of scientific progress," where ultimately the "potentially wrong hands of young scientists could be reformed into the right hands for the government's sanctioned violence."

MAPPING MATERIAL ACTIVISM

Most of these examples are forms of material making not in need of expensive scientific equipment and not necessarily framed as subversive or articulated around anti-establishment rhetoric. However, there are many types of sociopolitical forms of making that challenge domination in different ways, often also condemned as they attract practices that seek to escape state regulations, perhaps most apparent in the debates around darknets, DIY weapons production, and meth labs.

Other constructive practices explicitly challenge legal boundaries but tie such work to public virtues. Examples can be the building of independent internet services in rural areas left out of commercial infrastructure, autonomous encrypted communication networks among squatters, alternative community schooling, dumpster diving and freegan food distribution, turning squats into housing coops and community land trusts, and, not least, controversial maintenance and repairs when much products are inaccessible and protected by regulations and warranties. Yet the troubles still multiply. Kids selling cookies or lemonade on the stoop can be illegal for many reasons, not least on taxes and food safety. The content of dumpsters belongs to the property owner and cannot be freely taken and distributed. Collecting rainwater from the rooftop is illegal in many US states. Many sustainable practices are stifled by regulations, also repairs or the reuse of building materials. Not least, the Digital Millennium Copyright Act (DMCA) of 1998 severely restricts how consumer goods can be used and repaired, as it is illegal to circumvent digital rights management (DRM), regardless of the intent. This has effects as more and more products include digital components and software, making almost any form of tinkering and even repair illegal.[16]

---

[16] For examples of controversies and resistance in construction and repair, see Söderberg and Daoud (2012); Toupin (2016); Svensson et al. (2018).

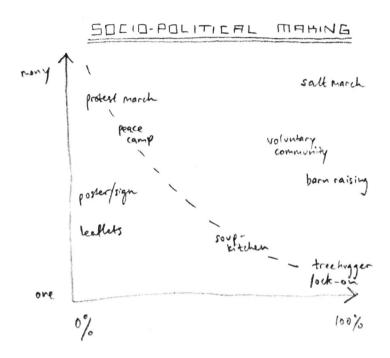

SOCIO-POLITICAL MAKING

many

protest march

peace camp

salt march

voluntary community

barn raising

poster/sign

leaflets

soup kitchen

treehugger lock-on

one

0% 100%

If we use the same diagram of agency and affect to map out various classic activist practices, it is possible to see similar dynamics play out where certain material practices run into state trouble.

Many types of activism involve mobilization of people, done legally by handing out leaflets and making signs for protests. Yet, when people increase the material agency, they may run into increasing legal gray zones (a soup kitchen needs to comply with food regulation, a march or a peace camp requires permits, access to property, etc.).

When actors increase their agency and use their bodies and tools to affect material agency, trouble arises; with more illicit agency mobilized and among a large population, then state designations are at risk of being overrun. An important example of mass DIY activism is the 1930 Salt March in the

Indian independence struggle, where masses of participants used their own agency to explicitly challenge the laws of the British colonial rule.[17]

The diagram is only schematic but can be helpful to display forces crucial to the material agency used in activism. The main point is to show the positioning of material agency that brings it to cause trouble. Historical, social, and geographic context makes a big difference that has to be considered. Doing a sit-in in one's garden is different from doing it at the military base entrance. Staying in bed as a protest works best if you are John Lennon and Yoko Ono. Blocking the gates of a community garden is different than locking oneself to a railroad intersection or the gates of a prospective nuclear waste site. Notably, such actions also exist as media images, narratives, and imitations. They are not merely material. Actions ripple through culture and the social body. Their impact may be an inspiration for action as much as affect, they may work as nudges toward action and mobilization as much as practical changes of the material environment. Yet, as modes of actions, they break cynic submission and challenge participants to advance their claims to control. They are makings of worlds that simultaneously unmake opposing undesired worlds.

Again, it is not only a matter of the size of the public but where the strategic making takes place and how it mobilizes material agency as means and ends. It is the agency of new making that suggests and brings new worlds into reality. But most makers have a lot to learn from the CIA: utilize inactivity, move into proximity with state space, increase the pressure on state matter, and keep escalating the efforts by mobilizing more material affect. Who dares wins. As Donna Haraway has it, corrosive skepticism cannot be midwife to our new stories.[18]

---

[17] Another example can be the hundreds of thousands of poor and landless people of *Movimento dos Trabalhadores Sem Terra* (*MST*), the landless workers' movement, who have occupied land in Brazil for more than thirty years of struggle for land reform and a self-sustainable way of life for the rural poor. On occupied land, they have set up communities and started to grow food, basing their work on ideas of fair distribution, gender equality, cooperative and organic farming (Sørensen 2016).

[18] Haraway (1981).

12 Make It Simple

Screws hold the world together. They are practical fasteners with a material ctrl-Z function scripted into their physical constitution: turn the screw clockwise and it holds the world together, turn the screw counterclockwise and it undoes what previously seemed immovable and permanent. In their banal quotidian ways and following strict protocols and standards, screws and nuts and bolts hold together the fissures across the tangible realms that make up the world we live in. Where different parts meet, there are screws. And the screw heads give the user access to construct as well as deconstruct, or make and unmake, the world.

No wonder then screws are drawn into so many conflicts. Thread standards and metric or imperial scales we encounter in the local hardware store. Still, there are also more obfuscated agendas around thread-gauging system, tolerance classes, and material compositions, and not least the heads that give access to their magical material properties.

Screws are just one of the many political interfaces of the world. This is why you may see so many types of screw heads around the everyday. Some screwheads are designed to be accessible, while others embody an arms race between those with authority to use them and those without. You find tamper-resistant screws, such as Security Torx, which looks just like a standard Torx but has a post in the center of the head to make it inaccessible to the bits you get in the standard set (or five-lobed variants, sometimes also with a center post). You may spot these kinds of screwheads on public transport. The screws on your computer may also be of an odd shape, signaling you should keep away from unmaking them, while also turning the signal into an obstacle for disobeying the warranty.

Screwheads embody the authority of access. This makes tamper-resistant screwheads common in controlled environments such as prisons. Much of the work at installing infrastructure in such environments is concerned with minimizing tampering; after attaching a piece of furniture or equipment, the work is then about sanding down screw heads and restricting the profile of the screw from unsanctioned interference. Look around your everyday world. You can see where authority is required in the forms of special screwdrivers to gain access to interfere with the material interfaces of the designed environment. Elevators and subway cars, computers and technical gadgets, screws point you to the material boundaries of agency and authority.

Nevertheless, also screwheads have their justice machines. Get creative, file down, and modify bits from a cheap set, and you can access many of the safety heads. Or, if you are in tight spaces with no access to hardware, gently heat up the handle of a standard BIC pen with a lighter or over the stove and then push it into the slots of the screwhead. The plastic will melt into the slot of the head, and if the screw is not too tight the pen will work well enough as a screwdriver. When it comes to tinkering, the pen may sometimes be as mighty as the screwdriver.

MAKING ACTION SPACES

Everyday tools equip its user to intervene, construct, deconstruct, and reconstruct their world, changing it according to their will. Expanding and amplifying the capacities of the body, tools can be virtuous as well as dangerous things, and

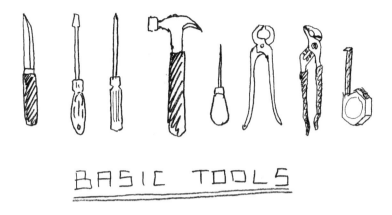

BASIC TOOLS

they are created to allow certain things to be operable to the user while not others. In a very rudimentary way, tools offer the possibility to question the distribution of agency and authority. In that way, we can see tools as primitive justice machines.

A Swedish introductory book about home repairs I have kept since childhood suggests an essential toolbox should include the following: fixed blade knife, screwdrivers (flat-head and Phillips), claw hammer, scratch awl, carpenter's pincers, groove-joint pliers, tape measure. The book suggests a next step up would include adding an adjustable wrench, combination pliers, a small handsaw, and then more. Introductory textbooks on craft and repairs suggested much the same tools around the 1900s, and today an internet search would recommend something similar.[1]

---

[1] You can sense the book is a bit dated as the focus is still a lot on nails (claw hammer and carpenter's pincers); today a (cordless) drill would probably be in the current version as screws have basically replaced nails in many home improvement projects. Vise grips is a good thing to have around. What tools are most practical and educational has been subject to long debate. When it comes to educational shop class, Doug Stowe (2005: 80) sums up some of the controversies around using knives in children's Sloyd education in the 1890s, where, for example, British educators argued the chisel being a better educational tool, whereas Scandinavian educators suggested the knife

Since we rarely take on the world bare-handed, a set of tools of some sort is essential to a practical approach to the world. Tools give access to the world. A screwdriver to open a black box, a hammer to shape the world, or a needle and thread for simple repairs. When used successfully, tools reveal how malleable and hackable the everyday living environment is. And with each new skill and with the right tools, the surrounding world seems open for more and more modification and manipulation. A bit of practical homesteading adds a tiny room of independence amid designed systems, or it can even be a form of crafty superpower, not least romanticized in the autonomous off-gridder or tiny-house-dweller.[2] Of course, many practical people make and repair their things, and every toolbox in the wardrobe or little workbench in the garage speaks of this. This approach is the norm across the planet, while consumer societies are the exception. So it is encouraging that the internet keeps expanding the treasure chest of videos and DIY manuals to support everything from fixing your leaking toilet, repairing bikes, glasses, or washing machines, or building a house using only primitive stone-age technologies, all the way to DIY dentistry and knee surgery. Sharing such methods across the globe exposes how unequal the distribution of services and goods is and how dearly primitive justice machines are needed.

So much of design and making deals with the banal level of life, and while a metaperspective on these dealings is essential, the way most people encounter design is still on an everyday level of matter. For most people, primitive designs make up their everyday world and the everyday space of activity. Handling and

---

allowed more organic and less mechanical work. The debate also echoed classism as the knife was a tool for the rural population, whereas the chisel was a historically preferred instrument of craftsmen and guilds.

[2] This can be seen not least in the enduring romantic call of Thoreau's *Walden* ([1849] 2008), the examples of Helen and Scott Nearing that inspired a generation of back-to-the-land activists after the Second World War, and the books on self-sufficiency that have been bestsellers since the 1970s. Also the current resurgence of making craft mindfulness counterculture echoes similar traits.

repairing your WC, glasses, or door offers a basic grounding in the everyday.

I call these tangible worlds of everyday engagement "action spaces."[3] Our action spaces are those zones of interactivity where distributed potentiality is related to our abilities to affect, manipulate, and control the outcomes. With the skill of swimming, the element of water opens as an action space, a space where my agency was severely limited before I acquired that skill. With sewing, we can change our looks without necessarily following what the brands say or what is available in the stores; and with carpentry, the walls and structure of our house soften to become something I can shape. With some basic skills in electricity, we can turn off the main switch and repair some broken fixtures. As we increase our action spaces, the world we can change grows, and thus the reach of our agency and power also increases, while authorities have less material influence over us. As geographer J. K. Gibson-Graham puts it, "If to change ourselves is to change our worlds, and the relationship is reciprocal, then the project of history-making is never a distant one but always right here, on the borders of our sensing, thinking, feeling, moving bodies."[4]

An action space is a room for agency that connects matter and meta. With an expanded action space and manipulation of matter, I can impose my will onto the public realm and the meta. I can learn how to work on the mechanical parts and configurations on my moped or electric scooter, which have the dark matter of meta imposed into their engines and transmissions in the form of speed regulations capping the effect of the vehicle. The material potential of the scooter is suppressed through matter, imposing the meta of speed limits into its mechanical parts. By disassembling the scooter, replacing some parts, I can "liberate" the potential of the scooter's matter, but by doing so, I challenge and transgress the meta. But as I do so, I also run into trouble.

---

[3] The term's usage in this way was introduced when applied to fashion in von Busch (2008).

[4] Gibson-Graham (2006: xvi).

Look carefully and you will find how the struggles over the boundaries of action spaces are ever present; *who is allowed to do what, where*? It may concern how and where a child drops Lego pieces across the kitchen floor to the frustration of parents ("keep your toys in your room!"). It may be the conflicting zones of influence between two neighbors, of who should pick up the trash, cut the hedge along the shared property line, or who gets to park their car where. It may concern the struggle between the janitor and the noisy street vendor in front of the house, squatters taking over a building, or whole neighborhoods hijacking the electrical infrastructure of the municipality. In some cases, the negotiations are between subjects with the meta being cultural patterns and traditions; at other times the meta of state regulation is more present where a state functionary comes to represent and uphold the meta boundaries.

As people increase the potential to manipulate our physical world, they start running into trouble where the negotiation between matter and meta needs to be remade. I wish to impose my will onto the wood to join two pieces, but the nail bends. Or the hem frays on my latest sewing project. The parents don't like the oversized treehouse in the garden. The neighbor complains about the new shed I built in our yard. The recycled wooden beams used to extend the house are not certified as construction lumber, thus putting my house insurance at risk. The electrical wiring I did in the garage was not properly inspected. The repair I did on the car challenged the terms of the warranty. The illustration I made for the book is based on a copyrighted one. The moonshine I make with my neighbor in the garage is not really legal. The DIY surgery equipment overrides patents.[5]

---

[5] It is easy to think trouble starts with damaging stuff, but it may just as well emerge from illicit construction (Webb et al. 2009), unregulated sustainable practices (Hren 2011). A playful example of the latter can be the French urban exploration group Untergunther who in 2005 set up a secret workshop under the Panthéon famous dome to repair the antique clock that had been left to rust in the building since the 1960s. The Centre of National Monuments took legal action against the group. The discussion on legal versus illegals forms of making has been raging intensively over the last decades, especially when

Action spaces easily become zones of conflict as manifested interests clash. It is in the act of making that matter and meta create inherent frictions and where these conflicts become apparent and tangible. It does not take long before my making runs into trouble, without me necessarily striving to be a troublemaker. The same matter and practices may be used by Robin Hood as well as the mafia, by Gandhi as well as oppressors. And far too often, the same actor and practice, seen with different methods, perspectives, and positions, can be praised or condemned with equal fervor.

MAKING CALISTHENICS

It may be easy to conclude that the activist's creation of action spaces must run into trouble to be effective. In my modest opinion, we should first practice with less conflict and perhaps with somewhat banal aspirations. Start by scratching your immediate itch to get a feeling for where the lines of conflict are drawn. Stay small and make sure you can press ctrl-Z if needed, then escalate and get your work pulsating.

At Sätergläntan, an institute for folk crafts in the middle of Sweden, together with six other crafters, we set out to use greenwood crafts to modify the local commuter train station. During one day, we used traditional woodcrafts and tools to create a series of seating devices to extend the few benches along the platform. The action got us excited, and we worked with several variations of seating and added decorative carvings and patterns. The result looked rough but also inviting with its tried-and-tested greenwood expression. In the end, the "hacks" of the extended benches stood out in clear contrast to the minimalist public furniture. But there was more going on

---

it concerns software code. Code is a very interesting instance where matter and meta overlap, not least debated around copyrights, cracking, and not least cryptocurrencies. For more discussions on the productive elements of constructive and collaborative peer production, see the endlessly fascinating *Journal of Peer Production*.

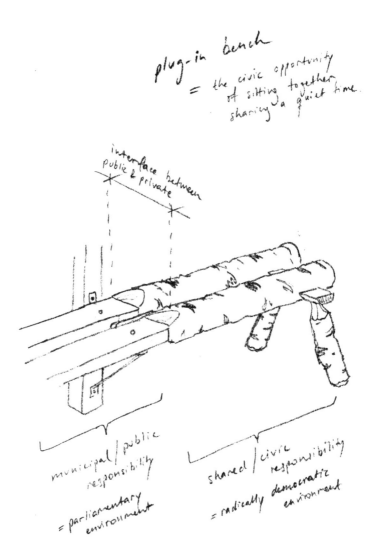

plug-in bench
= the civic opportunity
of sitting together,
sharing a quiet time.

interface between
public & private

municipal/public
responsibility

= parliamentary
environment

shared/civic
responsibility

= radically democratic
environment

with these straightforward additions to the communal seats. As we got together to work on these simple craft objects, we got captivated by a feeling of common purpose. Our skills that would otherwise mainly serve our own interests or be part of our work could easily come to serve the public good. Rather than discuss politics, we were making politics.

In many ways, it was in the collaborative work to make these extensions of public benches that my thoughts on the primitive making of justice machines got started. While they were not addressing an injustice per se, they were manifestations of how rudimentary crafts, without surplus technology, can come to address communal needs in a very tangible way. After a day of work, we all could testify to the use of our shared labor, sit down and utilize the extended seating spaces. It was an immediate testament to the "can-do" pragmatic negotiations of shared making. Taking the initiative to rectify or harmonize a public need, the crafted plug-in benches spoke of a particular political action space we seldom explore and work in. It was not barn-raising, but we all got a taste of the public use of how craft skills could unify a sense of common purpose that I, at least, had experienced all too seldom in design education. It was as if I had too rarely experienced the real communal and democratic use of making, to share with fellow makers the work of using craft to fully being at service to the community, finding a shared objective and hands-on building for the public good. Together, with hands-on crafts, we were taking responsibility for an extended part of the public realm, yet in a way that still plugs into the formal structures of state meta.

Under the everyday works of design, designers are driven to servility; we come to desire "to be of use," even if this is most often limited to the service of the client or the discipline itself in the form of exhibits, competitions, projects, or research. The client tells us what needs to be done, or we set out to research and predict what the client wants users to desire. In either case, under the regular division of labor, designers serve to create more servitude. Under default-designed obedience, servility makes users anticipate desires, making obedience an expression of gratitude while also stripping both designers and users of interfaces to give back to the community. In the division of labor, it is always someone else's job to fix things, repair, and build our commons. In the end, all too often, the function of design is to make the user justify the current order and arrangements, so much better if it comes at a low price and looks cool. This is the surplus obedience built into design, an excess beyond original functionality: how each person comes to obey more than is genuinely required by the situation of submission. With surplus obedience, the possibility to take power stays abstract and scary.[6]

Primitive making offers a minimal subordination under meta organization, bringing the locus of control closer to the workbench. It is ascetic in the Greek sense of ascetic, as a form of "exercise." It is the striving toward minimal obedience, or minimal submission to the scripted use, to find the appropriate matters of manifestation an alternative reality. It does not renounce technology or sacrifice it but makes the execution of orders the least complete. It obeys as badly as possible. Ascetic means primitive and appropriate in that it tries to minimize its alignment with surplus statehood; it uses minimal surplus technology, minimal surplus meta, and minimal surplus subordination. It is ascetic obedience that discourages alignment and acceptance.

Primitive making is also ascetic in that it offers a sensibility to how democratic crafts can help build tangible ways to create and maintain a shared world of our own making. Making our world tangible, it celebrates the local knowledge, common sense, and creativity of our fellow beings. As it sometimes emerges in tension with state designations, it is an embodiment of anarchist ethical possibilities. It offers something akin to the "ethical calisthenics" that Scott argues we need to train in the everyday.[7] To Scott, ethics is a bit like gymnastics. Or perhaps more like parkour or free-running, turning the quotidian into an unexpected yet adventurous obstacle course. We need to practice it to stay in shape, breaking the law a little here and there to keep ethically alert for the time when greater ethical considerations and risk-takings are needed. But like physical

---

[6] For a longer discussion on surplus obedience, see Gros (2020).
[7] Scott (2012b).

calisthenics, it must stay grounded in the local context and situation. It is exercises that don't rely on anything but a person's own body weight. It is an applied ethical training on one's own life, to rid oneself of surplus obedience, stop providing or aligning with the signs, and give more to power than it demands. *Making calisthenics* is the ethical calisthenics of the workshop. It opens physical space, action spaces, through state space. But it is also an ethical space; the landscape is unlocked for new dynamics of movement, even though the layout is the same as before. Call it Nakatomi crafts.

The task ahead is to train our making calisthenics more often. Making can manifest participatory subordination in a multitude of ways. Most design briefs follow the demands of the meta to then shape matter to put something on the market. When designers try to address a political problem, the suggested fix follows a similar route: here is a problem, and here is a thing that can fix it—take it or leave it. *Designers propose* and construct themselves out of contested situations. On the other hand, political activists usually focus on stopping the problem, protesting, and mobilizing to create enough impetus to address the contested issue. *Protesters oppose* and mobilize to stop problems. It is not always true, but in general, protesters obstruct injustices from taking place, while designers create band-aids and soup kitchens.

Making calisthenics binds oppositions and propositions together in the same gesture and matter. Feminist Barbara Deming suggested that the two modes of action must be combined into a method for which she used the metaphor of the "two hands," actions that both try to stop an injustice while in the same gesture also pointing to the alternative. It both opposes and proposes. The resistance suggested by Deming strives to frame and reform the relationship between activist and opponent or, more precisely, to make sure the activity reforms the guiding principles between opponents:

> The more the real issues are dramatized, and the struggle raised above the personal, the more control those in nonviolent rebellion begin to gain over the adversary. For

> they are able at one and the same time to disrupt everything
> for him, making it impossible for him to operate within the
> system as usual, and to temper his response to this … They
> have as it were two hands upon him—the one calming him,
> making him ask questions, as the other makes him move.[8]

One hand calms, slows down, stops, closes down agency.
Another hand moves, builds, and opens up agency. If we think in
matter, one hand uses itself to become a speed bump, the other
hand connects and is a strategic tool of capacities.

STAY MATTER!

So, it's time to end these ramblings. Let's spend less time on
this text and move to the workshop. I hope to finish with some
words of encouragement.

I am an old metal-head, perhaps you have noticed. It often
sounds raw, but it is a music culture that encourages and respects
primitive instrument crafts as much as elaborate technique. The
first album I bought was Black Sabbath's *Born Again*; dark,
heavy, with a lot of humor and tongue-in-cheek devilishness,
tricksy while also explicitly corny. There is a greeting you
sometimes hear between metal fans: "stay metal!" A bit quirky,
sure. But I also think it is a fun way of affirming a shared
perspective between people in an otherwise quite introverted
and gloomy scene. And if there are metal-heads, should there
not also be matter-heads? With heads full of matter, they keep
their hands on the meta. Perhaps the greeting between matter-
heads in the workshop should simply be "stay matter!"

Perhaps this sounds too kittenish for academia, but we should
not miss the many similarities between making and music. The
magic happens when it is made together and shared. There is
a certain charm when both are hammered out in the garage

---

[8] Deming (1971: 207).

or stitched and patched up with a sense of rebellion between participants. A similar dynamic occurs in the workshop. We may think of the lonely tinkerer, but the workshop is often a shared space of labor. Tools shift hands, care has to be taken to keep the edges sharp, surfaces clean, and cables untangled. There is something communal in the workshop, and we should not forget it is also a place where justice is practiced. As Richard Sennett points out:

> The workshop spawned an idea of justice, that the things people make cannot be seized from them arbitrarily, and it enjoyed a kind of political autonomy, at least in Greece, since artisans were allowed to make their own decisions about how best to practice their craft.[9]

More so, as a cultural site, the workshop has also been the testing ground for social contracts, in mutual obligations between unequal partners, as in guilds, or as sites for social reform. It allows for tangible cooperation in more complex ways than institutions normally regulate and administer. "Political cooperation has to be humanly fine-tuned, through rituals of mutual respect; shared interests alone will not make it prosper."[10] Like the musicians, it is in the shared cooperation the result becomes real. Only by earning the experience from practical activity, the joinery will match up, and all can share the whole.

Even if starting in solitude, making physical things can turn a common project tangible. Don't underestimate this material capacity. It makes tangible that we can improve and repair the material conditions of our world, or even that we can build another shared world together. Think of it as civic crafts; together, we *build common deliberation.* If it is on the boundaries of what is designated or allowed, it offers us an opportunity to discuss how we want our world to be, despite the current manifestations of state matter.

---

[9] Sennett (2012: 57).
[10] Ibid., 62.

The future is rendered tangible, discussable, and this deliberation is not meta, but we can test it together. After working in concert, we can sit down on our plug-in bench together. If you are so inclined, we can also taste the latest batch of moonshine. In whose interest do we make this future, and how does this redistribute agency and power? Where do we redraw the boundaries, and how do we decide it is the right thing? Most probably, things did not turn out the way we hoped. We may need to take a step back, shrink the issue, and try again. But let's work strategically; this is making calisthenics after all.

To distill some of the words into a list to keep in the toolbox, I think of civic crafts like this:

It is *material*; make civic tangible, gather a public around a practical example, stay concrete. It is *prefigurative*; make it visionary, make it simple, emphasize practice and training, balance obstructive and constructive means—propose while you oppose. It is *democratic*; make it easy to access, modify and reproduce; it is locally available and cheap; it inspires more action. It *mobilizes*; make objectiles that assemble capacities toward a shared goal/effort, build on small wins to build trust and continuity. It is *strategic*; make it realize means and ends, make it not merely "provocative," but challenge unjust boundaries and laws, be realistic—others will strive to undermine your efforts. Be *primitive*; make it quick, easy, and inviting, minimize surplus waste, technology, subordination. Be practical, be material.

Perhaps today, one of the most critical elements of this type of primitive making can be to *heal societal distrust*. New publics and politics can be tested, and chasms overcome, if we set out to create local tangible results or constructive cross-boundary objects. Together we gather around making to practice togetherness. The potential in primitive making is its grounding in matter, recursive immediacy, and closeness to the locus of control. Here, at this instance, we are not delegating the task ahead, not asking for meta guidance. We carve out a space of responsibility as well as possibility to practice material ethics. We are governing here. There is no waiting to take action, but an acceptance that change has to start small, and if that doesn't work, shrink and go even smaller. Primitive making does not delegate but invites participation and works toward a common goal that all contributors can experience. Yes, it is tricky, and we run into all kinds of trouble. It is messy. There will be disagreements and conflicts. We need to respect each other. Some of us will be self-serving. Others want to pick fights. Some results will undoubtedly be used against us. To minimize misunderstandings, make sure means and ends meet.

In the end, the basic hand tools of the workshop may not look impressive. The outcome may seem primitive too. There is not much gloss here. Most design students quickly move on to 3D renderings, process diagrams, and the higher seminars. But for those who spend much time by the workbench, I hope some of these examples could encourage more hands-on engagements with both matter and meta, sociopolitical materials and hardwood politics, means and ends. After a hard day's work, it is time to start testing a more elegant and purposeful democratic chair.

There is a lot to improve here. Don't wait around to get meta-smart or feel frustrated by the mundane possibilities of your limited toolbox: you'll learn something different about making as well as society with the hammer and at the workbench than with the TV remote or smartphone.

Get on it. Have fun. I look forward to seeing your take on the justice machine. Until then, *stay matter!*

REFERENCES

Abbey, Edward ([1975] 2006), *The Monkey Wrench Gang*, New York: Harper.

Adamson, Glenn (2013), *The Invention of Craft*, London: Bloomsbury.

Adamson, Glenn (2018), *Fewer, Better Things*, London: Bloomsbury.

AdHack, Manifesto, Vyvian Raoul, and Matt Bonner (2017), *Advertising Shits in Your Head: Strategies for Resistance*, London: Dog Section Press.

Agamben, Giorgio (2009), *What Is an Apparatus?*, Stanford: Stanford University Press.

Ahmed, Sara (2010), "Orientations Matter", in Dana Coole and Samantha Frost (eds.), *New Materialisms: Ontology, Agency, and Politics*, Durham: Duke University Press, 234–57.

Akrich, Madeleine (1992), "The Description of Technological Objects," in Wiebe Bijker and John Law (eds.), *Shaping Technology/Building Society: Studies in Sociotechnical Change*, Cambridge: MIT Press, 205–24.

Alinsky, Saul (1971), *Rules for Radicals: A Pragmatic Primer for Realistic Radicals*, New York: Vintage Books.

Amnesty International (2012), *"I Wanted to Die": Syria's Torture Survivors Speak Out*, London: Amnesty International.

Anderson, Chris (2012), *Makers: The New Industrial Revolution*, London: Random House.

Andreas, Peter (2013), *Smuggler Nation: How Illicit Trade Made America*, Oxford: Oxford University Press.

Andreas, Peter (2020), *Killer High: A History of War in Six Drugs*, Oxford: Oxford University Press.

The Art Journal Illustrated Catalogue: The Industry of All Nations (1851), London: George Virtue.

Attfield, Judy (2000), *Wild Things: The Material Culture of Everyday Life*, Oxford: Berg.

Bari, Judi (1994), *Timber Wars*, Monroe: Common Courage Press.

Bari, Judi (1997), "Revolutionary Ecology," *Capitalism Nature Socialism*, 8(2): 145–9.

Bayat, Asef (1997), *Street Politics: Poor People's Movements in Iran*, New York: Columbia University Press.

Bayat, Asef (2010), *Life as Politics: How Ordinary People Change the Middle East*, Stanford: Stanford University Press.

Bennett, Jane (2004), "The Force of Things Steps toward an Ecology of Matter," *Political Theory*, 32(3): 347–72.

The Berkeley International Liberation School (1972), *Beat the Heat: A Radical Survival Handbook*, San Francisco: Rampart Press.

Berrigan, Dan (1970), *The Trial of the Catonsville Nine*, Boston: Beacon Press.

Bestor, Arthur (1950), *Backwoods Utopias: The Sectarian and Owenite Phases of Communitarian Socialism in America 1663–1829*, Philadelphia: University of Pennsylvania Press.

Boggs, Carl (1977), "Marxism, Prefigurative Communism and the Problem of Workers' Control," *Radical America*, 6 (Winter): 99–122.

Bogost, Ian (2012), *Alien Phenomenology, or What It's Like to Be a Thing*, Minneapolis: University of Minnesota Press.

Bollier, David, and Silke Helfrich (2019), *Free, Fair and Alive: The Insurgent Power of the Commons*, Gabriola Island: New Society Publishers.

Boudin, Kathy, Brian Glick, Elanor Raskin, and Gustin Reichbach (eds.) (1969), *The Bust Book: What To Do Until the Lawyer Comes*, New York: Grove Press.

Bourriaud, Nicolas (2002), *Postproduction: Culture as Screenplay, How Art Reprograms the World*, New York: Lukas & Sternberg.

Braidotti, Rosi (2000), "Teratologies," in Ian Buchanan and Claire Colebrook (eds.), *Deleuze and Feminist Theory*, Edinburgh: Edinburgh University Press, 156–72.

Brantlinger, Patrick (1996), *Fictions of State: Culture and Credit in Britain, 1694–1994*, Ithaca: Cornell University Press.

Brinkley, Joel (1984), "C.I.A. Primer Tells Nicaraguan Rebels How to Kill," *New York Times*, October 17, section A, page 1.

brown, adrienne maree (2017), *Emergent Strategy: Shaping Change, Changing Worlds*, Chicago: AK Press.

Brown, Tim (2009), *Change by Design: How Design Thinking Transforms Organizations and Inspires Innovation*, New York: Harper Business.

Budds, Diana (2016), "Poäng: The Little-Known History of Ikea's Most Famous Chair," *FastCompany*, September 1, https://www.fastcompany.com/3063312/poaeng-the-little-known-history-of-ikeas-most-famous-chair (accessed December 30, 2020).

Burke, Peter (1992), *The Fabrication of Louis XIV*, New Haven: Yale University Press.

von Busch, Otto (2008), *Fashion-able, Hacktivism and Engaged Fashion Design*, Gothenburg: ArtMonitor.

von Busch, Otto (2017), "Resistant Materialities and Power Tools: Dynamics of Power and Resistance in Everyday Consumerism," *Journal of Resistance Studies*, 3(2): 66–88.

von Busch, Otto, and Per Herngren (2016), *Mode & motstånd: dialoger om befrielse och civil olydnad, imitation och politik*, Göteborg: Korpen.

Bussolini, Jeffrey (2010), "What Is a Dispositive?," *Foucault Studies*, 10: 85–107.

Casemajor, Nathalie, Christian Coocoo, and Karine Gentelet (2019), "Openness, Inclusion and Self-Affirmation: Indigenous Knowledge in Open Knowledge Projects," *Journal of Peer Production*, 13, April, http://peerproduction.net/issues/issue-13-open/peer-reviewed-papers/openness-inclusion-and-self-affirmation/ (accessed December 30, 2020).

Chenoweth, Erica, and Maria Stephan (2011), *Why Civil Resistance Works: The Strategic Logic of Nonviolent Conflict*, New York: Columbia University Press.

Chia, Robert, and Robin Holt (2009), *Strategy without Design: The Silent Efficacy of Indirect Action*, Cambridge: Cambridge University Press.

Churchill, David (2015), "The Spectacle of Security: Lock-Picking Competitions and the Security Industry in Mid-Victorian Britain," *History Workshop Journal*, 80(1): 52–74.

Cohen, Lizabeth (2001), "Citizens and Consumers in the US in Century of Mass Consumption," in Martin Daunton and Matthew Hilton (eds.), *The Politics of Consumption*, Oxford: Berg, 203–22.

Cook, Alice, and Gwyn Kirk (1983), *Greenham Women Everywhere: Dreams, Ideas, and Actions from the Women's Peace Movement*, London: Pluto Press.

Coperthwaite, William (2007), *A Handmade Life: In Search of Simplicity*, White River Junction: Chelsea Green.

Corbett, Sarah (2017), *How to Be a Craftivist: The Art of Gentle Protest*, London: Unbound.

Crawford, Matthew (2009), *Shop Class as Soulcraft: An Inquiry into the Value of Work*, New York: Penguin (published in the UK as *The Case for Working with Your Hands* by Viking, 2010).

Creasman, Allyson (2004), "Side-Stepping the Censor: The Clandestine Trade in Prohibited Texts in Early Modern Augsburg," in Mark Crane, Richard Raisewell, and Margaret Reeves (eds.), *Shell Games: Studies in Scams, Frauds, and Deceits (1300–1650)*, Toronto: CRRS Publications, 211–38.

Dant, Tim (2019), "Guns and Morality: Mediation, Agency and Responsibility," in Tom Fisher and Lorraine Gamman (eds.), *Tricky Design: The Ethics of Things*, London: Bloomsbury, 69–80.

Dauvergne, Peter, and Genevieve LeBaron (2014), *Protest Inc.: The Corporatization of Activism*, Cambridge, MA: Polity.

De Certeau, Michel (1984), *The Practice of Everyday Life*, Berkeley: University of California Press.

DeLanda, Manuel (1991), *War in the Age of Intelligent Machines*, New York: Zone.

DeLanda, Manuel (1997), *A Thousand Years of Nonlinear History*, New York: Zone.

DeLanda, Manuel (2006), *A New Philosophy of Society: Assemblage Theory and Social Complexity*, London: Continuum.

DeLanda, Manuel (2016), *Assemblage Theory*, Edinburgh: Edinburgh University Press.

Deleuze, Gilles (2006), *The Fold*, London: Continuum.

Deleuze, Gilles, and Felix Guattari (1987), *A Thousand Plateaus: Capitalism and Schizophrenia*, Minneapolis: University of Minnesota Press.

Deming, Barbara (1971), *Revolution & Equilibrium*, New York: Grossman.

Denzin, Norman, Yvonna Lincoln, and Linda Tuhiwai Smith (eds.) (2008), *Handbook of Critical and Indigenous Methodologies*, Los Angeles: Sage.

Detienne, Marcel, and Jean-Pierre Vernant (1991), *Cunning Intelligence in Greek Culture and Society*, Chicago: University of Chicago Press.

DiSalvo, Carl (2012), *Adversarial Design*, Cambridge: MIT Press.

Eagleton, Terry (2016), *Materiality*, New Haven: Yale University Press.

Ehrenreich, Barbara, and Deirdre English (1973), *Witches, Midwives, and Nurses: A History of Women Healers*, New York: Feminist Press.

Federici, Silvia (2004), *Caliban and the Witch*, New York: Autonomedia.

Fisher, Tom (2019), "Concealed Trickery: Design and the Arms Industry," in Tom Fisher and Lorraine Gamman (eds.), *Tricky Design: The Ethics of Things*, London: Bloomsbury, 23–44.

Flood, Catherine, and Gavin Grindon (eds.) (2014), *Disobedient Objects*, London: V&A Publishing.

Flusser, Vilém (1999), *The Shape of Things: A Philosophy of Design*, London: Reaktion.

Follis, Luca, and Adam Fish (2020), *Hacker States*, Cambridge: MIT Press.

Fordyce, Robbie (2015), "Manufacturing Imaginaries: Neo-Nazis, Men's Rights Activists and 3D Printing," *Journal of Peer Production*, 6, January, http://peerproduction.net/issues/issue-6-disruption-and-the-law/peer-reviewed-articles/manufacturing-imaginaries-neo-nazis-mens-rights-activists-and-3d-printing/ (accessed December 30, 2020).

Foreman, Dave, and Bill Haywood (1987), *Ecodefense: A Field Guide to Monkeywrenching*, Tucson: N. Ludd.

Forty, Adrian (1986), *Objects of Desire: Design and Society 1750–1980*, London: Thames and Hudson.

Foucault, Michel (2007), *Security, Territory, Population: Lectures at the College De France, 1977–78*, London, Palgrave Macmillan, 126–45.

Freedom Fighter's Manual (1984), New York: Grove Press.

Fuad-Luke, Alastair (2009), *Design Activism: Beautiful Strangeness for a Sustainable World*, London: Earthscan.

Geuss, Raymond (2001), *Public Goods, Private Goods*, Princeton: Princeton University Press.

Geuss, Raymond (2008), *Philosophy and Real Politics*, Princeton: Princeton University Press.

Gibson-Graham, J. K. (2006), *The End of Capitalism (As We Knew It): A Feminist Critique of Political Economy*, Minneapolis: University of Minnesota Press.

Goldfarb, Jeffrey (2006), *The Politics of Small Things: The Power of the Powerless in Dark Times*, Chicago: University of Chicago Press.

Graham, Stephen, and Nigel Thrift (2007), "Out of Order: Understanding Repair and Maintenance," *Theory, Culture and Society*, 24(1): 1–25.

Gros, Frédéric (2020), *Disobey! A Guide to Ethical Resistance*, London: Verso.

Guldi, Jo (2012), *Roads to Power: Britain Invents the Infrastructure State*, Cambridge: Harvard University Press

Hamdi, Nabeel (2004), *Small Change*, London: Earthscan.

Hamdi, Nabeel (2010), *The Placemaker's Guide to Building Community*, London: Earthscan.

Haraway, Donna (1981), "In the Beginning Was the Word: The Genesis of Biological Theory," *Signs*, 6(3): 469–81.

Harvey, Simon (2016), *Smuggling: Seven Centuries of Contraband*, London: Reaktion.

Havel, Vaclav (1985), "The Power of the Powerless," in John Keane (ed.), *The Power of the Powerless: Citizens against the State in Central-Eastern Europe*, London: Hutchinson, 10–59.

Hein, Hilde, and Carolyn Korsmeyer (1993), *Aesthetics in Feminist Perspective*, Bloomington: Indiana University Press.

Hemmings, Jessica (2018), "Rereading and Revising: Acknowledging the Smallness (Sometimes) of Craft," *Craft Research*, 9(2): 273–86.

Herngren, Per (1993), *Path of Resistance: The Practice of Civil Disobedience*, Philadelphia: New Society Publishers.

Herzog, Don (2006), *Cunning*, Princeton: Princeton University Press.

Hill, Dan (2012), *Dark Matter and Trojan Horses: A Strategic Design Vocabulary*, Moscow: Strelka Press.

Hill, Julia Butterfly (2000), *The Legacy of Luna: The Story of a Tree, a Woman, and the Struggle to Save the Redwoods*, San Francisco: Harper San Francisco.

Hobsbawm, Eric (1959), *Primitive Rebels*, Manchester: Manchester University Press.

hooks, bell (2000), *All about Love: New Visions*, London: Women's Press.

Hornborg, Alf (2016), *Global Magic: Technologies of Appropriation from Ancient Rome to Wall Street*, New York: Palgrave Macmillan.

Hren, Stephen (2011), *Tales from the Sustainable Underground: A Wild Journey with People Who Care More about the Planet Than the Law*, Gabriola Island: New Society.

Hyde, Lewis (1998), *Trickster Makes This World*, New York: Farrar, Straus and Giroux.

Illich, Ivan (1973), *Tools for Conviviality*, New York: Harper & Row.

Ingham, Geoffrey (2004), *The Nature of Money*, Cambridge, MA: Polity.

Ingham, Geoffrey (2020), *Money: Ideology, History, Politics*, Cambridge, MA: Polity.

Ingold, Tim (2013), *Making: Anthropology, Archaeology, Art and Architecture*, London: Routledge.

Jackson, Richard (2015), "How Resistance Can Save Peace Studies," *Journal of Resistance Studies*, 1(1): 18–49.

Jennings, Chris (2016), *Paradise Now: The Story of American Utopianism*, New York: Random House.

Johnson, Steven (2006), *The Ghost Map*, New York: Riverhead.

Karras, Alan (2010), *Smuggling: Contraband and Corruption in World History*, Lanham: Rowman and Littlefield.

Katsiaficas, Georgy (2006), *The Subversion of Politics: European Autonomous Social Movements and the Decolonization of Everyday Life*, Oakland: AK Press.

Kelty, Christopher (2005), "Geeks, Social Imaginaries, and Recursive Publics," *Cultural Anthropology*, 20(2): 185–214.

Kelty, Christopher (2008), *Two Bits: The Cultural Significance of Free Software*, Durham: Duke University Press.

Kilcullen, David (2013), *Out of the Mountains: The Coming Age of the Urban Guerrilla*, London: Hurst.

Kline, Ronald (2000), *Consumers in the Country: Technologies and Social Change in Rural America*, Baltimore: Johns Hopkins University Press.

Kline, Ronald (2003), "Resisting Consumer Technology in Rural America: The Telephone and Electrification," in Nelly Oudshoorn and Trevor Pinch (eds.), *How Users Matter: The Co-construction of Users and Technology*, Cambridge: MIT Press, 51–69.

Kokko, Sirpa (2009), "Learning Practices of Femininity through Gendered Craft Education in Finland," *Gender and Education*, 21(6): 721–34.

Korsmeyer, Carolyn (2002), "Feminist Aesthetics," in Lorraine Code (ed.), *Encyclopedia of Feminist Theories*, Abingdon: Routledge.

Krawiec, Kimberly (2009), "Foreword—Show Me the Money: Making Markets in Forbidden Exchange," *Law and Contemporary Problems*, 72(3): i–xiv.

Kullenberg, Christopher (2015), "Citizen Science as Resistance: Crossing the Boundary between Reference and Representation," *Journal of Resistance Studies*, 1(1): 50–76.

Lahiji, Nadir (ed.) (2016), *Can Architecture Be an Emancipatory Project? Dialogues on Architecture and the Left*, Alresford: Zero Books.

Larabee, Ann (2015), *The Wrong Hands: Popular Weapons Manuals and Their Historic Challenges to a Democratic Society*, Oxford: Oxford University Press.

Large, Joanna (2019), *The Consumption of Counterfeit Fashion*, Cham: Palgrave Macmillan.

Larkin, Brian (2013), "The Politics and Poetics of Infrastructure," *Annual Review of Anthropology*, 42: 327–43.

Lasn, Kalle (1999), *Culture Jam: The Uncooling of America*, New York: Eagle Brook.

Latour, Bruno (1988), "How to Write the Prince for Machines as Well as for Machinations," in Brian Elliott (ed.), *Technology and Social Process*, Edinburgh: Edinburgh University Press, 20–43.

Latour, Bruno (1992), "Where Are the Missing Masses? The Sociology of a Few Mundane Artifacts," in Wiebe Bijker and John Law (eds.), *Shaping Technology/Building Society: Studies in Sociotechnical Change*, Cambridge: MIT Press, 225–58.

Latour, Bruno (1994), "On Technical Mediation," *Common Knowledge*, 3(2): 29–64.

Latour, Bruno (2005), *Reassembling the Social: An Introduction to Actor-Network-Theory*, Oxford: Oxford University Press.

Le Guin, Ursula (2016), "Freedom," in *Words Are My Matter: Writing about Life and Books, 2000–2016*, Easthampton: Small Beer Press.

Le-Mentzel, Van Bo (ed.) (2012), *Hartz IV Moebel*, Ostfildern: Hatje Cantz Verlag.

Lietaer, Bernard (2001), *The Future of Money: A New Way to Create Wealth, Work and a Wiser World*, London: Century.

Lohmann, Larry (2012), 'Beyond Patzers and Clients: Strategic Reflections on Climate Change and the 'Green Economy'", *Development Dialogue, What Next, 3*, September, 295–326.

Lynn, Conrad (1967), *How to Stay Out of the Army: A Guide to Your Rights under the Draft Law*, New York: Monthly Review Press.

MacAskill, William (2015), *Doing Good Better: How Effective Altruism Can Help You Make a Difference*, New York: Gotham Books.

Maeckelbergh, Marianne (2011), "Doing Is Believing: Prefiguration as Strategic Practice in the Alterglobalization Movement," *Social Movement Studies*, 10(1): 1–20.

Manaugh, Geoff (2016), *A Burglar's Guide to the City*, New York: Farrar, Straus & Giroux.

Mantena, Karuna (2012), "Another Realism: The Politics of Gandhian Nonviolence," *American Political Science Review*, 106(2): 455–70.

Margolin, Victor (2002), *The Politics of the Artificial: Essays on Design and Design Studies*, Chicago: University of Chicago Press.

Mari, Enzo ([1974] 2002), *Autoprogettazione?*, Mantova: Corraini.

Markussen, Thomas (2013), "The Disruptive Aesthetics of Design Activism: Enacting Design between Art and Politics," *Design Issues*, 29(1): 38–50.

Marres, Noortje (2012), *Material Participation: Technology, Environment and Everyday Publics*, Basingstoke: Palgrave.

Marres, Noortje, Michael Guggenheim, and Alex Wilkie (eds.) (2018), *Inventing the Social*, Manchester: Mattering Press.

Mau, Bruce (2004), *Massive Change*, London: Phaidon.

McCay, George (2011), *Radical Gardening: Politics, Idealism & Rebellion in the Garden*, London: Frances Lincoln.

McGoey, Linsey (2019), *The Unknowers: How Strategic Ignorance Rules the World*, London: Zed Books.

Meadows, Donella (1999), *Leverage Points: Places to Intervene in a System*, Hartland: The Sustainability Institute, http://www.

donellameadows.org/wp-content/userfiles/Leverage_Points.pdf (accessed December 30, 2020).

Minahan, Stella, and Julie Cox (2007), "Stitch'nBitch: Cyberfeminism, a Third Place and the New Materiality," *Journal of Material Culture*, 12(1): 5–21.

Mongoven, Ann (2009), *Just Love: Transforming Civic Virtue*, Bloomington: Indiana University Press.

Monteiro, Mike (2019), *Ruined by Design: How Designers Destroyed the World, and What We Can Do to Fix It*, San Francisco: Mule Books.

Naidu, M. V. (2006), "Gandhian 'Practical-Idealism': Nonviolence," *Peace Research*, 38(2): 35–69.

Naylor, Robin (2014), *Counterfeit Crime: Criminal Profits, Terror Dollars, and Nonsense*, Montreal: McGill-Queens' University Press.

Neustadt, Robert (2014), "Music, Guns, and Peace," *UTNE Reader*, July 21, https://www.utne.com/arts/music-guns-and-peace (accessed December 30, 2020).

New York Times (1984), "C.I.A. Linked to Comic Book for Nicaraguans," October 19, section A, page 1.

Nijhuis, Michelle (2003), "How the Five-Gallon Plastic Bucket Came to the Aid of Grassroots Environmentalists," *Grist Magazine*, 23 July, http://grist.org/article/the19/ (accessed December 30, 2020).

Nodder, Chris (2013), *Evil by Design: Interaction Design to Lead Us into Temptation*, Indianapolis: John Wiley.

O'Donnel, Darren (2008), *Social Acupuncture*, Toronto: Coach House Books.

O.M. Collective (1971), *The Organizer's Manual*, New York: Bantam.

Ottinger, Gwen (2010), "Buckets of Resistance: Standards and the Effectiveness of Citizen Science," *Science, Technology and Human Values*, 35(2): 244–70.

Pacey, Arnold (1999), *Meaning in Technology*, Cambridge: MIT Press.

Peebles, Gustav, and Ben Luzzatto (2019), "More Precious Than Gold: How a Carbon-Based Cryptocurrency Might Save Our Planet," *Public Seminar*, September 19, https://publicseminar.org/essays/more-precious-than-gold/ (accessed December 30, 2020).

Peukert, Detlev (1987), *Inside Nazi Germany: Conformity, Opposition, and Racism in Everyday Life*, New Haven: Yale University Press.

Pfaller, Robert (2003), "Little Gestures of Disappearance: Interpassivity and the Theory of Ritual," *Journal of European Psychoanalysis*, 16: 3–16.

Pirsig, Robert (2006), *Zen and the Art of Motorcycle Maintenance*, New York: Harpertorch.

Popper, Nathaniel (2019), "How a Bitcoin Evangelist Made Himself Vanish, in 15 (Not So Easy) Steps," *New York Times*, March 12, https://www.nytimes.com/2019/03/12/technology/how-to-disappear-surveillance-state.html (accessed December 30, 2020).

Puig de la Bellacasa, Maria (2017), *Matters of Care: Speculative Ethics in More Than Human Worlds*, Minneapolis: University of Minnesota Press.

Ratto, Matt (2011), "Critical Making: Conceptual and Material Studies in Technology and Social Life," *Information Society: An International Journal*, 27(4): 252–60.

Ratto, Matt, and Megan Boler (eds.) (2014), *DIY Citizenship: Critical Making and Social Media*, Cambridge: MIT Press.

Record, Isaac, ginger coons, Dan Southwick, and Matt Ratto (2015), "Regulating the Liberator: Prospects for the Regulation of 3D Printing," *Journal of Peer Production*, 6, January, http://peerproduction.net/issues/issue-6-disruption-and-the-law/peer-reviewed-articles/regulating-the-liberator-prospects-for-the-regulation-of-3d-printing/ (accessed December 30, 2020).

Rejali, Darius (2007), *Torture and Democracy*, Princeton: Princeton University Press.

Ricketts, Aidan (2012), *The Activists' Handbook: A Step-by-Step Guide to Participatory Democracy*, London: Zed Books.

Riker, William (1986), *The Art of Political Manipulation*, New Haven: Yale University Press.

Robinson, Kim Stanley (2012), *2312*, New York: Hachette.

Roitman, Janet (2005), *Fiscal Disobedience: An Anthropology of Economic Regulation in Central Africa*, Princeton: Princeton University Press.

Rorabaugh, William (1979), *The Alcohol Republic: An American Tradition*, New York: Oxford University Press.

Rose, Hilary (1983), "Hand, Brain, and Heart: A Feminist Epistemology for the Natural Sciences," *Signs*, 9(1): 73–90.

Sandel, Michael (1996), *Democracy's Discontent: America in Search of a Public Philosophy*, Cambridge: Belknap.

Sandel, Michael (1998), *Liberalism and the Limits of Justice*, Cambridge: Cambridge University Press.

Scarry, Elaine (1985), *The Body in Pain: The Making and Unmaking of the World*, Oxford: Oxford University Press.

Schüll, Natasha (2012), *Addiction by Design: Machine Gambling in Las Vegas*, Princeton: Princeton University Press.

Scott, James (1985), *Weapons of the Weak: Everyday Forms of Peasant Resistance*, New Haven: Yale University Press.

Scott, James (1986), "Everyday Forms of Peasant Resistance," in James Scott and Benedict Kerkvliet (eds.), *Everyday Forms of Peasant Resistance in South-East Asia*, London: Cass, 5–35.

Scott, James (1990), *Domination and the Arts of Resistance: Hidden Transcripts*, New Haven: Yale University Press.

Scott, James (1998), *Seeing Like a State: How Certain Schemes to Improve the Human Condition Have Failed*, New Haven: Yale University Press.

Scott, James (2009), *The Art of Not Being Governed: An Anarchist History of Upland Southeast Asia*, New Haven: Yale University Press.

Scott, James (2012a), "Infrapolitics and Mobilizations: A Response by James C. Scott," *Revue francaise detudes americaines*, 1: 112–17.

Scott, James (2012b), *Two Cheers for Anarchism: Six Easy Pieces on Autonomy, Dignity, and Meaningful Work and Play*, Princeton: Princeton University Press.

Scott, James (2013), *Decoding Subaltern Politics: Ideology, Disguise, and Resistance in Agrarian Politics*, New York: Routledge.

Sennett, Richard (2008), *The Craftsman*, New Haven: Yale University Press.

Sennett, Richard (2012), *Together: The Rituals, Pleasures and Politics of Cooperation*, New Haven: Yale University Press.

Shah, Aashit (2004), "UK's Implementation of the Anti-Circumvention Provisions of the EU Copyright Directive: An Analysis," *Duke Law & Technology Review*, 1(22): 1–19.

Shales, Ezra (2017), *The Shape of Crafts*, London: Reaktion.

Sholette, Gregory (2010), *Dark Matter: Art and Politics in the Age of Enterprise Culture*, London: Pluto.

Shove, Elizabeth (1999), "Constructing Home: A Crossroads of Choices," in Irene Cieraad (ed.), *At Home: An Anthropology of Domestic Space*, Syracuse: Syracuse University Press.

Simon, Herbert (1996), *The Sciences of the Artificial*, Cambridge: MIT Press.

Snyder, Gary (1990), *The Practice of the Wild*, San Francisco: North Point.

Söderberg, Johan (2010), "Misuser Inventions and the Invention of the Misuser: Hackers, Crackers and Filesharers," *Science as Culture*, 19(2): 151–79.

Söderberg, Johan (2016), "DIY Research in the Psychonaut Subculture: A Case of Unwanted User Innovation," in Sampsa Hyysalo, Torben Elgaard Jensen, and Nelly Oudshoorn (eds.), *The*

New Production of Users: Changing Innovation Collectives and Involvement Strategies, New York: Routledge, 297–324.

Söderberg, Johan, and Adel Daoud (2012), "Atoms Want to Be Free Too! Expanding the Critique of Intellectual Property to Physical Goods," *triple*, 10(1): 66–76.

Sørensen, Majken Jul (2016), "Constructive Resistance: Conceptualising and Mapping the Terrain," *Journal of Resistance Studies*, 1(2): 49–78.

Spelman, Elizabeth (2002), *Repair: The Impulse to Restore in a Fragile World*, Boston: Beacon Press.

Star, Susan Leigh (1999), "The Ethnography of Infrastructure," *American Behavioral Scientist*, 43(3): 377–91.

Starhawk (1979), *The Spiral Dance: A Rebirth of the Ancient Religion of the Great Goddess*, San Francisco: Harper & Row.

Stowe, Doug (2005), "The Sloyd Knife," *Woodwork*, August, 80.

Strange, Jason (2020), *Shelter from the Machine: Homesteaders in the Age of Capitalism*, Champaign: University of Illinois Press.

Suttler, David (1970), *IV-F: I Guide to Draft Medical, Psychiatric, and Moral Unfitness Standards for Military Induction*, New York: Grove Press.

Svensson, Sahra, Jessika Luth Richter, Eléonore Maitre-Ekern, Taina Pihlajarinne, Aline Maigret, and Carl Dalhammar (2018), "The Emerging 'Right to Repair' Legislation in the EU and the US," *Proceedings from Going Green–Care Innovation*, Vienna, Austria, November 27–29.

Thoreau, Henry David ([1849] 2008), *Walden, Civil Disobedience and Other Writings*, New York: W.W. Norton.

Thrift, Nigel (2004), "Movement-Space: The Changing Domain of Thinking Resulting from the Development of New Kinds of Spatial Awareness," *Economy and Society*, 33(4): 582–604.

Toupin, Sophie (2016), "Gesturing towards 'Anti-Colonial Hacking' and Its Infrastructure," *Journal of Peer Production*, 9, September, http://peerproduction.net/issues/issue-9-alternative-internets/peer-reviewed-papers/anti-colonial-hacking/ (accessed December 30, 2020).

Traganou, Jilly (ed.) (2021), *Design and Political Dissent: Spaces, Visual, Materialities*, New York: Routledge.

Traugott, Mark (2010), *The Insurgent Barricade*, Berkeley: University of California Press.

Trentmann, Frank (2016), *Empire of Things*, New York: Harper.

Tronto, Joan (1993), *Moral Boundaries: A Political Argument for an Ethic of Care*, London: Routledge.

Turner, Mandy (2015), "Peacebuilding as Counterinsurgency in the Occupied Palestinian Territory," *Review of International Studies*, 41(1): 73–98.

Unger, Roberto (2007), *The Self Awakened: Pragmatism Unbound*, Cambridge, MA: Harvard University Press.

Vaneigem, Raoul (2012), *The Revolution of Everyday Life*, Oakland: PM Press.

Vattimo, Gianni (2012), "Dialectics, Difference, Weak Thought," in Gianni Vattimo and Pier Rovatti (eds.), *Weak Thought*, Albany: SUNY Press, 39–52.

Verbeek, Peter-Paul (2005), *What Things Do: Philosophical Reflections on Technology, Agency, and Design*, University Park: Pennsylvania State University Press.

Verbeek, Peter-Paul (2011), *Moralizing Technology: Understanding and Designing the Morality of Things*, Chicago: University of Chicago Press.

Vinthagen, Stellan (2015), *A Theory of Nonviolent Action: How Civil Resistance Works*, London: Zed Books.

Virilio, Paul (1995), *Bunker Archeology*, New York: Princeton Architectural Press.

Vossoughi, Shirin, Paula K. Hooper, and Meg Escudé (2016), "Making through the Lens of Culture and Power: Toward Transformative Visions for Educational Equity," *Harvard Educational Review*, 86(2): 206–32.

Webb, Justin, Laszlo Tihanyi, Duane Ireland, and David Sirmon (2009), "You Say Illegal, I Say Legitimate: Entrepreneurship in the Informal Economy," *Academy of Management Review*, 34(3): 492–510.

Weil, Simone (2002), *Gravity and Grace*, New York: Routledge.

Wenger, Etienne (1998), *Communities of Practice: Learning, Meaning, and Identity*, Cambridge: Cambridge University Press.

Whitehead, Mark (2018), *Neuroliberalism: Behavioural Government in the Twenty-First Century*, Abingdon: Routledge.

Wilkinson-Weber, Clare, and Alicia DeNicola (eds.) (2016), *Critical Craft: Technology, Globalization, and Capitalism*, London: Bloomsbury.

Winner, Langdon (1980), "Do Artifacts Have Politics?," *Daedalus*, 109(1): 121–36.

Yates, Luke (2014), "Rethinking Prefiguration: Alternatives, Micropolitics and Goals in Social Movements," *Social Movement Studies*, 14(1): 1–21.

Yomango (2008), "Whatever Happened to Yomango? Fifteen Answers to a Questionnaire", European Institute for Progressive Cultural Politics, September, cited in Otto von Busch (2017), "Resistant Materialities and Power Tools: Dynamics of Power and Resistance in Everyday Consumerism," *Journal of Resistance Studies*, 3(2): 66–88.

Zuboff, Shoshana (2019), *The Age of Surveillance Capitalism: The Fight for the Future at the New Frontier of Power*, London: Profile Books.

Zukin, Sharon, and Max Papadantonakis (2017), "Hackathons as Co-optation Ritual: Socializing Workers and Institutionalizing Innovation in the 'New' Economy," in Arne Kalleberg and Steven Vallas (eds.), *Precarious Work* (Research in the Sociology of Work, Volume 31), Bingley: Emerald Publishing, 157–81.

INDEX